COLUMBIA CRITICAL GUIDES

George Eliot

Adam Bede
The Mill on the Floss
Middlemarch

EDITED BY LUCIE ARMITT

Consultant editor: Nicolas Tredell

COLUMBIA UNIVERSITY PRESS   NEW YORK

Columbia University Press
Publishers Since 1893
New York
Editor's text copyright © 2000 Lucie Armitt

First published in the Icon Critical Guides series in 2000 by Icon Books Ltd.

Library of Congress Cataloging-in-Publication Data

George Eliot : Adam Bede, The Mill on the Floss, Middlemarch / edited by Lucie Armitt.
    p. cm.—(Columbia critical guides)
    ISBN 0–231–12422–8 (cloth)—ISBN 0–231–12423–6 (paper)
    1. Eliot, George, 1819–1880. Adam Bede. 2. Eliot, George, 1819–1880. Mill on the Floss. 3. Eliot, George, 1819–1880. Middlemarch. 4. Midlands (England)—In literature. I. Eliot, George. II. Armitt, Lucie. III. Series.

                                                    2001042377

For Scott and Bethany Grace

Contents

NOTES ON THE TEXT

The critical material chosen for inclusion here reflects much of what I believe to be the most interesting scholarship published on Eliot during the last thirty-five years. Occasionally this is at the expense of one or two more established names (most notably Barbara Hardy and Gordon Haight), but their work is extensively reproduced elsewhere.[1]

The number of *Critical Heritage* collections available on Eliot[2] also makes the need for a separate chapter specifically dedicated to the early reviews less important here than to many volumes in this series. For this reason I have chosen, instead, to include extracts from such reviews as and when they directly impinge upon the issues raised. In addition, to ease any difficulties surrounding the cross-referencing of material I have taken the liberty of standardising all page references to the primary material throughout. The editions to which these refer are: *Adam Bede* (abbreviated to *AB* on many occasions), edited by Beryl Gray (London: Everyman, 1994); *The Mill on the Floss* (*MF*), edited with an Introduction and Notes by A.S. Byatt (Harmondsworth: Penguin Classic, 1985); and *Middlemarch* (*M*), edited by Margaret Harris and Judith Johnston (London: Everyman, 1997).

CHAPTER ONE

Introducing Eliot: Then and Now

GEORGE ELIOT'S critical reputation has had a chequered history from the start. A bright beginning was made possible by Mary Ann(e) (or Marian) Evans shielding her true identity, at first pretending to be a clergyman friend of her life-long partner, George Henry Lewes (who carried out all the publishing negotiations on her behalf). Controversy and outrage accompanied her career, however, once Victorian society uncovered the real writer behind the veil. There were a few important literary allies: she was delighted when Charles Dickens corresponded with her on the subject of *Adam Bede*:

■ I know nothing so skilful, determined, and uncompromising. The whole country life that the story is set in, is so real, and so droll and genuine, and yet so selected and polished by art, that I cannot praise it enough to you . . .

I cannot close this note without touching on two heads. Firstly . . . if you should ever have the freedom and inclination to be a fellow labourer with me, it would yield me a pleasure that I have never known yet and can never know otherwise . . . Secondly, I hope you will let me come to see you when we are all in or near London again, and tell you – as a curiosity – my reasons for the faith that was in me that you were a woman, and for the absolute and never-doubting confidence with which I have waved all men away from *Adam Bede*, and nailed my colours to the Mast with 'Eve' upon them.[1] □

Another ally is Mathilde Blind who, in her 1883 book on Eliot's work, described Eliot as 'stand[ing] supreme and unrivalled' in 'her own peculiar field . . . the novel of English provincial life' and published her study as part of a series called 'Eminent Women'.[2]

Far better known, however, is Leslie Stephen's 1902 study in which, despite describing *The Mill on the Floss* as 'clearly the most interesting of all [Eliot's] books', he goes on to assert that 'she was too thoroughly feminine to be quite at home in the psychology of the male animal. Her women are . . . unerringly drawn . . . but when she draws a man, she has not the same certainty of touch.' Hence, he concludes, 'George Eliot did not herself understand what a mere hairdresser's block she was describing in Mr Stephen Guest. He is another instance of her incapacity for pourtraying [sic] the opposite sex.' This from a critic who perceives no hint of irony in publishing his study of George Eliot in a series called 'English Men of Letters'.[3]

In the same year Edith Wharton, writing primarily in direct response to Stephen, oscillates between extremes in describing Eliot as having 'started in life with the worst style – or with the greatest lack of style – that ever hampered a writer of genius', and goes on to qualify this observation further by asking us to '[c]ompare the laboured and ineffective attempt to describe a fat man in the person of Mr Casson (the innkeeper in *Adam Bede*) with the brief and masterly strokes which put before us such figures as Mr Brooke, Dorothea [and] Sir James Chettam . . . *Middlemarch* abounds in vivid portraits drawn in half-a-dozen lines.'

Most surprising for us, however, is the observation with which Wharton opens her review:

■ Mr Leslie Stephen has performed an invaluable service, not so much to the genius of George Eliot, which may well trust its case to posterity, as to those among her admirers who resent the momentary neglect into which she has fallen.[4] □

In fact, it is not until Virginia Woolf's celebration of her style in 1919 that most critics perceive Eliot to have been finally resurrected.

■ The beauty of those first books, *Scenes of Clerical Life, Adam Bede, The Mill on the Floss*, is very great. It is impossible to estimate the merit of the Poysers, the Dodsons, the Gilfils, the Bartons, and the rest with all their surroundings and dependencies, because they have put on flesh and blood and we move among them, now bored, now sympathetic, but always with that unquestioning acceptance of all that they say and do, which we accord to the great originals only. The flood of memory and humour which she pours so spontaneously into one figure, one scene after another, until the whole fabric of ancient rural England is revived, has so much in common with a natural process that it leaves us with little consciousness that there is anything to criticize. We accept; we feel the delicious warmth and release of spirit which the great creative writers alone procure for us. As one comes back to the books after years of absence they pour out, even against our expectation, the same store of energy and heat, so that we want more than anything to idle in the warmth as in the sun beating down from the red orchard wall. If there is an element of unthinking abandonment in thus submitting to the humours of Midland farmers and their wives, that, too, is right in the circumstances. We scarcely wish to analyse what we feel to be so large and deeply human. And when we consider how distant in time the world of Shepperton and Hayslope is, and how remote the minds of farmer and agricultural labourers from those of most of George Eliot's readers, we can only attribute the ease and pleasure with which we ramble from house to smithy, from cottage parlour to rectory garden, to the fact that George Eliot makes us share their lives, not in a spirit of condescension or of curiosity, but in a spirit of sympathy. She is no satirist. The movement of her mind was too slow and cumbersome to lend itself to comedy. But she gathers in her large grasp a great bunch of the main elements of human nature and groups them loosely together with a tolerant and wholesome understanding which, as one finds upon re-reading, has not only kept her figures fresh and free, but has given them an unexpected hold upon our laughter and tears. There is the famous Mrs Poyser. It would have been easy to work her idiosyncrasies to death, and, as it is, perhaps, George Eliot gets her laugh in the same place a little too often. But memory, after the book is shut, brings out, as sometimes in real life, the details and subtleties which some more salient characteristic has prevented us from noticing at the time . . . Thus one can muse and speculate about the greater number of George Eliot's characters and find, even in the least important, a roominess and margin where those qualities lurk which she has no call to bring from their obscurity.[5] □

Most famous of all is Woolf's assertion that *Middlemarch* is a 'magnificent book' and 'one of the few English novels written for grown-up people'.[6] The rest of the twentieth century seems to have been led by her opinion for, as I will now come on to argue, its currency has been proved all over again via the medium of television.

In 'Televising "Middlemarch"',[7] David Gervais examines the relationship between Eliot's written/original text of 1874 and its visual serialisation in the highly acclaimed 1993 television drama series. Though wary of the implied reductionism involved in the translation of this complex narrative work into a series of screen images for a mass audience, he nevertheless pays homage to the merits of the form.

■ It goes without saying that the new serial is impeccably made: the BBC's mastery in the genre is acknowledged all over the world (as the serialisation rights will no doubt confirm). The fact that 'Middlemarch' had a budget of over £6,000,000 (roughly the same as the comparable film of *Howard's End*) is proof that the corporation is well aware of this.

There is by now, of course, a very long tradition of classic serials on BBC television and radio. Originally, the term meant simply the serialisation of a classic but, by now, it has an under-meaning: that the serial itself is in some way classic, a contribution to 'culture' . . . But what exactly do we get for our money?[8] □

There is nothing surprising about Gervais's ambivalent opening to his article. It is what we would expect from an academic publishing in the journal *English*. Those of us reading the article are likely to share the same views, automatically nodding our assent before moving on to read something else more obviously contentious, having enjoyed this comfortable dip into shared territory in exactly the same way we (and Gervais) enjoyed watching the serial as 'light-relief'. But there are aspects of Gervais's approach in this passage that are well worth pausing over, because for all his claims that the television serialisation must always be doing something different to the original text, it is ironic that he raises here precisely the same issues as Eliot's original raised at its first point of publication.

We have to remember that *Middlemarch* itself was initially published in serial form in five bi-monthly and three monthly instalments between December 1871 and December 1872, prior to its eventual publication as a single volume in 1874. As with the television series, this was as much an economic as an aesthetic decision. Eliot wished to reach as broad an audience as possible, and serialisation was the best way for her to do it. As a nineteenth-century reviewer of the serialised *Middlemarch* put it:

■ We are disposed to maintain that no story gets so well apprehended, so completely mastered in all its aspects, as one which, written as a whole, is published in parts . . . it is the only way in which human life itself . . . can be studied. There you are not allowed to see the beginning, middle, and end at a sitting . . . , but must usually become perfectly familiar with the human elements of a story before you see them even begin to combine into a plot.[9] □

It is not, however, merely reader-reception that is at stake here. Notice how, in Gervais's previously quoted remark, he slips swiftly and seamlessly from concerns about aesthetics to those of economics. '[W]orld-wide' reception is, after all, as much involved with circulating currency as it is with satellite link-ups. Brian Spittles[10] expands on a similar theme by spelling out in precise terms the true financial equation for nineteenth-century readers.

■ In Eliot's period the most common, although not the only, form of novel publication was in three volumes at a price of half a guinea each, which meant a complete novel cost thirty-one shillings and sixpence (£1.52½p). All prices are, of course, significant only in relation to incomes. The two largest single groups of employees were agricultural workers, who accounted for approximately 20% of the working male population; and domestic servants, who comprised over a tenth of female employees. At the time Mudie set up his Select Library the pay of agricultural labourers, according to the statistics researched by the historian J.H. Clapham, was not generous: 'In ten northern counties the average wage was 11s. 6d. . . . In eighteen southern counties the average was 8s. 5d.'[11] This would put the national annual average wage at around £25, which meant a novel cost three weeks' full income.

Domestic workers were paid even less in actual cash. The social historian Frank Huggett has recorded a typical household some years later: 'Frances Marlow came as a nurserymaid at £7 a year in 1864 and left in 1876 . . . by which time she had become a £20-a-year lady's maid.'[12] In addition she would have received board and accommodation, but it was still not an income that allowed luxuries such as books, even if Frances Marlow had had time and education to read them.[13] □

Spittles's statistics demonstrate that Gervais is placing the contemporary serialisation of *Middlemarch* at the centre of precisely the same issues that Eliot addressed in constructing her original community of Middlemarch. Throughout this Readers' Guide to three of Eliot's 'Midlands' novels, *Adam Bede, The Mill on the Floss* and *Middlemarch*, we will find critics analysing the role of currency, information networks, mobility and origins as some of the core concerns of Eliot's *oeuvre*. It strikes me as wholly fitting (more in keeping with the novel than we might credit) that the serialisation has managed to raise the same issues, but in a different historical context.

Eliot's own juxtaposition of differing narrative chronologies is one of her most characteristic textual practices. In each of these novels we find that the time in which the action is set is superimposed upon that within which it is written. *Adam Bede*, first published in 1859, is set in the years 1799–1807; *The Mill on the Floss*, first published in 1860, is set in the 'not very remote' past,[14] and *Middlemarch* is set in the decade spanning the late 1820s and '30s, forty to fifty years prior to volume publication. Although some critics have diagnosed, in this recurring tendency, an atavistic desire for nostalgia and escapism, others have identified a predilection for deliberate cultural clashing which would have been evident to a nineteenth-century reader, though perhaps less so to an increasingly distant one of the twenty-first century. As Alan W. Bellringer observes of *The Mill on the Floss*:

■ The mill is . . . a lot more than an adjunct to a picturesque rural house. It is an example of early industry, a human artefact, which had replaced a half-timbered building damaged in the floods three generations back and with a malthouse added . . . Though the mill can survive its disintegration, its rebuilding is not a 'thorough repair' to those who have known it in the past. The human present does not grow seamlessly from the past, but is divided from it by change and loss.[15] □

Again this returns us to Gervais's argument.

■ Can one expect a modern television audience to be interrogating its own experience when it watches a 'classic serial'? . . . *Inspector Morse* [for example] . . . make[s] a viewer ask questions about society and may be more disturbing, despite its being more entertaining and not improving. When I find myself more emotionally gripped by the latter than the former I wonder whether serials from nineteenth-century novels, however well-intentioned and however well-made, aren't intrinsically a form of escapism . . .'[16] □

Few apparently random juxtapositions could be more jarring than *Middlemarch* versus *Inspector Morse* (until, of course, we remember that the Oxford location for the latter helps to provide a 'cult' academic audience presumably equally nostalgic for idealised 'times-past' as those readers who read Eliot for atavistic gratification). Nevertheless, the disjunction is once again fitting. *Middlemarch* is, as I have said, a novel about currency, and tied up in that phrase are not just circulations of money, but issues of presentness ('current'-cy). Not just the technological realities of television, but also its illusory quality in comparison with what we these days call 'hard-copy' (paper and ink), help to ensure that all televisual texts exist only in the present for the viewer, even if we know they are stored away on tape in the BBC archives and brought out as repeats and/or videos as and when the commercial possibilities make it attractive to do so.

What of this final charge of escapism? For Gervais, this claim is explicitly set up as popularity versus élitism; I have suggested it is also about economics. But the terms of his larger argument actually situate the question far more implicitly in the traditional academic argument of mimesis versus metaphor, or realism versus modernism. Here he questions the nature of the representation offered in the television series.

■ First of all, we get a seamless patchwork of beautifully finished images: Georgian Stamford, shorn of all signs of the twentieth century, glows warmly as the handsome young Dr Lydgate inspects its bustling street-market; two elegant young ladies wearing black riding hats canter over the fields on thoroughbred horses; Mr Farebrother pots antique billiard balls at the Green Dragon as the thick voiced locals expostulate on his prowess; Mr Bulstrode cants in uneducated tones in a study burnished with calf-bound books; Mrs Cadwallader's outlandish dress steals our attention from what she has to say; every conversation seems to be punctuated by horses trotting across the screen (it is even clear that Fred Vincy's isn't a thoroughbred). All this, in its way, is spot on . . . You are tempted to say that you are made to feel just what it must have been like to live in Middlemarch. Then you remember the novel. What, one wonders, will anyone who picks it up after seeing the serial have left to imagine? Won't such a reader have the sense of knowing everything about this world already? – its varied surface, its ins and outs, its deeper tones. Will we still be able to hear, in George Eliot's own phrase, the sound of the grass growing and the squirrel's heart-beat? For the fact is that what we have been watching is not an interpretation of *Middlemarch* or a version of it but an adaptation. In an adaptation what matters is not so much to understand a book, though that may help, as to find an exact equivalent for as much of it as possible. It is like one of those copies of masterpieces which one sometimes sees students making in art galleries: it is not the real thing but, in some ways and to some spectators, it can become more interesting than the real thing. Will the copyist get just the right shade of red for the man's hat, we wonder? Copying, of course, can be a valuable thing – think how much Cézanne learnt from it – but would we want to call it 'classic'? It would be churlish not to salute the authenticity of a series like 'Middlemarch' but I want also to suggest that its authenticity is the most inauthentic thing about it.

. . . [A]lterations, I believe, are strictly off-limits to anyone setting out to make a good 'classic serial'. The cardinal sin is to tamper with it in any way; the object to be as faithful to it as possible . . . ['Middlemarch'] is painfully faithful and parades its authenticity on every possible occasion but what is such faithfulness worth?

One obvious answer is that it helps us to understand what nineteenth-century England was like. Clearly, it does do this. Just to see all those well-groomed horses trotting in and out helps us to feel what life was like before the motor-car. So, too, the dresses and the furnishings and so on – all caught with picturesque exactness. But is this the nineteenth century? It seems to me that there is an abstract, historical thing which we call the nineteenth century as if it were impossibly remote from us, like the Pyramids, and this the 'classic serial' can create to perfection. There is also a striving, struggling, self-divided nineteenth century which such a serial can also convey if it is intelligent, as this 'Middlemarch' is: Dorothea's doubts and aspirations, for example, are there for us to sympathize with. But all this is only a part of the past, even so. In *Middlemarch* itself we are always conscious that this is an earlier time, the period of agitation over Reform, as seen from the perspective of the narrator forty years later. This distance is not the same as the kind of distance that evokes, say, our wondering amusement at Rosamond Vincy's arch dress-sense and golden ringlets. The narrator may also think of such things as quaint – dated, provincial – but they lie much closer to him than to us, as part of the past out of which he himself has been made. The novel is as much about the presence of the past as its pastness.[17] □

Such 'fake' authenticity is, however, characteristic of literary realism too. As a nineteenth-century text, first published in 1859, Eliot's *Adam Bede* is situated quite firmly within the heyday of classical realism – a term usually perceived to be synonymous with the aim for absolute verisimilitude. What we will find, however, particularly in chapter three of this Readers' Guide, is that such purported authenticity is only ever an ideological mask for veiling some issues and revealing others. There is also, of course, a further social context to consider, which is that dictating reader reception. Realist novels are still the most popular in terms of sales figures, but such fiction can be presumed to be 'frivolous' and primarily associated with railway station book-stands set up to sell books to travellers looking for something to pass the time. Here we encounter another of the many ironies of history (or chronological juxtaposition). Originally it was the coming of the railways (seen in *Middlemarch* as a great social evil) that proved invaluable to the economic rise and stability of the novelist – as Eliot herself would have been only too well aware. This is a layer of irony often overlooked by even informed readers of *Middlemarch*, although it is not lost on Spittles, for whom networks of transportation and circulation (including those relating to reading and book-lending) are intrinsically connected in relation to Eliot's work. He observes: 'In 1819 . . . the railway had not even been invented, but by 1880 over 14,000 miles of track existed in Britain alone, and the railway had become the great nineteenth-century symbol of economic, scientific and technological progress across almost the whole globe.'[18] Expanding on the connection with the practice of reading, he continues:

■ The development of the railways was perhaps, somewhat surprisingly, the first important influence on early Victorian reading habits. By the 1840s railway travel was expanding very rapidly. In 1838 only 500 miles of track were in operation, by 1848 5,000 miles were in use, and most of the increase was due to passenger rather than freight transport . . . Railways were faster, cheaper and more comfortable than horse-drawn coaches – although comfort is a relative concept, which in this context emphasizes the awful discomfort of most coach journeys. Despite their comparative speed trains were still quite slow, and journey times therefore long – but it was generally possible to read in order to alleviate the boredom of travel. This factor opened up new markets for novels. It is not coincidental, either, that W. H. Smith's railway station bookstalls, stocked with journals and magazines carrying stories and serializations of novels, became a feature of the traveller's culture from the 1840s. During Eliot's writing lifetime perhaps the two strongest influences on the writer's market-place were the circulating libraries, and the many magazines and journals that serialized fiction. Books were relatively expensive and one way of reading them was through the services of a private library, the largest of which, Mudie's Select Library, was founded, significantly during the railway boom, in 1842 . . .

Before the widespread availability of libraries such as Mudie's the reader of the long novel – such as Henry Fielding's or Jane Austen's – usually needed three attributes: money, time and education. The development of cheap, or free, libraries obviously curtailed the importance of the first necessity – although the possession of, or access to, some kind of wealth was also relevant to the consideration of time. The typical labourer, railway worker or servant at their job for 70 or 80 hours a week had little leisure, or energy, for reading even if they could get hold of the books. Provision for education was also limited, although it expanded considerably during Eliot's lifetime.[19] □

This question of mass popularity versus nineteenth-century social privilege takes on a new dimension for the modern-day reader, whose idea of mass entertainment is less likely to reside within the covers of books and more likely to take shape in the form of soap opera. In 'The "Soaping" of *Middlemarch*', Bernard O'Keefe goes further than Gervais in claiming not only that the televisual 'Middlemarch' does not compare with the novel, but also that it became a debased form of soap opera: at least in the eyes of the media.

■ *The Daily Mail*, presumably intending to praise, ambiguously comments that 'enough drama was packed into last night's final episode of the superb *Middlemarch* to keep *EastEnders*, *Coronation Street* and *Brookside* going for months'. Mark Lawson in the *Independent* describes the readings of Featherstone's and Casaubon's wills and Rosamond's miscarriage as scenes with 'exact parallels in popular television serials from *Dallas* downwards', while in the *New Statesman* Chris Baldick develops the analogy further:

Taking a small community beset by infighting, gossip, marital breakdown and failing medical services, in which everyone is related to, or owes money to, or is being blackmailed by, everyone else, George Eliot laced together a dozen different intrigues into a new kind of fictional plot. She inadvertently became the godmother of *Neighbours*.

Such critics are responding to what television does best, namely telling a story . . . However, in doing so, it simplifies and reduces many of the novel's effects.[20] □

Of course O'Keefe is right, but so are the journalists and critics cited – and not just about the television series. Just as soap opera is neatly divided up into a series of short and fragmented episodes (thus allowing us to divide our own time up into neat and discrete viewing moments), so *Middlemarch*, the novel, is neatly divided up into eight Books, helping us to dip in and out of it while maintaining a sense of reader orientation. Similarly, where soap opera often functions as a tapestry of ever-shifting multiple plots, often subordinate to a central plot of any one or a series of episodes, so Eliot's novel functions by moving between a series of plots that are only ever partially brought together by the end. Because *Middlemarch* centres around a community rather than any one character, the plot is potentially incapable of closure. The response of its first reviewers therefore drew a distinction between the experience of reading *Middlemarch* as serialised fiction, which they felt 'focused on suspense, and the plot', and subsequently reading the entire novel as one volume, 'allow[ing] contemplation of the subtleties of the work as a whole'.[21] For those who remain unconvinced of the analogy with modern-day soap opera, consider the following point made by Carol Martin in response to a reviewer of the period.

■ Dreaming about Borthrop Trumball . . . or avenging Dorothea by appropriating her husband's name may seem to violate the line between text and audience, but that is precisely the point. As they became entangled with the characters, [nineteenth-century] serial readers experienced a mixture of frustration at delayed gratification along with the pleasure and suspense that came from treating the characters as if they were real. Reviews show that they were conscious of this blurring of the line between fact and fiction . . . , [one reviewer in *The Manchester Examiner and Times* coming] to regard the pleasure of gossiping about the characters during the intervals between parts as compensation for this mode of publication.[22] □

Making *Middlemarch* both popular and 'serious' was the dual benefit of publishing in serial form prior to volume publication. But not all novels were deemed suitable for serialisation, as Eliot was made all too well aware while negotiating the serialisation of *Adam Bede* and *The Mill on the Floss*. As Martin observes:

■ Serialization, despite its potential for great monetary rewards, at times threatened [Eliot's] power to present her 'own conception of life and character' . . . As a result . . . *Adam Bede* and *The Mill on the Floss* . . . were published first in the standard Victorian three-volume format, even though they were originally planned for serialization . . .

. . . [I]t is uncertain how *Adam Bede* would, from an artistic standpoint, have borne serialization. The plot seems to develop slowly, and slow development is inimical to serial fiction's requirement for frequent climactic endings, especially in a magazine like Blackwood's that featured relatively short instalments . . . Nonetheless, the structure of the early parts of *Adam Bede* suggests that Eliot not only attended to the larger canvas of three-volume publication but planned her instalment breaks to include the drama requisite in a serial's smaller units . . . These breaks show that despite the cumulative impression of a slowly unfolding plot, the individual parts would have evoked suspense effectively and drawn readers back for future instalments. The excitement of the love affair would have sustained interest through [B]ook 2, and [B]ook 3 would have had the sensation of Hetty's pregnancy and the child murder to keep readers returning . . . [23] □

It is well known, however, that literary criteria were not the only ones affecting such commercial decisions. Equally important to Eliot's publisher, John Blackwood, was the scandal that accrued around the woman behind the books. Mary Ann Evans had chosen to live out of wedlock with a married man, George Henry Lewes. Both were shunned by many in 'respectable' society. While pseudonymous publication in serial form was acceptable, Blackwood feared that revelation of the real identity of the woman behind the pseudonym would be commercially disastrous for his magazine. Alexander Welsh[24] summarises the biographical elements of the controversy thus:

■ The embarrassing but triumphant revelation of the identity of George Eliot took place in an appropriately unintended way. The Leweses were in effect blackmailed, without so much as a threatening letter, by the complacency of a nearly total stranger named Joseph Liggins, who permitted people to believe that *he* was George Eliot. Blackmailers, after all, do not wish to reveal the secret they can profit by – they do their best one way or another to exploit someone else's need to keep a secret hidden. The payoff for Liggins was enjoyment of the glory of authorship. The Leweses had not dreamed, nor Blackwood either, of the secret being manipulated by a third party.[25] At first all three were amused that someone named Liggins professed to have written *Scenes of Clerical Life* and *Adam Bede*, but they became upset and unnerved when other outsiders conceived the idea of raising charity for Liggins, who was said to have received no pay for these books from the publisher – as indeed he had not. The Liggins rumor arose as early as June 1857 and was eventually given space in *The Times* in April 1859: two months later George Eliot, who was writing *The Mill on the Floss*, determined to keep her secret no longer. It was an altogether amusing, exasperating, and instructive episode. Even Lewes, who knew his way in the writing and publishing business very well, found himself much more deeply involved than he could have expected. Following Scott's precedent he had advocated lying, when necessary, to defend Marian's pseudonym; but the Liggins affair drew him in deeper. Over the signature of 'George Eliot' he wrote to *The Times*, 'Allow me to ask whether the act of publishing a book deprives a man of all claim to the courtesies usual among gentlemen?'[26] Lewes of course knew that he was not George Eliot, knew also that George Eliot was not a gentleman, and that the courtesies usual among gentlemen did not apply in the realm of print and publicity. Blackwood took the matter more calmly, since his personal pride was not threatened if the motive of concealment should be said to be the illicit marriage; but he was deeply worried about the reputation of his magazine and about future sales of books by George Eliot. He and the author were in negotiations over *The Mill on the Floss*, and she did not mistake, or take very kindly to, his nervousness about the revelation of her identity. Their differences were resolved to Blackwood's satisfaction mainly by his promising himself that he could continue to admit the name 'George Eliot' in books but not in *Blackwood's Magazine*.[27] Nevertheless, the falsehood of Liggins's supposed authorship would be publicly linked to the falsehood of George Eliot's supposed marriage. As a reviewer of Cross's *Life* complained, 'It is no more true that the author of *Adam Bede* was Mrs Lewes than it is true that the author of *Adam Bede* was Mr Liggins.'[28] □

Nevertheless, Martin reminds us, the different nature of the narrative of *The Mill on the Floss* may have made this decision advantageous in the end. *The Mill on the Floss* lacks the regular narrative climaxes so necessary to an episodic structure.

■ Most of the exciting moments early [on] . . . come from Maggie's disobedience to small behests . . . [A]t least [*Adam Bede*] featured the novelty of a woman preacher, a sudden death by drowning, the supernatural rapping of the willow wand, disappointed love, and a possible seduction, along with a modicum of silver-fork appeal in the Irwines and Donnithornes.

> . . . *Adam Bede* is 'more interesting', but *The Mill on the Floss* is 'better constructed', agrees *The Morning Post*. We never 'love any of the characters portrayed but we know them all . . .'[29] □

A different type of writing is also employed in *Middlemarch*, but this time, as we have seen, it was better suited to serialisation. Instead of frequent narrative climaxes early on in the text, a gradual accretion of interest in Dorothea Brooke is built up – largely deriving from her obviously ill-fated marriage early on – which carries the narrative forward. Once other threads are gradually woven into the tapestry the reader is ensnared like a fly in a web. It is, of course, later on, when serial readers' interest might well otherwise have started to flag, that the introduction of Raffles provides the necessarily sensationalist element that carries the novel forward to its conclusion. Robert B. Heilman offers a useful structural breakdown of *Middlemarch* in terms of its piece by piece construction:

■ Dorothea Brooke dominates the first nine and a half chapters as she progresses to the altar with Casaubon; observers' comments on this affair introduce us indirectly to six supporting characters. Then Lydgate dominates the next eight and a half chapters, which also identify people important in his later life. From the Casaubons to Lydgate looks like a big shift in focus. Yet Eliot does not crudely drop the honeymooners, saying, 'We will now take a look at the stay-at-homes.' Rather she sneaks us across an invisible borderline between the newly-weds and others so smoothly that we hardly notice the process. Chapter 10 describes a big dinner just before the wedding. This is the right occasion for Eliot to use more intensely her method of having friends and neighbours discuss the principals: in doing this, the townspeople portray Dorothea and Casaubon further, introduce and sketch themselves, and reflect community tone. We are given almost a tape-recording of random party chatter, but beneath the air of randomness a controlled process directs our attention. Some speakers compare Dorothea with Rosamond Vincy; others, noting Casaubon's unrobust look, talk of illness and thus naturally allude to the town's new physician, Lydgate. Then it is Lydgate who opens Chapter 11, and he thinks about a subject continued from the party discussion: the difference between Rosamond and Dorothea. From this Eliot slips easily into portrayals of Rosamond and the other Vincys, including Fred Vincy and hence his girl, Mary Garth; and so on, until we have met Mary, Featherstone and his household, Bulstrode, and the hospital problems that involve Bulstrode, Lydgate, and Farebrother. These details may be tedious, but we need them if we are to see clearly how Eliot, without palpable break or rude leap from one topic to another, has taken us adroitly, imperceptibly, from one love-affair to the making of two different ones and to the supporting casts of some size. We have been gliding along a continuum of segments of a community-in-action, segments as of now independent or loosely connected, but appearing serially for one initial inspection as if they were panels of a polyptych.[30] □

So far we have concentrated primarily upon plot, a focus made largely inevitable by our discussion of reader reception and serialisation. However, other aspects of the narrative structure contribute to a reader's understanding too. Passages of description, for example, work especially hard in Eliot's writing to place us within particular contexts of reading, create deliberate relief or tension, or encode key themes and ideas. The following passage from Chapter 2 of *Adam Bede* illustrates this strategy perfectly.

■ The Green lay at the extremity of the village, and from it the road branched off in two directions, one leading farther up the hill by the church, and the other winding gently down towards the valley. On the side of the Green that led towards the church, the broken line of thatched cottages was continued nearly to the churchyard gate; but on the opposite, northwestern side, there was nothing to obstruct the view of gently-swelling meadow, and wooded valley, and dark masses of distant hill. That rich undulating district of Loamshire to which Hayslope belonged, lies close to a grim outskirt of Stonyshire, overlooked by its barren hills as a pretty blooming sister may sometimes be seen linked in the arm of a rugged, tall, swarthy brother; and in two or three hours' ride the traveller might exchange a bleak treeless region, intersected by lines of cold grey stone, for one where his road wound under the shelter of woods, or up swelling hills, muffled with hedgerows and long meadow-grass and thick corn; and where at every turn he came upon some fine old country-seat nestled in the valley or crowning the slope, some homestead with its long length of barn and its cluster of golden ricks, some grey steeple looking out from a pretty confusion of trees and thatch and dark-red tiles. It was just such a picture as this last that Hayslope Church had made to the traveller as he began to mount the gentle slope leading to its pleasant uplands, and now from his station near the Green he had before him in one view nearly all the other typical features of this pleasant land. High up against the horizon were the huge conical masses of hill, like giant mounds intended to fortify this region of corn and grass against the keen and hungry winds of the north; not distant enough to be clothed in purple mystery, but with sombre greenish sides visibly specked with sheep, whose motion was only revealed by memory, not detected by sight; wooed from day to day by the changing hours, but responding with no change in themselves – left for ever grim and sullen after the flush of morning, the winged gleams of the April noonday, the parting crimson glory of the ripening summer sun. And directly below them the eye rested on a more advanced line of hanging woods, divided by bright patches of pasture or furrowed crops, and not yet deepened into the uniform leafy curtains of high summer, but still showing the warm tints of the young oak and the tender green of the ash and lime. Then came the valley, where the woods grew thicker, as if they had rolled down and hurried together from the patches left smooth on the slope, that they might take better care of the tall mansion which lifted its parapets and sent its faint blue summer smoke among them. Doubtless there was a large sweep of park and a broad glassy pool in front of that mansion, but the swelling slope of meadow would not let our traveller see them from the village green. He saw instead a foreground which was just as lovely – the level sunlight lying like transparent gold among the gently-curving stems of the feathered grass and the tall red sorrel, and the white umbels of the hemlocks lining the busy hedgerows. It was that moment in summer when the sound of the scythe being whetted makes us cast more lingering looks at the flower-sprinkled tresses of the meadows. [*AB*, pp. 16–17] □

In Eliot's use of the pastoral landscape, we find pictorial realism and symbolism merging. This scene is laid out in the form of a painting, with clear demarcation lines of foreground, layers of middle distance and background. In narrative terms these correspond to the movement of the plot, beginning with the choice that any character must make between taking up one of two roads constituting a forked path which will take him/her on a 'heavenly' journey via the church, not just to salvation, but also happy marriage, or winding slowly but surely downwards into the valley (of death). This binary divide sums up, from the start, the differing fates that will befall the novel's two heroines, Dinah Morris and Hetty Sorrel respectively, both of whom are woven into this scene in clandestine ways. The Green, from which the passage emanates, is more than the original location for Dinah's preaching in the novel; it almost stands in as a figure of speech representing her in her absence. Hetty Sorrel has not yet been encountered in the text, but her arrival is foreshadowed in the progression of the passage.

Leaving the Green (and Dinah) behind, we journey with the traveller through an increasingly sensualised piece of description via which, in the cumulative combination of phrases such as 'gently-swelling' and 'gently-curving' (suggestive of breasts), 'dark masses' (suggestive of hair), 'pretty confusion' (suggestive of that particular childlike naivety that so attracts both Arthur and Adam to Hetty), not to mention, of course, the 'parting crimson glory' that surely evokes the sexual organs of the aroused woman, this landscape is both feminised and eroticised without the need for the explicit comparison with the 'pretty blooming sister . . . linked in the arm of a rugged, tall, swarthy brother'. But undercutting the idealised sensuality of this passage is what awaits – namely 'the sound of the scythe being whetted', which 'makes us cast more lingering looks at the flower-sprinkled tresses of the meadow'. In other words this beauty will be hacked down in its pride, while in the background the 'more advanced line of hanging woods' seem to represent a gibbet coming to meet its prey – that 'prey' being, most obviously, the 'tall red (Hetty) sorrel' – that flower to be scythed.

The reader's position within the passage is also important. Implicitly, our stand-in is the traveller who surveys all before him. It is in this passage that we are first encouraged to become interested in this figure. But almost immediately he is forgotten, later to be recalled like a thread on a spool, tying together the long, encyclopaedic narrative, disappearing at the end of Chapter 2, not to return until Chapter 32 and then, again, in Chapters 39 and finally 45, 'In the Prison', where his true identity is revealed as Colonel Townley the magistrate [*AB*, p. 421]. Later on in her career, in *Middlemarch*, we will find such incomers viewed with increasing suspicion, a point that might well help to complicate the apparent authority with which this character is endowed in *Adam Bede*.

Such is this note of authority that some critics conflate this persona with that of the narrator – much as the narrator of *The Mill on the Floss* is personified in the first chapter of that text as an avuncular storyteller cum day-dreamer. But limitations to Colonel Townley's perceptions are built into this passage from the start (signalled, as so often in Eliot's writing, by his name, suggestive of only limited understanding of 'country ways'). Hence, although we begin by seeing what he sees, Eliot makes it clear that elements of the description available to the reader are hidden from his view: 'Doubtless there was a large sweep of park and a broad glassy pool in front of that mansion, but the swelling slope of meadow would not let our traveller see them from the village green.'

Even if we do not read this travelling stranger as the narrator, he is similar to the narrator in functioning as a masculine manifestation of George Eliot's presence within the text, standing in, paradoxically, for the *woman* writer as 'indefinable, alienated, a freakish outsider'.[31] Joining him are the two main female characters of the novel – both orphans: Dinah, who 'comes out o' Stonyshire, pretty nigh thirty mile off' [*AB*,

p. 15], and Hetty, who will be expelled from this community to the other side of the world, the initial portent of which is signalled in Chapter 24, as class schisms become apparent to her at the 'Health-Drinking':

- [A] moment of chill daylight and reality came across [Hetty's] dream: Arthur, who had seemed so near to her only a few hours before, was separated from her, as the hero of a great procession is separated from a small outsider in the crowd. [*AB*, p. 258] ☐

Thus she exchanges the red cloak of Little Red Riding Hood, 'tripping' through the forest with 'a small basket under her arm' [*AB*, p. 121], for the scarlet garb of Nathaniel Hawthorne's adulterous heroine, Hester Prynne, in his novel *The Scarlet Letter*, published nine years before Eliot's own.[32] In doing so Hetty journeys alone 'away from the familiar to the strange' [*AB*, p. 351].

That the reader should be encouraged to identify with the traveller is clearly appropriate insofar as we journey, like him, through the landscape of the text, taking in information *en route*. But we need to pay heed to the limitations of his view, as it is these that help to identify the more interrogative aspects of Eliot's writing. A typical realist text often works very hard to conceal its presence as an aesthetic construct in order to facilitate our involvement. It is perhaps for this reason that, when we consider a novel such as *Adam Bede*, we find a complex interweaving of narratorial visibility and invisibility in terms of the structure, and this opens up the realist mode to rather more interesting textual possibilities. Look, for example, at the opening paragraph.

- With a single drop of ink for a mirror, the Egyptian sorcerer undertakes to reveal to any chance comer far-reaching visions of the past. This is what I undertake to do for you, reader. With this drop of ink at the end of my pen, I will show you the roomy workshop of Mr Jonathan Burge, carpenter and builder, in the village of Hayslope, as it appeared on the eighteenth of June, in the year of our Lord 1799. [*AB*, p. 5] ☐

Here Eliot deliberately situates the presence of the implied author within (as opposed to beyond) the frame of the story. In doing so she overtly reminds us that this is a fabrication at the same time that her words here imply a mimesis (through the motif of the mirror) which claims to reflect upon a 'life-like' experience. Nor should we overlook the fact that the title of this chapter is 'The Workshop', or that we go on to be treated to a passage of carpentry involving frames and their (in)completion. Eliot sets up here, from the start, two competing frames: one offering a window on the narrative and integrating within it an implied author as its creator;

the second relates purely to plot. Hence, the title 'The Workshop' refers simultaneously to Jonathan Burge's business and the place from which the writer herself, as artisan, crafts texts. Within this same paragraph she informs us that narrative time is retrospective, a narrative device that, in itself, makes claims for 'truth' in the sense of documentation of past events. And yet all this, of course, is a trick which reminds us that her comparison with the 'sorcerer' is not an arbitrary one. In reminding us of her trickery at the same time as she seduces us with the verisimilitude of her fictions, Eliot draws attention to the precarious role played by narrative authority within realism.

Critical opinion cannot agree on the status of Eliot's narrators – or even their gender. According to Dorothea Barrett, for example:

■ [The] narrator [of *The Mill on the Floss*] is chameleon-like, *she* shifts and changes, and *her* attitude to Maggie, like the *Middlemarch* narrator's attitude to Dorothea, is in flux [my emphasis]. Nevertheless, her identification is with Maggie, in relation to whom she 'seems to function as Maggie's more powerful *alter ego*'.[33] □

For U.C. Knoepflmacher, however, this same narrator is:

■ [a] comical, bookish gentleman . . . forced to hold on to his armchair in his study in the first chapter . . . [and becoming] a helpless observer of Maggie's agonies in the novel's tragic conclusion.[34] □

The most sensible stance seems to be that adopted by Alan W. Bellringer, who simply acknowledges the inability to identify consistently any one narrative voice or persona at work. The example he gives here relates to *Adam Bede*.

■ Although George Eliot's commentary may seem to carry more weight than the story . . . it is hard to pin it down to anything authoritative. It more frequently abjures authority than insists on its privileged role as truth told in the voice of the writer.

The multiple focus of the narrator goes with an ambiguity of *status* which is even more bewildering if taken too seriously . . . [Certain] proleptic[35] observations locate the narrator in the fictional Loamshire, which seems confirmed when we learn that when she is abroad she sees things which remind her that she is 'not in Loamshire' [*A B*, p. 344]. Yet she is apparently a socialising city-dweller too, to whom 'it would be a pleasant variety' to see country-dancing sometimes instead of 'low dresses and large skirts' [*A B*, p. 270]. By way of complete contrast, she also belongs to Shepperton, often listening to the opinion of [Mr Gedge], the landlord of the Royal Oak there [*A B*, p. 175]. Now

Shepperton is not only in a different district from Loamshire it is in another novel, *Scenes of Clerical Life*! Some of this ubiquitousness can be reconciled with singleness of identity, no doubt, but the main impression of the narrator we receive is one of volatility.[36] □

This deliberate inconsistency fuels Eliot's narrators' complex depictions of character. Compare *Middlemarch*, for example, with Jane Austen's *Emma* (1816). On the opening page of Austen's text we read: 'Emma Woodhouse, handsome, clever, and rich, with a comfortable home and happy disposition, seemed to unite some of the best blessings of existence; and had lived nearly twenty-one years in the world with very little to distress or vex her.'[37]

The ironies of this sentence are present (albeit in a nuanced fashion) from the start, conveyed in the cautiously wry narrative voice adopted. This young woman will, we immediately surmise, irritate as much as beguile us and will consistently do so throughout. The narrator's opinion of Dorothea Brooke, as revealed by the opening passage of *Middlemarch*, is rather more difficult to definitively 'read'.

■ Miss Brooke had that kind of beauty which seems to be thrown into relief by poor dress. Her hand and wrist were so finely formed that she could wear sleeves not less bare of style than those in which the Blessed Virgin appeared to Italian painters; and her profile as well as her stature and bearing seemed to gain the more dignity from her plain garments, which by the side of provincial fashion gave her the impressiveness of a fine quotation from the Bible, – or from one of our elder poets, – in a paragraph of today's newspaper. [*M*, p. 7] □

The first sentence seems neutral rather than ironic in tone and has clarity and conciseness in its favour. We are less sure than the narrator of the precise 'kind of beauty' meant, but we trust our guide and await further information. However, the second, complicated, overlong sentence, makes us far less sure of our ground. Why, we might ask ourselves, does the narrator choose the convoluted phrase 'sleeves not less bare of style than' over the clearer, and surely preferable, 'sleeves as bare of style as'? The answer lies in the nuance suggested by the circumlocution. While the second option might imply a judgement made by the narrator and of which Dorothea could be unaware, the first suggests a more self-conscious identification. Just as we have to peruse the phrase carefully to work out its trickery, so Dorothea (it is suggested) has perused the precise effect her own image produces. The self-consciousness of her piety is therefore already suggested, without being *too* definitively revealed. The final clause of the sentence makes us more wary still.

Dorothea's costume, we are told, rather than reflecting 'provincial fashion', endows her with the 'impressiveness of a fine quotation from the Bible'. The analogy between fashion and the Bible is a bizarre one in itself, but an even stranger disjuncture follows. Only once that quotation is resituated 'in a paragraph of today's newspaper' does the comparison hold true.

J. Hillis Miller chooses to read this oddly situated opening as an early caution to the reader to tread carefully where Dorothea is concerned. She is, he interprets, 'born out of her time', a feature not necessarily to her credit as it suggests inauthenticity.[38] The overall effect of this opening is, on the one hand, to reinforce the saintly identification Dorothea is given in the Prelude, while taking away that saintliness on the other. The perpetuation of such ambiguity is a key element in Dorothea's characterisation. If she is too good to be true we will simply tire of her. She will (and does) prove interesting primarily at those moments when the serene mask slips to reveal a fictively 'real' woman underneath. This more complex identification also explains the particular choice of St Theresa as Dorothea's muse. As Hilary Fraser reminds us, Saint Theresa was not just 'a founder and reformer of religious communities', but also a woman torn between 'self-sacrifice and sensuality in her ecstasy'.[39]

A similar lack of clear-cut narrative guidance defines the manner in which characters collectively interrelate in this novel. Knoepflmacher picks up on this point, choosing the following passage from Chapter 10 as illustration of his argument.

■ If to Dorothea Mr Casaubon had been the mere occasion which had set alight the fine inflammable material of her youthful illusions, does it follow that he was fairly represented in the minds of those less impassioned personages who have hitherto delivered their judgments concerning him? I protest against any such conclusion, any prejudice derived from Mrs Cadwallader's contempt for a neighbouring clergyman's alleged greatness of soul, or Sir James Chettam's poor opinion of his rival's legs, – from Mr Brooke's failure to elicit a companion's ideas, or from Celia's criticism of a middle-aged scholar's personal appearance. I am not sure that the greatest man of his age, if ever that solitary superlative existed, could escape these unfavourable reflections of himself in various small mirrors; and even Milton, looking for his portrait in a spoon, must submit to have the facial angle of a bumpkin. [*M*, p.75] □

Knoepflmacher continues:

■ Nearly all of the characters in *Middlemarch* are highly opinionated. Indeed, 'opinion' – like 'point of view' – is one of the words most frequently repeated in the novel. Each opinion, we discover, possesses some truth; yet each opinion is also one-sided. In the first ten chapters of the novel Dorothea's hasty idealization of Mr. Casaubon is counterbalanced by the opinions of those who see the clergyman in a totally different light . . . The reader is slightly baffled. Whose point of view is he to adopt? The soulful Dorothea's or the sensual Celia's? . . . At the end of [Chapter 2] the omniscient narrator . . . offers a glimpse into Sir James' condescending view of Casaubon . . . [but does so] as an indictment of his limited perspective rather than as a view endorsed by the narrator. Only after briefly considering [several more] point[s] of view . . . does the narrator sum up the indictments made against Casaubon [in Chapter 10] . . . [40] □

There is, however, another issue brought to light by this unstable and unfixed narrator, and that is his/her relationship to the role played by gender in nineteenth-century writing. Note the ironies underlying Elizabeth Weed's reading of the relationship between unstable narrative voices and the implied gendering of the text in the context of *The Mill on the Floss*.[41]

■ In order to accept th[e] authority [of Eliot's narrator in *The Mill on the Floss*] . . . one must accept the fiction of George Eliot the male novelist, a fiction which, in turn, permits the fiction of the (male) omniscient narrator . . .

The difficulty the reader has accepting these fictions stems from the fact that he knows and remembers that behind George Eliot there is a woman. Moreover, he may know that behind the fiction of Maggie Tulliver there is the life of Mary Anne Evans with which it shares certain characteristics. If he knows this, he finds that the already ambiguous stance of the narrator in the first chapter becomes even more ambiguous. As Lynne Roberts comments in her analysis of the opening scene, the emphasis on memory in the first chapter 'suggests that the narrator is going to tell her [*sic*] own story, the story of her childhood and her past', but unexpected spatial and temporal shifts put that conventional narrative use of memory into question.[42] In the first pages the narrator moves . . . through several levels of time and space, with the result that at the end of the chapter the reader remains uncertain of the precise relationships existing between the narrator and the setting he (she?) has just described and between him (her?) and the little girl standing by the water.

The ambiguities regarding gender, in particular, are never really clarified. As the novel progresses and the narrator takes on a masculine identity, the reader may either forget the questions raised by the opening scene, or assume he has misread the chapter. The problem does not go away, however, for just as Mary Anne Evans remains behind George Eliot and the narrator, so does the first chapter remain anterior to the rest of the book.

Not only does one have difficulty at times *not* remembering that George Eliot is a fiction, and not only does one have trouble at times accepting the convention of the male narrator, but one also has problems with the author's use of Maggie as heroine of the book. Although Eliot gives considerable attention to the character's particular problems as a female, it is clear nonetheless that Maggie's experience is meant to be seen as generally analogous to the experiences of the other characters in the novel, male as well as female. In other words, Maggie has a synecdochic function in the novel: she, a young girl, stands for man, for human beings in general. When Maggie cuts her hair in anger and then immediately regrets her act and bursts into sobs, the narrator takes the opportunity to comment on the generality of the experience of adults forgetting the importance of the tragedies of childhood, thereby reinforcing Maggie's synecdochic role. It is at this point, however, that he chooses to express himself as an unequivocally male (human) narrator who addresses himself to a male (human) reader by referring to 'our youth and manhood,' and common problems with frocks, trousers, and tails [*MF*, pp. 122–3]. Following as it does Maggie's very particular act of defiance against her female condition, this passage from the particular to the 'general' seems a jarring one.[43] □

Most significant of all, however, is Weed's own admission, added in the following note.

■ Equally jarring, from my point of view, is my own use of the generic 'he' when referring to the reader of the novel. Having sacrificed my feminist convictions to stylistic simplicity, I have wittingly introduced yet another element into the play of genders, and may have, perhaps unwittingly, contributed to the dismantling of my own paper.[44] □

This brings us on to the subject of textual authority in relation to gender more generally.

George Eliot's reputation with regard to gender and, in particular, feminism tends to be coloured for twenty-first-century readers by the apparently negative stance she adopts in her early essay 'Silly Novels by Lady Novelists' (1856).[45] First published in the *Westminster Review*, one of the points of contention aimed at this essay by modern-day feminists is that the woman who was to become known as George Eliot wrote the essay anonymously, failing to disclose her own sex in the process. One key question raised by the tantalising ambiguity of the title is whether Eliot was criticising the silly writing produced by some women as a phenomenon likely to pour scorn on other, genuinely talented, women writers, or suggesting that all female novelists were 'silly women' capable of writing nothing better. In all honesty, the tone of the essay shifts uneasily between the two, never fully or consistently making clear which stance it is adopting. Take, for example, the following passage.

■ The epithet 'silly' may seem impertinent . . . but we use this epithet advisedly. If, as the world has long agreed, a very great amount of instruction will not make a wise man, still less will a very mediocre amount of instruction make a wise woman. And the most mischievous form of feminine silliness is the literary form, because it tends to confirm the popular prejudice against the more solid education of women.[46] □

One obvious question raised by this passage is to whom the pronoun 'we' refers. Sheltering behind the formal editorial convention is an anonymity that is surely inferred to be masculine, particularly in conjunction with the following.

■ We are aware that the ladies at whom our criticism is pointed are accustomed to be told, in the choicest phraseology of puffery, that their pictures of life are brilliant, their characters well drawn, their style fascinating, and their sentiments lofty. But if they are inclined to resent our plainness of speech, we ask them to reflect for a moment on the chary praise, and often capatious blame, which their panegyrists give to writers whose works are on the way to becoming classics. No sooner does a woman show that she has genius or effective talent, than she receives the tribute of being moderately praised and severely criticised. By a peculiar thermometric adjustment, when a woman's talent is at zero, journalistic approbation is at the boiling pitch; when she attains mediocrity, it is already at no more than summer heat; and if ever she reaches excellence, critical enthusiasm drops to the freezing point.[47] □

In fact, George Eliot appears to have been a writer profoundly at odds with her own gender, experiencing it as a monstrous obstacle/deformity to literary success. As Gilbert and Gubar comment: '[S]elf-definition necessarily precedes self-assertion: the creative "I AM" cannot be uttered if the "I" knows not what it is.'[48]

During the nineteenth century, the woman writer was forced to wrestle with perceptions (including self-perceptions) of her identity as a monstrous usurper, taking upon herself the authority 'rightfully' belonging to the father. Eliot's means of apologising is to inscribe her writerly paranoia within the narrative of her own text. For nineteenth-century women writers such as George Eliot, then, the concept of author/ity is one masked by a feeling of illegitimacy, insecurity and a lack of self-awareness as author/ity of the text that makes any straightforward relationship with a narrative 'I' intrinsically problematic.

Precisely how, then, does this anxiety of authorship manifest itself in *Adam Bede*? Here the voice of authority is quite self-consciously constructed as a masculine presence, our perceptions of characters being filtered, not through the eyes of a woman (as we might expect from a woman writer), but through the eyes of a man. Thus Eliot, depicting Hetty at work in the Poysers' dairy, opens Chapter 7 with a description of the dairy, only to continue: 'But one gets only a confused notion of these details when they surround a distractingly pretty girl of seventeen, standing on little pattens and rounding her dimpled arm to lift a pound of butter out of the scale' [*AB*, p. 77] and, more explicitly in Chapter 27, poses the rhetorical question: 'What man of *us*, in the first moments of a sharp agony, could ever feel the fellow-man who has been the medium of inflicting it, did not mean to hurt us?' [*AB*, pp. 286–7 – my emphasis]. Hetty Sorrel, of course, steals the show, despite Eliot's desperate attempts to make this the novel of the eponymous hero.

The very relationship between the title of the novel and the characters also contributes to such authorial paranoia. Unlike Austen's *Emma*, Burney's *Evelina* or *Camilla*, or Charlotte Brontë's *Jane Eyre*, Mary Ann Evans combines the joint assignations of legitimacy to her offspring by handing it over to her fictive, authorial 'father' George Eliot on the one hand, and stamping it with the nomenclature *Adam Bede* on the other. But readers are never fully convinced by either technique. We have already seen the inconsistency with which the purportedly masculine implied author speaks. Repeatedly stressing Adam's tremendous physical prowess, his earthy masculinity and his 'masterly' execution of his work, Eliot tries simply too hard to persuade us just how manly this man is. As Elizabeth Weed demonstrates, there are similar difficulties with *The Mill on the Floss*.

■ *The Mill on the Floss*, [despite] . . . its fictitious male author and fictional male narrator, finds itself ungrounded, decentered, by its female elements. Style is indeed dismantled by writing, as George Eliot is dismantled by Maggie Tulliver and Mary Anne Evans. And if the author takes such pains to assure us that the destructive and violent elements of the novel can be contained within it, it is perhaps because she herself is aware that containment is impossible . . . The narrator who speaks to the reader so fraternally of 'our youth and manhood', and who guides that reader to the resolution and closure of the novel, is also the narrator of the first chapter, that elusive figure of indeterminate gender who, far from establishing discrete categories, puts the temporal, spatial, and narrational elements of the novel into question and declares his/her love of fluidity and 'moistness'. [*MF*, p. 54][49] ☐

However, there is another level of complexity relating to gender that derives from the use of consolationist narrative endings and the disappointment so many feminist critics associate with Eliot's depiction of female characterisation. According to Dorothea Barrett in *Vocation and Desire*, one of the most impressive aspects of positive female characterisation in Eliot's work is the sense of literal and figurative largeness with which they are endowed: 'Dorothea's beautiful hands, for example, are large' and her identification with 'St Theresa of Avila, Don Quixote, Santa Clara, Cleopatra, Ariadne, and the Madonna' has the effect of 'qualify[ing] and modify[ing the] . . . passivity of the Virgin Mary' in relation to the 'power and activity of the classical female deities'. She observes: 'Most of George Eliot's heroines walk quickly as an indicator of their energy and lack of self-consciousness, and one gets the feeling that they are all metaphorically in advance of their companions . . .'[50] However, equally typical is Eliot's apparent insistence that these same characters capitulate to a conformity not found in her own relationship with Lewes.

Feminist critical opinion largely subdivides into two categories: those readers disappointed by the nature of the capitulations at the ends of Eliot's novels; and those who read the obvious falsity of such endings as innately subversive in itself. Kristin Brady falls into the second of these categories.

■ An important focus of the final chapters [of *Adam Bede*] is the restoration of the Poyser family to its former state of patriarchal stability, with Dinah conveniently replacing Hetty as the mediating link between Mr Poyser and Adam Bede (Poyser apologises to Adam after learning of Hetty's arrest, and Adam initiates his courtship of Dinah while seated in Poyser's three-cornered chair). Any satisfaction one might find in this union is undermined, however, by the rigid narrowness of the Poyser parents, who have from the beginning been implicated in Hetty's fate . . .

From this perspective, curious details in the description of the Poyser household seem appropriate. In Chapter 49, where the family is seen restored to happiness, their 'timid feminine' cows are shown being driven into the milking yard by an excited and aggressive male bulldog, and the animals are made fearful and confused by 'the tremendous crack of the waggoner's whip, the roar of his voice, and the booming thunder of the waggon'. The 'vicious yellow cow' which had kicked over a pail of milk (like Hetty, she has broken the rules governing female commodities) is seen undergoing the 'preventive punishment of having her hinder-legs strapped'. In the same scene, Totty is clutching a doll 'with no legs and a long skirt', which her brother later takes away 'with true brotherly sympathy . . . amusing himself by turning Dolly's skirt over her bald head, and exhibiting her truncated body to the general scorn – an indignity which cut[s] Totty to the heart'. Buried in the texture of the pastoral description of Hall Farm, these references to intimidation, constriction and exposure reveal a repression of the feminine at the very basis of the Poyser family structure.

That this repression will be extended into Adam Bede's family is also subtly indicated, not only by Adam's patriarchal name and his close association with Martin Poyser, but also by the repeated references to his views, paralleling those of the Poysers, about women preaching (he is also quoted – in his old age and hence after the novel's happy closure – as attributing to women ignorance of 'math'-matics and the natur o' things' [AB, p.172]). It is established in the first chapter of the novel that Adam is against the practice, and although he tells Dinah when he proposes to her that he will allow her to continue it, he eventually – as if giving vent to the same fear of a feminine threat in Methodism as that felt by the men in the Red Lion – expresses strong support of the Conference decision to abolish female preaching. Significantly, Adam's view is different from that of Eliot's own uncle, who, in proposing to her aunt (the original of Dinah Morris), emphasised that her marriage would not interfere with her preaching and who joined the Arminian Methodists with her so that she could continue to preach after the Conference had banned such activity for women.[51] In these terms, it is significant that Adam is the only man whose 'dark penetrating glance' can create in Dinah Hetty-like blushes and 'self-consciousness' [AB, p.109]. The *lack* of self-consciousness that had deflected the invasive gaze during her preaching is obliterated by Adam, whom Dinah twice calls a 'patriarch' [AB, pp.86, 312]. It is fitting, therefore, that the Epilogue of *Adam Bede* should focus not only on the marriage of Adam and Dinah, but also on the revival of the male friendship between Adam and his own patron in the class system, Arthur Donnithorne: with this recon-ciliation, the male power structure has been fully restored.

The symmetry of this restoration is undermined, however, by the presence at the end of the novel of so many supernumerary figures whose positions within the patriarchal structures of the Poyser and Bede families are tenuous or incomplete. In all of these characters, female and male, a repression of the feminine signals an absence or lack in their lives, even as they form relationships and 'marriages' that mirror patriarchal power structures. There is Bartle Massey, whose misogyny disguises his own maternal attitude to Adam and whose unspecified victimisation in the sexual market-place has been revealed in the scene when he goes to console Adam. There is 'quiet

Mary Burge, the bridesmaid' [*AB*, p.505], whose future . . . will be confined to taking care of her ailing father. There is Mr Irwine, who has forgone any sexual relationships in order to support his maiden sisters and to act as submissive servant . . . There is Lisbeth Bede, whose continuing position of powerlessness in relation to both her husband and her elder son finds expression in her querulous and helpless female language. And there is her own submissive servant, Seth Bede – in her view less than 'half the man' his brother is [*AB*, p.43] – who from the beginning had offered complete freedom to Dinah and who is made 'silent' by Adam on the 'standing subject of difference' between them, the issue of women preaching . . . Seth's solitary presence at the end of *Adam Bede*, like that of the other characters whose desires remain unfulfilled, exposes the suppression that is required to maintain patriarchy. For the standard romance plot to work, Eliot's narrative reveals, supernumerary desires must be marginalised, the female voice that deflects the male gaze must be silenced, and the unjustly punished Medusa, with her anguished face, must be banished.[52] □

A similar stance is adopted in relation to *The Mill on the Floss*. Brady reminds us that, at the start of the novel, Maggie is '"gone nine" – a year younger than Hetty Sorrel when she was taken in by the Poysers', but, whereas the intervening years between this stage and that of the action of *Adam Bede* are erased from the reader's view, *The Mill on the Floss* plays them out before our eyes:

■ Maggie's position in the Tulliver household is, moreover, a variation of Hetty's anomalous role in the Poyser family. Though she is not an orphan, Maggie is, like [Hetty] . . . less than a full family member because of what patriarchy perceives to be her deficiencies . . . [53] □

Like the ending of *Adam Bede*, Brady reminds us that the consolatory epitaph to *The Mill on the Floss* comprises the words 'not of Maggie herself or even of Eliot's narrator, but of unnamed surviving members of the community of St Ogg's who chose the inscription'.[54] It is, therefore, another forced conclusion, one sufficiently uncomfortable for the disparities between surface and sub-text to be revealed. Again, similar reservations accompany her reading of *Middlemarch*.

■ . . . a predictable outcome of Will's worship of Dorothea is her subordination to him in their marriage, described in the Finale as one in which her 'wifely help' is 'absorbed into the life of another' so that she is 'only known in a certain circle as a wife and mother'. In this relationship . . . Dorothea is described as happy, but the narrator also dwells at some length on 'the conditions of an imperfect social state' that have kept her from pursuing her original public aims. Will, on the other hand, finds happiness in his private life while also becoming 'an ardent public man'. His son, moreover, acquires even more scope for development than his father had: in the Finale, much attention is given to the question of whether or not Brooke will cut off the entail; his decision not to do so makes Dorothea's son the heir of the Brooke estate who, when he is grown, has the freedom to decide not to represent Middlemarch in Parliament because he thinks 'that his opinions [have] less chance of being stifled if he remain[s] out of doors'. This son, in other words, has not only the freethinking tendencies of his father but also the wealth of a member of the gentry, inherited from his mother, and the masculine freedom to choose one career over another. His happy fate combines the best aspects of his parents' lives without their limitations.

The same range of opportunity and choice presumably is not available to Dorothea's second child, however, who is mentioned only in a vague reference to 'the two cousins' of 'dubiously mixed' blood who visit Celia's children at Tipton. Though this child's gender is never made explicit, the fact that the first is called 'Dorothea's son', not her 'elder son', implies that the second is a daughter. Significantly, the fate of this second and secondary child is a notable absence in the novel's Finale. Like her mother's influence, which the narrator both laments and celebrates as 'incalculably diffusive', this child is associated only with the 'unhistoric acts' that benefit the world but leave their performers in 'unvisited tombs'. The existence of this child thus emerges as one of several details that contribute to a disturbing doubleness in the novel's Finale: while presenting a happy closure to the romance plot and so fulfilling the generic expectations created by such a narrative structure, the Finale simultaneously reminds the reader of those aspirations the romance plot by definition suppresses or excludes. It is possible, in fact, that Dorothea's second child and presumed daughter is among those referred to in the Finale's darkest statement: 'But we insignificant people with our daily words and acts are preparing the lives of many Dorotheas, some of which may present a far sadder sacrifice than that of the Dorothea whose story we know.' In this conclusion to the novel's penultimate paragraph, the narrator's use of 'we' adds to self-accusation a strong charge against both the romance form itself and the patriarchal culture that demands a 'sacrifice' in some form from all of its women.

This emphasis in the Finale on 'the lives of many Dorotheas' may also be a reference back to the other women in the novel whose fates have also been interpreted in terms of the romance plot. Even Rosamond Vincy, for example, the figure from the rising middle class whose characterisation simultaneously epitomises and satirises the

ideal romance heroine, unknowingly pays a price for the perverse fulfilment ascribed to her at the end of the novel. Rosamond's very
destructiveness is the result of her unquestioning acceptance of her
feminine fate and her similarly unreflective adherence to middle-class
aspirations about rising financially and socially through marriage.
From the first mention of her in the novel, when she is discussed as a
sexual object by the men at the Brooke dinner-party, Rosamond is presented as a successful player of feminine roles who enjoys the
appropriating male gaze. As a result, even her suffering is trivial and
clichéd. As the narrator reports of the ten days during which Lydgate
stays away from the Vincy household, 'Poor Rosamond lost her
appetite and felt as forlorn as Ariadne – as a charming stage Ariadne
left behind with all her boxes full of costumes and no hope of a coach'
[M, p.268]. This cynical image stands in startling contrast to that of the
desolate Dorothea standing in front of Ariadne's statue in Rome,
oppressed by the baffling sense that neither her yearning for affection
nor her desire for masculine knowledge can be satisfied by her marriage. The contrast points up the main difference between the two
women: that Dorothea's desires extend beyond what patriarchy has
ascribed to women, while Rosamond's do not.[55] □

Ironically, however, once we see these two characters placed alongside
each other, we recall a description of the typical 'silly lady novelist's'
heroine given by Eliot herself in her essay.

■ She is the ideal woman in feelings, faculties, and flounces. For all
this, she as often as not marries the wrong person to begin with,
and she suffers terribly from the plots and intrigues of the vicious
[husband]; but even death has a soft place in his heart for such a
paragon, and remedies all mistakes for her just at the right moment
. . . [T]he tedious husband dies in his bed requesting his wife, and
as a particular favour to him, to marry the man she loves best, and
having already dispatched a note to the lover informing him of
the comfortable arrangement. Before matters arrive at this desirable
issue our feelings are tried by seeing the noble, lovely, and gifted
heroine pass through many *mauvais moments*, but we have the
satisfaction of knowing that her sorrows are wept into embroidered pocket-handkerchiefs, that her fainting form reclines on the
very best upholstery, and that whatever vicissitudes she may
undergo . . . she comes out of them all with a complexion more
blooming . . . [56] □

This descriptive passage could almost be seen to place Dorothea (from
'She is the ideal woman' to 'comfortable arrangement') back to back

with Rosamond (from 'our feelings are tried' to 'complexion more blooming'). The distinction between the two lies in the levels of irony employed in each case. Dorothea's sickly saintliness is, we know, problematic: it is via her irritating self-control that we are encouraged to distance ourselves from her. And instead of the 'tedious husband' of Eliot's essay 'requesting his wife . . . to marry the man she loves best' and 'dispatch[ing] a note to the lover informing him of the comfortable arrangement', Casaubon festers jealous fantasies and destructive plots about Dorothea and her friendship with Will Ladislaw when he is alive, and leaves a written Last Will and Testament behind him after death disinheriting Dorothea should she join with him in marriage. That the ironies via which the all-too-perfect Rosamond Vincy are described are far more transparent simply serves here to remind us how similar these two apparently different women are. Brady also picks up on this encoded similarity.

■ The Ariadne image also suggests, however, that there are notable similarities between Dorothea and Rosamond, and these serve often to dramatise the extent to which both of them are able to seek fulfilment of their desires only through marriage. Like Dorothea, therefore, Rosamond fantasises about a married future that will correct all that is unsatisfactory in her life, only to choose a man who will fail to implement her plan. The first marriages of the two women are also similar. Lydgate, of course, is presented more sympathetically than Casaubon, but, like the older man, he expects that his marriage will give him additional time for his career and so looks forward to the end of courtship. Lydgate's condescending attitude toward women makes his choice of Rosamond a natural one: while she seeks a man who will elevate her socially, he looks for a woman who is 'polished, refined', and 'docile' [M, p.147]. For him, as for Casaubon, 'one of the prettiest attitudes of the feminine mind' is 'to adore a man's pre-eminence without too precise a knowledge of what it consist[s] in' [M, p.240]. For this reason, though Lydgate in his 'narrowed lot' [M, p.715] invites sympathy after he is defeated by Rosamond's 'studied negation' and 'inward opposition' to him [M, p.576], it is also apparent that he is paying the price for his patriarchal view of women. Attracted to them . . . for what he perceives to be 'the weakness of their frames and the delicate poise of their health both in body and mind' [M, p.582], he is mastered by a woman who uses her subordination as an instrument of power. The Lydgate marriage is thus a grotesque parody of the romantic ideal that requires the absorption of the woman's life in the man's. In these terms, it is significant that the references in the Finale to Rosamond's happiness with her second husband, while sardonically reported, do not include any of the qualifiers that are attached to

Dorothea's fulfilment in her second marriage: for Rosamond, the romance plot imposes no limitations on her desire precisely because her desire, so perfectly in accordance with her position in patriarchy, is itself so limited.

The third major focus of the romance plot in *Middlemarch*, the marriage of Mary Garth and Fred Vincy, appears to offer a simpler, more pastoral version of the courtship narrative than the Dorothea and Rosamond stories. Mary, indeed, who represents the lower middle class, stands in radical contrast with both of the other two women. Unlike Dorothea in her first marriage, she prefers to look down on her husband and assumes a maternal rather than a daughterly relationship with him. Unlike both Dorothea and Rosamond in their first marriages, moreover, she has no illusions about how her husband will transform her life. All of Mary's decisions are presented as compromises, choices of a lesser evil: she nurses Featherstone in order to avoid being a governess; when he dies, she arranges for a position in a school in York because she is *'less unfit* to teach in a school than in a family' [[*M*, p. 358] – emphasis added]; when Fred's prospects look unpromising, she resolves to remain, in defiance of the stereotype of the old maid, 'single and merry' [*M*, p. 738] and she finally marries Fred rather than Mr Farebrother, who can offer her 'new dignities and an acknowledged value of which she had often felt the absence', because she cannot allow any 'cheapening' of her original affection for Fred [*M*, p. 518]. The first three of these decisions are made in response to a realistic appraisal of her inferior financial and social position – in these terms, Mary's freedom is much more limited than that of Dorothea or Rosamond – but the choice of Fred over Farebrother . . . seems to reflect Mary's need to stand in a position of authority over her husband. As she says to her father, 'husbands are an inferior class of men, who require keeping in order' [*M*, p. 739] . . .

The irony directed at the marriage of Mary and Fred is generally mild, but the issue of how their values will be carried down into the next generation has serious implications. Mary is the mother of three sons and, the narrator comments, 'was not discontented that she brought forth men-children only'. The double negative here, however – in keeping with Mary's habit of making choices based not on positive benefits but on degrees of deprivation – emphasises her avoidance of discontent rather than any achievement of contentment. The comment is made all the more ironic, moreover, by its allusion to Shakespeare's Lady Macbeth, whose husband says these words to her after she has passionately urged him on to perform his role in the murder of Duncan: 'Bring forth men-children only!/For thy undaunted mettle should compose/Nothing but males' (1.7.73–75). Mary obviously has none of Lady Macbeth's violence, but the suggestion that bearing sons rather than daughters is a function of woman's masculine 'mettle' is disturbing, especially in light of the fact that Mary's book, written 'for her boys', is entitled 'Stories of Great Men, taken from Plutarch'. Such a book, which appeals to the ambitions of boys but not girls, seems a telling reflection of the consistent exclusion of Mary's own aspirations from her marriage. Eliot's personal notes on Plutarch, which mention 'heroic wifehood' in the Cleomenes story and allude to 'Plutarch's Interpretation Concerning the Virtues of Women', suggest all the more strongly that the presence of female subordination is a necessary condition for male greatness.[57] In their parents' marriage and in the narratives their mother writes down for them, this is the understanding of gender difference offered to Mary Garth's sons.

The same lesson is also imposed on Mary's younger siblings, Ben and Letty, who have been present in many of the Garth family scenes as representing still another version of the hierarchical sibling relationship seen in Maggie and Tom Tulliver . . . and Dorothea's unnamed children. Ben is seen from the first time he appears as an aggressive child obsessed with power: he uses Fred's whip to torment a cat, asks Mary to make with breadcrumbs the image of a peacock, and thinks his father is like Cincinnatus, whose heroism he has learned about from his educated mother. Letty, on the other hand, has a life that is continually 'checkered by resistance to her depreciation as a girl' [M, p. 511] and appears in the Finale, like Maggie, using the knowledge she has learned from books to defeat her brother's asser- tions about male superiority – only to be refuted by the 'oracular sentence' of a mother who prefers boys over girls.

The unmitigated frustration of Letty in the midst of the Finale's happy closure, like similar instances of discordance in the conclusions of Eliot's earlier fictions (her name echoes that of Hetty), serves not only to modify the reader's sense of satisfaction but also to draw atten- tion to the very assumptions and ideologies that underlie the romance plot and its conventional fulfilment. Thus both the limited happiness of the three married women and the frustration of Letty are based on the necessity within patriarchy that the feminine remain subordinate. As Eliot herself said of the Finale to *Middlemarch* in a letter to Sara Hennell, 'Expect to be immensely disappointed with the close of *Middlemarch*. But look back to the Prelude'.[58] □

This Readers' Guide moves on, in the next chapter, to a further consider- ation of Eliot's realist techniques before, in chapter three, examining the class-based implications of her work. In those two chapters *Adam Bede* is perhaps the dominant focus, although discussion of all three novels takes place. Chapter four is specifically dedicated to readings of *The Mill on the Floss* and, in particular, the role played by desire in that novel. The last two chapters focus primarily, though not exclusively, on *Middlemarch*. Chapter five outlines and examines Eliot's use of science and social science, while chapter six pulls together the major metaphors of her work, centring on the trope of the web or network.

CHAPTER TWO

Eliot in Relation to Literary Realism

FOR MANY readers (including, as we have seen in chapter one, Virginia Woolf), Eliot's fictions often stand or fall on the basis of readers' responses to relatively minor characters. Dominant among all of these is Mrs Poyser, in *Adam Bede*, who delights almost every critic with her acerbic turns of phrase, quick-witted speech and shrewish temperament. Indeed one might say that Mrs Poyser's kitchen, at the Hall Farm, lies at the core of the novel, not least because of its wealth of minor detail and her own perceived role as 'the voice of rural tradition'.[1]

Having already beckoned us into Broxton Parsonage in Chapter 5 ('We will enter very softly, and stand still in the open doorway' [*AB*, p. 51]), Eliot's narrator invites us to enter into Mrs Poyser's domain by 'Put[ting] your face to one of the glass panes in the right-hand window: what do you see?' [*AB*, p. 67]. These moments are simultaneously moments of invitation and exclusion. While drawing us closer they enforce the barriers to access. In fact they replicate the stance Alison Booth identifies with Eliot herself.

■ [Eliot] . . . assumed that a woman's disadvantage – which must become her strength – lay in her confinement to domestic life; her expertise must be in the detail of domestic experience, from counter-panes to courtship . . . But the woman writer . . . continued to grow restless indoors and to violate her threshold by stepping out. Strangely, Eliot . . . can be seen standing outside the door telling her [female character] how much more seemly she appears within her familiar environs.[2] □

Adam Bede is full of threshold moments, characters often being first greeted in doorways. This is where Mrs Poyser herself stands, watching the cows going for milking as she discusses Dinah's future with her. It is the stance adopted by Mr Casson, the pompous pub landlord, as he watches Dinah preaching on the village green; it is where Arthur rests and asks for

Adam's help as they both leave the Hermitage after the former's recuperation from their brawl over Hetty; it is where we first encounter Lisbeth Bede, standing on the 'doorstone' [*AB*, p.12], awaiting Adam's return, a stance she will later adopt as she waves Dinah off for what she believes to be the last time. Not the least significant of these scenes is the following threshold moment of the text, which takes place in Chapter 50.

■ [Dinah] heard Seth's step just outside the open door, towards which her back was turned, and said, raising her clear treble,

'Seth, is your brother wrathful when his papers are stirred?'

'Yes, very, when they are not put back in the right places,' said a deep strong voice, not Seth's.

It was as if Dinah had put her hands unawares on a vibrating chord; she was shaken with an intense thrill, and for the instant felt nothing else ... [*AB*, pp.465–6] □

Of course it is not Seth that waits on the threshold, but the 'ultra-manly' Adam with his 'deep strong voice'. That it is Adam and Dinah around whom this crucial threshold moment is woven should not surprise us. It functions as a powerful clue that the two characters will ultimately join each other in a joint crossing of the threshold into the realms of wedded bliss. And yet, as Eve Kosofsky Sedgwick cautions us,[3] we must be suspicious of Dinah's replication of Lisbeth's stance as we leave the text with Dinah straining her eyes at the doorway of the cottage, looking out for her husband – her new reason for life. On one level these moments of stasis suggest that, whatever happens, hearth and home will always be waiting. It is a reassuring reflection of rural 'real' life for patriarchs, but less promising for female readers.

The very fact that realist techniques move us towards a type of documentary perspective is sufficient to endow them with a sense of historical authenticity. But another characteristic of Eliot's writing contributes additionally to this, and this derives from the fact that she is often read as a regional novelist, a point of identification that tends to encourage readers (particularly, perhaps, readers of her own time) to accept the content of her novels not just as realism in a literary sense, but also as 'realistic' in the sense of 'true to life'. This connection may have contributed to the down-turn in Eliot's literary reputation in the early decades of the twentieth century for, as Q.D. Leavis observed in 1935, regional novels are often presumed to be 'some commonplace work of fiction made interesting to the Boots library public by a painstaking application of rural local colour'.[4]

It is also interesting to note how snobbishly scathing certain critics are about the Midlands. Leslie Stephen lists as one of his prejudices against Eliot's work the 'fact' that 'the Warwickshire landscape is not precisely stimulating . . . Shakespeare had the good fortune to migrate to the centre of intellectual activity [we take it he means London] at an early period'; Virginia Woolf is actually little better when she praises Eliot for her ability to 'make us share the lives of her Midland people, not in a spirit of condescension or curiosity, but in a spirit of sympathy'; and even the otherwise insightful Gillian Beer condescends to make the following point about the community of Middlemarch.

■ *Middlemarch* the book is something different from Middlemarch the town. It's worth emphasising this simple primary distinction because the inhabitants of Middlemarch within the book are so confident that Middlemarch is not only in the Midlands but in the Middle of the world; the book's expansiveness creates an effect of size for the town, so that Paris, Rome, and London look thin and small by comparison. But we as readers are made also to recognise its mediocrity. George Eliot, or Marian Evans, after all, escaped from Middlemarch. *The narrator's business in the novel is to remind us of worlds intellectual, aesthetic, spiritual, which do not naturally flourish in the provinces.*[5] □

Perhaps it is merely my personal identification with the Midlands as the place of my birth that causes my hackles to rise at such petty 'small-city' ignorance, but the larger point is, of course, that such opinions are inaccurate scholarship. 'The Midlands' is not *really* what Eliot is giving us and nor are Hetty Sorrel, Adam Bede, Arthur Donnithorne and Dinah Morris real people. They are words on a page – literary representations. We cannot 'live in' Eliot's Midlands or give the characters autonomy as individuals, however three-dimensional they may appear in print – even if Eliot's own narrator tries to persuade us to the contrary in Chapter 17 of *Adam Bede*.

■ And so I come back to Mr Irwine, with whom I desire you to be in perfect charity, far as he may be from satisfying your demands on the clerical character . . . I must believe that Mr Irwine's influence in his parish was a more wholesome one than that of the zealous Mr Ryde, who came there twenty years afterwards, when Mr Irwine had been gathered to his fathers. It is true, Mr Ryde insisted strongly on the doctrines of the Reformation, visited his flock a great deal in their own homes, and was severe in rebuking the aberrations of the flesh – put a stop, indeed, to the Christmas rounds of the church singers, as promoting drunkenness, and too light a handling of sacred things. But I gathered from Adam Bede, to whom I talked of these matters in his old age, that few clergy-men could be less successful in winning the hearts of their parishioners than Mr Ryde. [*AB*, p. 171] □

The obvious question in the mind of the reader on encountering this passage is what is its purpose? Mr Ryde's presence as a 'character' is restricted to this passage alone and he bears little real relevance to our view of Mr Irwine (for whom there are already sufficient foils in the text, not least Arthur Donnithorne). In my opinion, the only genuine function the passage serves is to entertain us with Eliot's own sleight of hand. In the guise of her avuncular narrator, she manipulates the historical juxtapositions employed by the text in order to suggest that Adam Bede has a real life beyond his story in this novel and is capable of conducting a conversation with a narrator beyond the text and beyond its own chronological scope. It also draws attention to the implied author's own privileged stance as 'a local' – inferring that not only can her narrator address the hero as 'our friend Adam Bede' (as s/he frequently does), but that the implied author herself is, indeed, these characters' 'friend'. It is a plea for authenticity, and perfect trickery for a chapter entitled 'In Which the Story Pauses a Little', designed purely to draw attention to the mechanics of realism. Unfortunately for Eliot it also draws attention to the *limits and limitations* of realism – and does so by overstepping them. Eliot cannot get away with this here, as the response of so many of my own students affirms.

I have said that George Eliot is often read as a 'regional writer' and that this tends to suggest her novels come as close to 'real life' as one can expect of a fictional medium. Her novels are also, predominantly, novels of the countryside, novels that self-consciously exploit the conventions of the pastoral tradition. Pastoral literature is dependent on far more than simply a rural setting. It is also dependent on a utilisation of idealisation, nostalgia, consolatory techniques of a number of kinds and certain reductive character stocktypes. Basically, then, it suggests a form of the simple or good life which is set up in contrast to the complex, difficult and rather unsatisfactory life that readers of literature know only too well and contributes to a sense of consolation and passive consumerism.

■ Arthur's shadow flitted rather faster among the sturdy oaks of the Chase than might have been expected from the shadow of a tired man on a warm afternoon, and it was still scarcely four o'clock when he stood before the tall narrow gate leading into the delicious labyrinthine wood which skirted one side of the Chase, and which was called Fir-tree Grove, not because the firs were many, but because they were few. It was a wood of beeches and limes, with here and there a light silver-stemmed birch – just the sort of wood most haunted by the nymphs; you see their white sunlit limbs gleaming athwart the boughs, or peeping from behind the smooth-sweeping outline of a tall lime; you hear their soft liquid laughter – but if you look with a too curious sacrilegious eye, they vanish behind the silvery beeches, they make you believe that their voice was only a running brooklet, perhaps they metamorphose themselves into a tawny squirrel that scampers away and mocks you from the topmost bough. It was not a grove with measured grass or rolled gravel for you to tread upon, but with narrow, hollow-shaped, earthy paths, edged with faint dashes of delicate moss – paths which look as if they were made by the free-will of the trees and underwood, moving reverently aside to look at the tall queen of the white-footed nymphs.

It was along the broadest of these paths that Arthur Donnithorne passed, under an avenue of limes and beeches. It was still afternoon – the golden light was lingering languidly among the upper boughs, only glancing down here and there on the purple pathway and its edge of faintly-sprinkled moss: an afternoon in which destiny disguises her cold awful face behind a hazy radiant veil, encloses us in warm downy wings, and poisons us with violet-scented breath. Arthur strolled along carelessly, with a book under his arm, but not looking on the ground as meditative men are apt to do; his eyes would fix themselves on the distant bend in the road, round which a little figure must surely appear before long. Ah! there she comes: first a bright patch of colour, like a tropic bird among the boughs, then a tripping figure, with a round hat on and a small basket under her arm, then a deep-blushing, almost frightened, but bright-smiling girl, making her curtsy with a fluttered yet happy glance, as Arthur came up to her. If Arthur had had time to think at all, he would have thought it strange that he should feel fluttered too, be conscious of blushing too – in fact, look and feel as foolish as if he had been taken by surprise instead of meeting just what he expected. Poor things! It was a pity they were not in that golden age of childhood when they would have stood face to face, eyeing each other with timid liking, then given each other a little butterfly kiss, and toddled off to play together. Arthur would have gone home to his silk-curtained cot, and Hetty to her home-spun pillow, and both would have slept without dreams, and to-morrow would have been a life hardly conscious of a yesterday. [*AB*, pp. 120–2] □

The sensuality and idealisation of the above passage, taken from Chapter 12, is clearly evident in the language used. Also intriguing is the manner in which the narrator frames his/her gaze in the guise of Arthur from the start of it, even before Arthur appears in the passage as the onlooker into the middle distance. His characteristically evasive stance on the (im)morality of his actions is there in the idealised image of the nymphs of the first paragraph. These clearly prefigure Hetty, not least in their potential metamorphoses into other forms. As Nina Auerbach observes:

■ Eliot enmeshes [Hetty] with similes linking her with lower forms of life; at various times [she] is associated with a pound of butter, kittens, small downy ducks, babies, rose-petals, a young calf, a butterfly, a blossom, a bud, a peach, a brooklet, a spaniel, a bird, a pet, a 'thing', a canary, a water-nixie, 'a pictur' in a shop-winder', a 'round, soft-coated pet animal', a brute, a 'Medusa-face', a stone and death.[6] □

True to type, here the nymphs do not turn into 'scamper[ing]' squirrels, but into another exotic transformation: 'a bright patch of colour, . . . a tropic bird among the boughs, then a tripping figure'. These nymphs appear as if spawned by the landscape and behave in a coquettish manner in order to waylay and ensnare an innocent passerby (though we know that Arthur has set up this encounter via his interrogation of Hetty as to the times and routes of her visits to 'Mrs Pomfret, the lady's-maid' [*AB*, p.81]). Cumulatively the effect is to suggest that he is not to blame for the incident. It is precisely the type of evasiveness that Arthur philosophises about in the later discussion scene with the Reverend Irwine in Chapter 16. The difference is that here altercation is literally written into the landscape. Instead of a host of nymphs it is, of course, Hetty who rounds the corner, dressed as Little Red Riding Hood. It is she, the passage confirms, who is at risk from this predator.

Other phrases are worthy of note, too. We begin with a reference to Arthur's shadow 'flitting', a choice of verb that seems unusual for a hapless aristocrat, until we take in the reference to the 'butterfly kiss' with which the passage ends. Arthur is flirtatious, like a butterfly, drifting from entertainment to entertainment. But 'flitted' also suggests something covert, secret and clandestine. Arthur knows he is trapping Hetty like a butterfly in an exhibition case. As the curtsy she gives on encountering him affirms, they are not equals, even if the ensuing description does its best to suggest that the two are rendered equal by the mutual attraction: 'he would have thought it strange that he should feel fluttered *too*, be conscious of blushing *too*' [my italics]. Only Arthur can end the liaison, even if Hetty were willing to do so, as the implications of such an enforced severence could prove very costly for the Poysers. Note also the double-take caused by the phrase 'It was still afternoon'. On the one hand this reinforces the sense of time weighing heavily on Arthur's hands, but also carries with it the suggestive phrase 'it was *a* still afternoon', evoking a sense of sultry heat that underlines the already sensuous visuality of the scene.

The fact that the 'delicious labyrinthine wood' is said to 'skirt' the

'Chase' conveys, again, the combination of prey and predator, mixing the gendering of both in a manner that infers more confusion than the mere reference to the maze of trees. Notice also the use of veil imagery. On the one hand this, alongside the reference to downy wings, reinforces the fairy imagery set up in advance by the allusions to nymphs. On the other hand it is a reinforcement of the coquetry of the gaze: luring on the adoring lover, only to cast the eyes down to deny one's involvement in the seduction. The larger question for our purposes is to what extent this is a passage of realist description and to what extent it is fantasy, pastoral idyllicism, or pure symbolism. The truth is, of course, that in order to take pleasure in the nostalgic escapism of true pastoral writing we must carry with us an awareness of the 'otherness' with which such passages are endowed, and which help to shore up the 'romance' they convey. But the pastoral tone of the passage also has another, ideological dimension in pursuing the dynamics of the Little Red Riding Hood mythology. Here Hetty is not just a symbol of 'simplicity', but also inferiority.

Ian Adam's article, 'The Structure of Realisms in *Adam Bede*',[7] argues that the realism of the novel is not challenged by its pastoral elements but operates hand in hand with them.

■ Whatever traps for the unwary lie in the term 'realism,' few would quarrel over its appropriateness for *Adam Bede*. The characters in the novel are ordinary in either social class or native endowment and frequently in both, its tragic action grows out of a commonplace seduction, and its setting is humble and representatively agrarian. Perhaps even more important is the treatment of these subjects: there is a high degree of consistency and historical accuracy in details of time and place, the background is richly and minutely crowded with particulars, and the account of characters' motives always stresses ordinary causes, rationally explicable. It is of course possible and probably valuable to qualify: one may argue that Adam is idealized, or that various rural discomforts are suppressed in the picture of Hayslope, or that the moral framework stands out at times too nakedly from a decent covering of detail. But such qualifications are themselves parasitic on the overall impression of realism which makes them salient. *Adam Bede* is a realistic novel.

The distinction between realism of subject and realism of procedure is an important one. The first may be said to lie in the choice of commonplace subject matter, and the second in the degree of accuracy and particularity with which it is rendered. There is sometimes debate over which of these essentially defines realism, with, I think, the better arguments going to those who support procedure over subject, but the debate is not relevant here. Both kinds of realism exist in *Adam Bede*, as they do in most realistic novels, detailed presentation tending to go hand in hand with the selection of a commonplace and usually unfamiliar and unconventional subject. Realism of subject in the novel has perhaps had the most thorough treatment, particularly in discussion of the rustic background and the 'unheroic' nature of the central characters. But definition of the kinds, functions, and significance of its realistic procedures is, it seems to me, much closer to a mere beginning.

There are many kinds of procedural realism in *Adam Bede*. The novel conforms to Ian Watt's description of realism as a 'general temper' which is 'critical, anti-traditional, and innovating' as particularly manifest in the use of a nontraditional plot, precise and discriminating references to time, and nontypifying names for characters.[8] One may atomize and discuss further: there is, for example, the crowded particularity of background and the stress on natural causality already mentioned. There is also the way in which the author denies not merely literary conventions but also her own, in the defeat of expectations created for us from her characters. They surprise us. For example, Mrs Poyser has always been severe with Hetty, yet it is she, not her husband, who is charitable when the news of Hetty's crime comes out. Or we might expect a redemption of Hetty through forgiveness of Arthur in her last words in the novel, but she tells Adam only that she will 'try' to forgive 'for else God won't forgive me.' Hetty is altered by suffering, but forgiveness is still (and understandably) more effort than fact, and the prudential calculus is not entirely eliminated. Or there are the well-known psychological correlatives which make particular the psychological states generally described: Hetty's narcissistic ritual in front of her mirror in [C]hapter 15, or Arthur's evasive horse ride to Norburne in [C]hapter 12. These are realistic; they are demonstrative. Similar are the illustrations of 'real' peasant life as seen in the dancing at Arthur's birthday feast, or in the skeptical reactions to Dinah's preaching, or in the antics of the harvest supper. My point is not to provide an exhaustive list of the procedural 'realisms' of *Adam Bede*, but to suggest their variety, before discussing three kinds which seem to me to have broad structural significance. I will begin with three illustrative quotations. In the first, Martin Poyser is going to church with his family to attend the funeral of Thias Bede.

> The damp hay that must be scattered and turned afresh tomorrow was not a cheering sight to Mr Poyser, who during hay and corn harvest had often some mental struggles as to the benefits of a day of rest; but no temptation would have induced him to carry on any field-work, however early in the morning, on a Sunday; for had not Michael Holdsworth had a pair of oxen 'sweltered' while he was ploughing on Good Friday? That was a demonstration that work on sacred days was a wicked thing; and with wickedness of

any sort Martin Poyser was quite clear that he would have nothing to do, since money got by such means would never prosper.

'It a'most makes your fingers itch to be at the hay now the sun shines so,' he observed, as they passed through the 'Big Meadow.' 'But it's poor foolishness to think o' saving by going against your conscience. There's that Jim Wakefield, as they used to call "Gentleman Wakefield," used to do the same of a Sunday as o' week-days, and took no heed to right or wrong, as if there was nayther God nor devil. An' what's he come to? Why, I saw him myself last market-day a-carrying a basket wi' oranges in't.' [AB, pp. 182–3]

This passage is leisurely in procedure. We follow Martin Poyser's eye as it glances over the damp hay in the fields; we hear, in a mixture of authorial information and Poyser reflection, of his scruples about Sunday work, and are treated to rural anecdotes which justify them. These anecdotes deal with characters who have no relation at all to any major action in the novel, yet the circumstantiality of presentation suggests that their nature and doings are richly known, that there could be further digression on them if Martin (or the author) chose to make it, just as we could learn more about the 'Big Meadow,' whose precise naming suggests further detail possible about its place in community lore and topography. The theme of the first paragraph, the wickedness of Sunday work, is repeated in the second, which gives us another anecdote, only this time the repetition is given in Martin's dialect, a bit of speech which enlivens with dramatic vividness but adds little in significant information to the passage. Such lazy procedure is appropriate for the Sunday and for the rich rural background of the novel. It is generous, vivid, static. It is not quite pictorial, for there is reflection here, the inner world of thought, and there is movement, though slow. Yet I think we may call it, roughly, a 'pictorial' realism.

In the second passage, George Eliot brings the reader up sharply on his complacent view of Methodism.

And this blessed gift of venerating love has been given to too many humble craftsmen since the world began, for us to feel any surprise that it should have existed in the soul of a Methodist carpenter half a century ago, while there was yet a lingering after-glow from the time when Wesley and his fellow-labourer fed on the hips and haws of the Cornwall hedges, after exhausting limbs and lungs in carrying a divine message to the poor.

That after-glow has long faded away; and the picture we are apt to make of Methodism in our imagination is not an amphitheatre of green hills, or the deep shade of broad-leaved sycamores, where a crowd of rough men and weary-hearted women drank in a faith which was a rudimentary culture, which linked their thoughts with the past, lifted their imagination above the sordid details of their own narrow lives, and suffused their souls with the sense of a pitying, loving, infinite Presence, sweet as summer to the houseless needy. It is too possible that to some of my readers Methodism may mean nothing more than low-pitched gables up dingy streets, sleek grocers, sponging preachers, and hypocritical jargon – elements which are regarded as an exhaustive analysis of Methodism in many fashionable quarters. [*AB*, p. 35]

The second passage has something in common with the first: a deeply felt and intimate relationship with the subject, which is reflected in the details of 'hips and haws of the Cornwall hedges' or the 'deep shade of broad-leaved sycamores' which vivify the comment. But these are part of comment, rather than of description, and their point is less to re-create the past than to enliven it as part of the strategy for readjusting the reader's awareness. This is a passage in which the historian hits out at our conventionally cynical notions about Methodism, and its procedure is not that of leisurely and digressive reminiscence but rather that of thought, in which statement of the cultural role of Methodism moves to culmination in an ironic address to the reader on his clichés. The realism is analytic.

In the third passage, Hetty contemplates her desolation and her resources.

It was then she thought of her locket and earrings, and seeing her pocket lie near, she reached it and spread the contents on the bed before her. There were the locket and earrings in the little velvet-lined boxes, and with them there was a beautiful silver thimble which Adam had bought her, the words 'Remember me' making the ornament of the border; a steel purse, with her one shilling in it, and a small red-leather case fastening with a strap. Those beautiful little earrings with their delicate pearls and garnet, that she had tried in her ears with such longing in the bright sunshine on the 30th of July! She had no longing to put them in her ears now: her head with its dark rings of hair lay back languidly on the pillow, and the sadness that rested about her brow and eyes was something too hard for regretful memory. Yet she put her hands up to her ears: it was because there were some thin gold rings in them, which were also worth a little money. Yes, she could surely get some money for her ornaments: those Arthur had given her must have cost a great deal of money. The landlord and landlady had been good to her; perhaps they would help her to get the money for these things. [*AB*, pp. 360–1]

The third passage neither explains or lulls. We are acutely involved in another human being's plight. Details are a function of her necessity, not of rhetorical strategy or the desire to establish a setting. The locket, earrings, the silver thimble serve both to underline the pathos of Hetty's resources and to remind us of another time, when, ironically, earrings seemed an adequate resource for dealing with the world, even when incompatibility held with Adam's practical gift of a thimble. Now they function like the shilling in the purse: a source of cash for Hetty's desperate and hopeless journey, underlining in their inadequacy her pathos and naïveté. There is no suggestion of leisure or stability, but rather of urgent pressures, as desperation narrows Hetty's concentration to spare details, and the clauses record the calculations by which she strives to maintain some shreds of security. This realism is dramatic.

The pictorial mode is that of the novel's lavish background of Loamshire and its centers of Hayslope village and the Hall Farm. It is dominant in the first three books of the novel, and renewed in the sixth, the final. We know from biographical information that its source lies in George Eliot's memories of childhood, but the clue is given stylistically as well in the lingering clauses and rich, affectionately rendered detail . . . the 'spots of time' through which memory may make up an Eden in individual consciousness. We are not surprised to find many echoes of *Paradise Lost* in *Adam Bede*.[9] Time recaptured, for both individuals and cultures, tends to take on qualities of fecundity and stability and permanence . . .

We usually think of these as being suggested by the inclusiveness of the realism, by its plenitude. Few novels are as lavish in their background as *Adam Bede*. In the most obvious sense this inclusiveness may be seen in the sheer variety of rural activities presented (and described in chapter headings), either those of work ('The Dairy,' 'The Workshop') or, more frequently, those of leisure ('Church,' 'The Harvest Supper,' 'Going to the Birthday Feast'). But even more importantly the inclusiveness is suggested by the nature and quality of the smaller formal elements which are framed and contained within those activities. There are first of all the many descriptive passages which act as static centers for the background. In these the author pauses for a survey of a particular scene or object of interest which she (at times oversolicitously) presents in detail for the reader. Sometimes it is a character rather than the author who does the viewing, but that makes little difference. Here is part of the scene which greets Adam and Hetty as they return to the farmhouse after one of the ironic love scenes of the early chapters.

The yard was full of life now: Marty was letting the screaming geese through the gate, and wickedly provoking the gander by hissing at him; the granary door was groaning on its hinges as Alick shut it, after dealing out the corn; the horses were being led out to watering, amidst much barking of all the three dogs, and many 'whups' from Tim the ploughman, as if the heavy animals who held down their meek, intelligent heads, and lifted their shaggy feet so deliberately, were likely to rush wildly in every direction but the right. Everybody was come back from the meadow; and when Hetty and Adam entered the house-place, Mr Poyser was seated in the three-cornered chair, and the grandfather in the large arm-chair opposite, looking on with pleasant expectation while the supper was being laid on the oak table. [*AB*, p. 212]

In such passages action stops and the viewer is dissolved in our sense of what is seen. Details are abundant and arranged compositionally so that even activities like shutting the granary door or leading the horses to watering are reduced and subordinated as parts of a whole, in slow motion, little different in function from the three-cornered chair or the grandfather in the large arm-chair. The subordination is reflected in the structure of the sentences. The sentence here is not the container of a single perception, nor do its clauses have that tightness of organization and progression of movement of a sentence based on the discriminations of argument or the stages of event. The sentence is rather the frame for a series of more or less equally emphasized perceptions. Its activity is the activity of the viewer's eye, focusing leisurely on a detail or series of details, and its only logic is to take everything in without losing the sense of the whole. In this, its structure is microcosmic of the larger structure of which it is part. It is all, so to speak, time to spare in the study of space richly filled. There are many such points of steady observation: one thinks of the famous survey of the Hall Farm in [C]hapter 7, the description of the congregation gathered for Thias Bede's funeral in [C]hapter 18, or of our view of the leisurely procession led by Arthur Donnithorne and Mr Irwine to the marquee from which the games of [C]hapter 25 are to be seen.

But there are other kinds of details than the visual. An abundance of local incident and anecdote gives us a rich sense of the population of Loamshire, suggesting through the outline of situation and story that its members too could be subjects of books. There is a recessive quality to such passages as those in which we are given Mr Poyser's opinion of Luke Britton's farming habits [*AB*, p. 134], or learn about Joshua Rann's feud with Will Maskery [*AB*, pp. 55–6], or hear of Bill's reasons for wanting to learn to write [*AB*, p. 221]. Then there are those famous details, the conversations at the Hall Farm over which Mrs Poyser presides with energy, randomness, and pungent illustration. And there are the details of minor narratives, of Seth's and Adam's courtships of

Dinah, of the consequences (or lack of them) of Dinah's preaching on the Green, or of the death of Thias Bede. These largely involve the main characters and may have certain links with the main action, but even more emphatically they function to suggest the normal life rhythms of Hayslope. They are like the 'news' of the small-town paper, not really news at all. Finally there is room for an abundance of explanatory comment, enlarging our awareness of implication and meaning. Such comment often enlarges to digressions: on 'realism' in [C]hapter 17, or on 'leisure' in [C]hapter 52; and there are as well numerous lesser digressions on subjects like whey cheese, peasant dancing, or the democratic seating arrangements at the Poysers' dinner table. Frequently the digressions are themselves defenses of inclusiveness, especially where it extends to the apparently insignificant, in rectors like the Reverend Mr Irwine who are not 'zealous' about 'doctrine,' or in lovers like Adam and Dinah whose language of courtship is banal [AB, p. 503].

There is inclusiveness in time as well as in space. The rural activities are suggestively presented as recurrent, as versions of social rites. Others like the group at Hayslope church have been there before for other funerals or other church activities. This is another Harvest Supper. Or there are rhythms more daily and seasonal than social: the noontime feeding of animals and men, the butter making, or the 'drowsiest time of the day' in the 'drowsiest time of the year' when we first visit the Hall Farm. Then, too, the frequent emphasis on objects visually perceived suggests durability in the very fact of solidity, an emphasis frequently reinforced by authorial reminders of historical depth. So we are made aware of the architectural persistence of Hayslope Church [AB, pp. 185–6], or of Hall Farm [AB, pp. 66–7], or even of the durability of such humble objects as Mrs Poyser's tablecloth, 'good homespun that would last for two generations' [AB, p. 212]. And more unobtrusively but more persistently, the same effect is achieved by a descriptive bias towards the definite over the indefinite article: in the passage quoted above, we note quiet stress on '*the* three-cornered chair' with '*the* large arm-chair opposite,' and dinner being laid on '*the* oak table' [Ian Adam's italics]. The anecdotal details also suggest continuity: the rivalry between Will Maskery and Joshua Rann or the dancing achievements of Wiry Ben function as community institutions, settled points of attention and discussion, in themselves and in their kinds as predictable rural topics as talk about the weather. And one could make similar observations about the conversations at the Hall Farm, which in both subject and manner suggest the security of long intimacy. If the inclusiveness in scope primarily conveys the sense of background richness, the inclusiveness in time suggests stability . . .

The sociologist in the novel merges with the historian who speaks throughout in details which not only ground the picture of rural life in a sense of fact, but also draw our attention away from the eternal human heart to the precise conditions which make its behavior explicable, which make it relative. Thus when we hear of the meal which Lisbeth has prepared for Adam in [C]hapter 4, its significance in plainness is underlined: 'Those were dear times, when wheaten bread and fresh meat were delicacies to working people' [AB, p. 44]. Or we are made aware of one reason why marriage is possible between Adam and Hetty: '[T]hose were times when there was no rigid demarcation of rank between the farmer and the respectable artisan' [AB, p. 91]. We also learn that among the several reasons for Adam's delay in marrying Hetty is 'the terrible sweep of paying for Seth's substitute in the militia' [AB, p. 199]. Similarly, Hetty's sense of guilt is defined as not merely deriving from her pregnancy but also from even more historically relative elements: the thought that she might have to seek charity from the parish, a disgrace linked in her mind with common beggary. '"The parish!" You can perhaps hardly understand the effect of that word on a mind like Hetty's, brought up among people who were somewhat hard in their feelings even towards poverty' [AB, pp. 359–60]. The 'rootless' Hetty, 'not only of a proud nature but of a proud class', shares some of her community's values, and not to her advantage . . .

. . . Among [the] many interrelated social values composing [this community's] code we note especially the importance of candor, the necessity of self-sacrifice, the regenerative power of sympathy, the dignity of labor, and the value of established leadership. It is now quite commonplace to point to the origins of such values in Carlyle, who was early admired by both George Eliot and George Henry Lewes, and selections of whose work were reviewed by George Eliot for the *Leader* on 27 October 1855, not long before the commencement of the writing of *Adam Bede*. And for George Eliot, as for Carlyle, this social code is more than a mere convention. It also represents a view of man in his ideal relations with reality; it represents the best possible accommodation he may make with Nature . . .

[Eliot's] authorial irony, surrounding especially Arthur but also Hetty and Adam, is portentous, for it indicates moral error, and that error is to transform the society of Hayslope into one altered by 'consequences.' Such alteration calls for another style, another 'realism' . . . [suitable to provide] the record of Hetty's flight, and that of the birth and abandonment of her child . . . This mode reveals the 'grim Stoniton streets,' the indifferent fall of the rain, the emptiness of daytime space and nighttime darkness. It is a mode which reveals a world opposite to that of the early books of the novel, and while this opposition is often made geographic, between Stonyshire and Loam-shire, the importance of the opposition is less accidental and literary, and the geographical distinction is, in any case, not at all accurate. Much of Hetty's journey takes place in 'woody Warwickshire' [*AB*, p. 356].

Time in this world is not slow, with an emphasis on the recurrence of rural rhythms, but fast, recording changes and emphasizing sequence. June 18, 1799, the opening day of the novel, spreads itself over four chapters, while one typical chapter here, [C]hapter 36, consumes seven days, five of them in one paragraph. Time no longer occupies space, a day several chapters, but space devours time, a chapter several days. The proportioning is representative, and must obviously change the impression left on the reader. He no longer perceives pictorial effects, those which come from the steady view of studied scene, but receives the cinematic, the sequence of image after image.

> At last she was among the fields she had been dreaming of, on a long narrow pathway leading towards a wood. If there should be a pool in that wood! It would be better hidden than one in the fields. No, it was not a wood, only a wild brake, where there had once been gravel-pits, leaving mounds and hollows studded with brushwood and small trees. She roamed up and down, thinking there was perhaps a pool in every hollow before she came to it, till her limbs were weary, and she sat down to rest. The afternoon was far advanced, and the leaden sky was darkening, as if the sun were setting behind it. After a little while Hetty started up again, feeling that darkness would soon come on; and she must put off finding the pool till tomorrow, and make her way to some shelter for the night. She had quite lost her way in the fields, and might as well go in one direction as another, for aught she knew. She walked through field after field, and no village, no house was in sight; but *there*, at the corner of this pasture, there was a break in the hedges; the land seemed to dip down a little, and two trees leaned towards each other across the opening. [*AB*, pp. 365–6]

The style here is not for time recaptured, but for time running out. The stress is on flux and motion, in the double activity of Hetty's mind and body. She is trying to find a pool for her suicide, and a utilitarian desire to identify and locate dominates her perceptions, as in rapid order pathway, wood, brake, gravel-pits, mounds, and hollows pass before her eyes. Verbs of activity govern her motions: she roams, starts up, goes, walks, loses her way up and down through field after field. And when she rests it is not the autumnal rest of watching 'the ooz-ings' hour by hour, as Grandfather Poyser watches the clock to detect 'a rhythm in the tick,' but a mere respite, a grudging tribute to exhaustion. Viewer [*sic*] does not dissolve here in our sense of what is seen; every detail refers us back to Hetty, with eye too practical, need too urgent, shock too imminent for any perception other than a glance, a classification, the occasional stray irrelevancy.

If with the pictorial realism the tendency has been for recurrence to spatialize time, to *keep* things before us, with this realism the tendency is opposite, to temporize objects. They are there, momentarily, for a brief purpose, then gone. In the section as a whole, for example, Hetty passes through many towns, but they mark her passage, not define her location. We have less a landscape than a map in which names assume greater reality than the entities from which they derive. The Hall Farm of the early part of the novel is a *presence*, but the towns through which Hetty passes, Stoniton, Ashby, Hinckley, Stony Stratford, Windsor, and Norton, are virtual abstraction. Who remembers them? I have mentioned that 'woody Warwickshire' as well as Stonyshire is an area of Hetty's passage and that there is scarcely any emphasis on the obvious topographical differences which exist between them. There is no time for it. Number also assumes importance in this section, as in maps, to mark distances ('almost a hundred miles from Windsor' [*AB*, p. 356]), but also, as in journeys, to mark time ('already five days since she had left Windsor' [*AB*, p. 365]), or, as in budgeting, to mark resources ('there were some buns in her basket – three' [*AB*, p. 366]). Food is not treated as it is in the novel's famous digression on whey cheese, but as part of the tragic countdown . . .

The 'realisms' discussed above do not exhaust the kinds of that elusive mode that might be found in the novel, but rather are dominant kinds. They have, as I have suggested, a structural significance, representing the background, causality, and action of the tragedy, being methods appropriate to the rendering of each. I want to argue their function in providing coherence to *Adam Bede*.[10] □

If it is, for Ian Adam, via the filter of landscape, the symbolism of the outside, rural life, that the various realisms of *Adam Bede* are conveyed, for Jerome Thale, in his discussion of *The Mill on the Floss*,[11] it is via a wealth of interior, domestic detail.

■ George Eliot presents a good deal of detail as causally connected to the formation of [her] characters. And that is not always an easy thing to do. Often enough these things can be a deterrent to effective characterization, a way of making characters the sum of their parts. A mass of detail is likely to produce a social history, not a full consideration of character . . .

The Mill on the Floss is . . . a presentation of the interaction of character, manners, and morals in a particular society. How it is all these things, and all of them at once, can be seen in its rich surface texture, its abundance of detail that is at once thematically relevant and part of the concreteness that satisfies our curiosity and convinces us that this world must be real. George Eliot had the fine discrimination which could make the world both spectacle and vehicle. The Dodsons (Tom and Maggie's maternal aunts), for example, are as significant as they are live. Touch them on their domestic side and you see closets, linen, wills, sugar tongs. These minutiae are in fact the outward signs of a code which embraces and penetrates every aspect of life for the Dodsons, and which arises from ethical and metaphysical attitudes.

> Mrs Glegg had doubtless the glossiest and crispest brown curls in her drawers, as well as curls in various degrees of fuzzy laxness; but to look out on the week-day world from under a crisp and glossy front, would be to introduce a most dreamlike and unpleasant confusion between the sacred and the secular. Occasionally, indeed, Mrs Glegg wore one of her third-best fronts on a week-day visit, but not at a sister's house . . . [*MF*, p. 108]

> When one of the family was in trouble or sickness, all the rest went to visit the unfortunate member, usually at the same time, and did not shrink from uttering the most disagreeable truths that correct family feeling dictated.

And there are rules to govern what one serves to company, what one accepts at strange houses, what quality of linen one provides.

These pieties of the Dodson life are more than an object of satire for George Eliot. It is part of the richness of her art that she is able to see the pieties from so many aspects. Aunt Pullet's correctness makes visits to her miserable for Tom and Maggie – they have to scrape their feet carefully on the second scraper, not the ornamental one, before they can enter her house. But the same kind of correctness makes Aunt Glegg defend Maggie after she has lost her character. In Mrs Tulliver, the 'weakest vessel,' the code is pathetic and absurd. When the family has been sold up she is unable to sleep nights thinking of her linen scattered all over England. Because she lacks her sisters' rigidity and clear-sightedness, one part of the code, the domestic, comes into conflict with another, the acceptance of fact. In the other sisters the strength of the code enables them to order their lives successfully. For them domestic rites and duties operate within larger sets of moral stringencies.

The Dodson code also has certain somber implications, not so immediately evident, but suggested through images of keys, locks, darkened closets, mould, and mildew . . . [Often] the note of mortality is muted by the humor and by the idyllic strain, but it comes through, ironically, in the images of death surrounding the code. 'Other women, if they liked, might have their best thread lace in every wash; but when Mrs Glegg died, it would be found that she had better lace laid by . . . than ever Mrs Wooll of St Ogg's had bought in her life, although Mrs Wooll wore her lace before it was paid for' [*MF*, p. 108]. The Dodson code, so exacting, and so demanding of continual self-denial, seems directed toward one thing – mortality. And it has its last triumph at death. 'Pullet keeps all my physic-bottles . . . . He says it's nothing but right folks should see 'em when I'm gone. They fill two o' the long store-room shelves a'ready – but . . . it's well if they ever fill three. I may go before I've made up the dozen o' these fast sizes.' The same motif appears in the discussions of one of the citadels of correct dealings with one's family, strictly equal distribution of inheritance, regardless of attachments or merit. Appealing to Tom's sense of family, Mrs Glegg says, "'As if I wasn't my nephew's own aunt . . . and laid by guineas, all full weight, for him – as he'll know who to respect when I'm laid in my coffin."' And again, "'There was never any failures, nor lawing, nor wastefulness in our family – nor dying without wills –" "No, nor sudden deaths," said aunt Pullet; "allays the doctor called in."'

Placed against the Dodsons are the Tullivers, chiefly Mr Tulliver. The huge mill-like man, with his strong passions and animal stubbornness, is the equal of the whole Dodson clan. If the images to characterize the Dodsons are linen, locks, mould, wills – images drawn from domesticity and mortality – those to characterize Mr Tulliver are the mill, the river, the outdoors, horses – images suggesting strength and elemental energy. We think of the Dodsons closed up in their houses fingering their keys and documents, but Mr Tulliver we picture swaggering about, superintending, looking like a man of substance.

In economic terms Glegg and Pullet are the old middle class who have more than they show, cautious families who have accumulated wealth slowly. Mr Tulliver is the man who appears more than he is. But economic categories will not do for Mr Tulliver; he is totally unfit for economic life. And this is at the root of the inadequacy of the Tulliver way. Mr Tulliver has too little control over himself, is too much the victim of his passions, to succeed either in the way of Mr Glegg or in the more spectacular way of Mr Deane, who has risen rapidly through a connection with capital. Mr Tulliver is even too restless and sanguine to be a laborer or an artisan. I do not think George Eliot is suggesting that he represents a way of life that is being destroyed by industrialism. In fact the immediate cause of his trouble is simply his insistence on going to law to defend what he thinks are his rights. Mr Tulliver's tragedy is that, in spite of so much generosity and commitment to life, he has so little control over himself that he cannot cope with life. Economics is only the most disastrous way in which his flaw manifests itself . . .

These two worlds, Dodson and Tulliver, are presented so fully and occupy so much of a book about Tom and Maggie because it is in terms of their *milieu*, especially their families, that George Eliot establishes Tom's and Maggie's characters. She may be concerned with heredity, but she uses it poetically or symbolically . . . Tom and Maggie are on the one hand merely focuses . . . of the conflict between different kinds of character in society. On the other hand, the society objectifies and magnifies those problems which Tom and Maggie must work out within themselves; it is only a projection, though a causally related one, of the individual's conflicts, enabling us to see the elements of the conflict largely and simply. Between Tom and Maggie and their world, between symbol and the thing symbolized, there is a certain equivocality. It is part of George Eliot's art that the novel is at once the story of Maggie and of two different ways of life. The emphasis and most immediate interest is of course that given by plot; the story is to be read first as about Tom and Maggie, and second as about the two ways of life, with Tom and Maggie as extensions and combinations, means of exhibiting the two ways and bringing them to test.[12] □

In a later essay Ian Adam perhaps offers a further rider to Jerome Thale's reading when he observes:

■ The Dodsons have virtually starved feelings into submission. Among the fixities of preoccupation with impeccable wills, domestic economies, pills and potions, the tight rolling of table napkins, the dangers of draughts, 'the thorough scouring of wooden and copper utensils', and the failings of neighbours, there is little room for [children's] play. The 'hereditary custom' of family ritual, sufficient unto itself, keeps order as firmly as the locked doors in Mrs Pullet's house keep rooms and wardrobes uncontaminated by human use.[13] □

The readings of Ian Adam and Jerome Thale are typical, in that so many critics of Eliot's work pay homage to her miniscule attention to detail. Henry Auster, for example, praises the 'technical minuteness' of *Adam Bede*, such as is demonstrated in her easy use of the vocabulary of joinery in Adam's recounting of the making of the screen for Lydia Donnithorne in Chapter 21.[14] For Joseph Wiesenfarth, it is Eliot's use of historical detail that is impressive.

■ In [*Adam Bede*], before dressing her characters in the fashion peculiar to the turn of the century, she read and took notes from Fairholt's

Costume in England. From hose to headgear Hetty Sorrel attempts to be a fashionable lady on a milkmaid's pay. She even manages to buy herself a pair of large earrings, which were all the rage in 1799 . . . '[15] □

U. C. Knoepflmacher combines both perspectives, this time in relation to *Middlemarch*, in situating its action within a wider context of current and historical affairs.

■ From the notebooks she kept it is clear that [Eliot] wanted all of [*Middlemarch's*] fictional events to be most carefully interspliced with the actual events alluded to in the course of her book. The allusions to the spreading cholera plague – like the allusions to Burke and Hare, two criminals who sold the bodies of their victims to medical schools, and to St. John Long, a quack physician tried for manslaughter – not only give us a concrete background for Lydgate's attempts to improve the state of medical science . . . but also allow us to establish the dates of purely fictional occurrences like Lydgate's creation of the New Fever Hospital.[16] □

At the same time, Knoepflmacher reminds us, Eliot is a writer of fiction, not a historian, the town of Middlemarch being 'a mythical community in the Midlands', not a real place.[17] Quentin Anderson, however, claims that Eliot's stance on realism has shifted by the time she comes to write *Middlemarch*, away from the documentary detail of novels such as *Adam Bede* and towards a sense of community less dependent upon external detail. Instead, we experience 'things felt and believed . . . [W]e know almost nothing of the appearance of Middlemarch itself, although our sense of the life of the town as a community is very full . . . '[18]

This is also affected by Eliot's increasing use of figurative Book titles, the most evocative of which is that of Book V, 'The Dead Hand'. Book IV has left us with a rare moment of gentle intimacy between Dorothea and Casaubon, as they walk, hand in hand, along the corridor to bed. The sense of closure and consolation conveyed by the chapter ending is, of course, immediately qualified as the reader turns the page, for the giving of the hand is, as Suzanne Graver reminds us, metaphorical as well as literal here, referring not just to the giving of hands in marriage, but to the fact that Casaubon 'attempt[s] to keep Dorothea's hand tied to his even after his death . . . [If the] joining of hands is emblematic of community . . . the dead hand is a synecdoche for organic perversion, for life become moribund.'[19] How revealing that this is the connecting Book which finally glues together the various strands of the text.

Carol A. Martin also reminds us of this interconnection by deconstructing, piecemeal, the elaborate construction of the narrative web that is *Middlemarch*.

■ By [B]ook 6, the several plot lines are thoroughly interwoven. Not only do Will and Mr Brooke frequent the homes and public places of Middlemarch, but Mr Farebrother lives at Lowick Parsonage and Lydgate is Dorothea's medical attendant. Farebrother receives Mary Garth and Fred Vincy as visitors, and Mr Garth supervises repairs at Lowick, Freshitt, and Tipton . . . What is striking is not only the inter-mingling, which Victorian readers expected by the later parts of a multi-plot novel; but the way in which, by [B]ook 6, Eliot has become skilled in framing her story as a whole. In [B]ook 2, reversing the order in [B]ook 1, one large section is entirely devoted to the Middle-marchers, then one section is devoted to the Casaubons. The ponderous historical framework at the beginning of [C]hapter 19 reveals Eliot's effort to bridge these two plots . . . Once she has joined the two novels [*Miss Brooke* and *Middlemarch*] and begins to write them as one, the char-acters' lives become linked and her 'bridges' are more natural . . . [20] □

But as all of these readings imply, realism is only one aspect of Eliot's narrative style, and not necessarily the one most responsible for her enduring reputation. Combined with it is a symbolic, metaphoric and intellectual framework of ideas that infuse Eliot's writing with a larger significance. This is reflected in much of the criticism on her work.

One influential example of such criticism is Dorothy Van Ghent's reading of the role played by analogy in *Adam Bede* and its relationship to mimesis.[21]

■ In Chapter 17 of *Adam Bede*, 'the story pauses a little' and George Eliot sets forth her aim as a novelist, an aim which she describes as 'the faithful representing of commonplace things,' of things *as they are*, not 'as they never have been and never will be'; and we are reminded of a similar aim as expressed by Defoe's Moll Flanders, who said, 'I am giving an account of what was, not of what ought or ought not to be.' It is the vocation of the 'realistic' novelist to represent life in this way; . . . but, as Defoe brought us to a consideration of the shaping changes which the 'real' undergoes as it is submitted to art, even to the most 'realistic' art, so George Eliot brings us back to the same consideration of the transforming effect of composition upon things-as-they-are. Her strongest effort, she says, is to avoid an 'arbitrary picture', and

> . . . to give a faithful account of men and things as they have mir-rored themselves in my mind. The mirror is doubtless defective; the outlines will sometimes be disturbed, the reflection faint or confused; but I feel as much bound to tell you as precisely as I can what that reflection is, as if I were in the witness-box narrating my experience on oath. [*AB*, p. 167]

We cannot avoid observing that the 'mirror' is at times defective, but since it is for the most part clear and well lighted we are not primarily concerned with the defects; more interesting is the analogy of the mirror itself – the novelist's mind as a mirror from whose 'reflections' of 'men and things' he draws his account. Men and things, then, do not leap to his page directly out of the 'real' but, before they get there, take a journey through the 'mirror.' But the mirror which the mind offers is not at all like other mirrors; even – leaving out of consideration defective glasses – very clear minds are not like very clear mirrors. Dangerous as analogies are, a spoon would be a better one, where, in the concave, as we tip it toward us, we see our head compressed and a half-moon scooped out of it on top as if it were a dime-store flowerpot for our viney hair, our body tapered to vanishing at the hips, and the whole upside down; or, in the convex, our eyelids are as large as foreheads, our forehead is as small as an eyelid, our cheeks hang down from our face like shoulders, and our shoulders hide under them like little ears. The 'mirror' of the mind shapes what it sees. It does not passively 'reflect' things-as-they-are, but creates things-as-they-are. Though we can clearly discriminate the quality of intention shown by a realistic art – and it usually reduces finally to a choice of materials from the field of the quotidian, the commonplace, the mediocre – yet its aim of veraciousness is necessarily one of veraciousness to what the artist sees in the shape-giving, significance-endowing medium of his own mind . . .

Technique is that which selects among the multitude of possible qualities, organizes them in the finite world of the novel, and holds them in a shape that can catch the light of our own awareness, which, without shapes to fall upon, is ignorant. Technique is like the concave or convex surface of the spoon, and the different turnings and inclinations to which it is liable; technique elongates or foreshortens, and while the rudimentary relationships of common experience remain still recognizable, it reveals astonishing bulges of significance, magnifies certain parts of the anatomy of life, of whose potentialities we had perhaps not been aware, humbles others. The massively slow movement of *Adam Bede* is one such shape-making technique.[22] □

J. Hillis Miller's article, 'Optic and Semiotic in *Middlemarch*',[23] shares Van Ghent's fascination with mirroring surfaces, but places them in a more sophisticated intellectual context. As the title of his essay suggests, the visual is a key theme in the novel, but it frequently works in a figurative as much as a literal manner and as symbol as well as theme. It is not just that the web connects, but that scrutiny is repeatedly inflicted upon the nature of the (social) fabric woven therein as it is held up to the light of communal attention. Bringing this process into line with the larger scientific concerns of the text, Hillis Miller observes that 'Study of the web requires constant changes of the lens in the systole and diastole of inquiry. Any conceivable observer in *Middlemarch* will be changing himself along with all the other changes and so will change what he sees.'[24] It is this last sentence that connects up scrutiny *within* the text with the nature of observation constructed by the realism *of* the text.

In figurative terms, therefore, the central model of *Middlemarch* is a spider's web in which, at each major junction of thread, stands a different character. From each individual's position we are given a full picture of their version of events and characters as if it were the full picture. But the distortions and contradictions in competing versions of events remind us that such 'truths' are simply fabric-ations.

■ Seeing, then, is for Eliot not a neutral, objective, dispassionate, or passive act. It is the creative projection of light from an egotistic center motivated by desire and need. This projected radiance orders the field of vision according to the presuppositions of the seer. The act of seeing is the spontaneous affirmation of the will to power over what is seen. This affirmation of order is based on the instinctive desire to believe that the world is providentially structured in a neat pattern of which one is oneself the center . . .[25] □

This stance is an important qualifier of Eliot's perspective on realism because it reminds us that, unlike the 'purer' forms of nineteenth-century realism, Eliot's draws attention to the inconsistencies of the narrative filter as a means of reminding us of the artifice of the work. She is not detailing history, she is spinning 'yarns'. This takes Hillis Miller onto the more complex issue of narrative subjectivity in relation to both characters and readers.

■ Superimposed on the models for the human situation of the objective scientist and the subjective perspectivist, interlaced with them, overlapping them in each of their expressions, is a model for the situation of the characters and of the narrator which says all human beings in all situations are like readers of a text. Moreover, if for Eliot all seeing is falsified by the limitations of point of view . . . [then] all interpretation of signs is false interpretation . . .

. . . [Hence] any passage [in *Middlemarch*] will reveal itself when examined closely to be the battleground of conflicting metaphors. This incoherent, heterogeneous, 'unreadable', or nonsynthesizable quality of the text of *Middlemarch* jeopardises the narrator's effort of totalization. It suggests that one gets a different kind of totality depending on what metaphorical model is used. The presence of several incompatible models brings into the open the arbitrary and partial character of each and so ruins the claim of the narrator to have total, unified, and impartial vision. What is true for the characters of *Middlemarch*, that 'we all of us, grave or light, get our thoughts entangled in metaphors, and act fatally on the strength of them' [*M*, p.76], must also be true for the narrator. The web of interpretative figures cast by the narrator over the characters of the story becomes a net in which the narrator himself is entangled and trapped, his sovereign vision blinded.[26] □

Hence, according to Hillis Miller, not just readers but also characters offer conflicting 'readings' of their own position in relation to the community of Middlemarch as a whole. *Middlemarch* is a novel in which characters repeatedly misread or misinterpret each other, try to delude or hood-wink each other, make mistakes which are not always rectified. The resulting effect upon the canvas which tries so hard to emulate reality is that pieces of the jigsaw will remain missing, misplaced, forced into posi-tion in a manner that will always resist closure or flawless mirroring. In effect, just as the opening of *Adam Bede* is a passage about authorial creativity, Hillis Miller reads *Middlemarch* as a novel about conflicting reading positions within and beyond its own frame.

Hillis Miller's is an interesting and suggestive interpretation, but it is not one endorsed by the seemingly more traditionally minded Baruch Hochman. In an essay satirically titled 'Recon/Decon/Structing *Middlemarch*',[27] Hochman takes sustained issue with Hillis Miller's article. For Hochman, Hillis Miller's approach is symptomatic of the ills of con-temporary literary theory and, more pragmatically, the manner in which he believes it to obstruct rather than facilitate the revelation of 'mean-ing', particularly in relation to literary realism. He opens thus:

■ Again and again, sophisticated readings, deconstructive or other-wise, direct close, corrosive attention to the language of the text and its psychic and cultural presuppositions. In doing so, they dissolve what once seemed the plain sense of its language, and obstruct entry into its world. It has perennially been the way of fiction to beckon us into the realm of imagined reality within which the action unfolds. To read a classic nineteenth-century novel is, among other things, to generate in one's head an imagined space within which to move, more or less as in a dream. To realize the world of *Middlemarch*, readers must be able to give themselves up with some trust to the language of the novel and to participate in the experience of its narrator and its characters. Such reading may be drubbed for its 'escapism' and its passivity. Yet it has been the gift of the great novelists to engage the 'naive', secluded, fantasy-prone reader in probing exploration of experience in the world.[28] □

Hochman is keen to stress that the type of reading (and reader) he is conceptualising is not one that is slavishly driven by the narrative voice or point of view of the text, but one that is capable of and willing to engage with that narrative voice and point of view in order to subject its assumptions and recommendations to scrutiny.

■ In short, there is every reason to interrogate a variety of elements in a text like *Middlemarch*. It seems likely that we will, in the current cultural climate, be impelled to contemplate the genesis of the text and its imputable purposes, to scrutinize it in terms of its duplicities of language, and to analyze its partialities in matters of class, gender, and ideology. And there seems to be no escape from the problematics of reading – that is, from the difficulty of determining single-mindedly what the novel is saying and what, finally, it is about or from the urge to challenge the designs it has on us.

Yet, even if we are committed to challenging texts and reading them against the grain, we must undergo some primary, some rudimentary, experience of them . . . To read against the grain, we must, to begin with, discern the grain.[29] □

At points Hochman's stance becomes almost tangibly irritable, taking issue with what he clearly feels to be the egotism of deconstructive readings that set themselves up as superior to the text upon which they prey. This accusation lurks in the background of his complaint about Hillis Miller himself, firstly when he contrasts the humility of the novel's narrative voice with what he regards as the inability of 'most of us critics' to 'listen' to a text, so determined are 'we' to clamour out our own opinions,[30] and secondly when he returns to Hillis Miller's reading of Eliot's own pier-glass analogy of Chapter 27, set out in the following famous passage.

■ An eminent philosopher among my friends, who can dignify even your ugly furniture by lifting it into the serene light of science, has shown me this pregnant little fact. Your pier-glass or extensive surface of polished steel made to be rubbed by a housemaid, will be minutely and multitudinously scratched in all directions; but place now against it a lighted candle as a centre of illumination, and lo! the scratches will seem to arrange themselves in a fine series of concentric circles round that little sun. It is demonstrable that the scratches are going everywhere impartially, and it is only your candle which produces the flattering illusion of a concentric arrangement, its light falling with an exclusive optical selection. These things are a parable. The scratches are events, and the candle is the egoism of any person now absent – of Miss Vincy, for example.

> Rosamond had a Providence of her own who had kindly made her more charming than other girls, and who seemed to have arranged Fred's illness and Mr Wrench's mistake in order to bring her and Lydgate within effective proximity. It would have been to contravene these arrangements if Rosamond had consented to go away to Stone Court or elsewhere, as her parents wished her to do, especially since Mr Lydgate thought the precautions needless. Therefore, while Miss Morgan and the children were sent away to a farmhouse the morning after Fred's illness had declared itself, Rosamond refused to leave papa and mamma. [*M*, pp. 236–7] □

The passage is, of course, directly a commentary on Rosamond's egotism, but critics have used it as a model for many aspects of Eliot's narrative stance in the text. For Hochman it seems to be Hillis Miller's own ego that is on trial. He continues: 'Miller notes that the candle of the analogy signifies the ego, with its projections, but so does the pier glass, which mirrors back the ego that contemplates it.' For Hillis Miller this optical paradox testifies to the undecidability of the text, which sets up oppositions in order to prevent passive reading positions from being adopted. For Hochman it reveals Hillis Miller's lack of common sense: 'When we look at the candle's effect on the surface of the glass, we do not see ourselves there; when we contemplate ourselves, we do not see the candle, the scratches, or the circles on the surface.'[31] At its most pointed, Hochman's stance can be rephrased as Hillis Miller's own inability to see the wood for the trees; but a more generous analysis reveals more clearly the crux of the disparity between these two critical positions. Focusing on Hillis Miller's fascination with the optical metaphors at work, Hochman argues that 'Miller reads the novel not as an action moving toward its crisis but as a tissue of language . . . whose elements may be related to each other . . . in isolation from developing characters and events . . . [This strategy] also serves to distance the reader from the novel's governing concerns.'[32] As the argument develops it becomes clear that the nature of the disputed territory (and the relevance of this debate to our own concerns in this chapter) derives from the novel's status as literary realism, a point that is really behind Hochman's objection to Hillis Miller's preoccupation with metaphor.

It is a long established critical paradigm that realism is metonymic rather than metaphoric in its relationship to representation. Where metaphor compares two conventionally different things (as in a *camel* being known as the *ship* of the desert), metonymy compares two things naturally connected. When, for instance, we ask if the kettle is boiling, we are really making an enquiry regarding the temperature of the water, not the kettle. The one is being used to stand in for the other, but the close and obvious proximity between *water* and *kettle* makes the substitution metonymic rather than metaphoric. The same might be said of the relationship between realist literature and the so-called 'real' life it represents. Realist narrative might be said to operate as a window-pane through which we are encouraged to view representations of the world through an 'undistorted' lens. The one (realist narrative) is in close proximity with the other (real life). Other literary modes (particularly those of an avant-garde or more experimental nature) may deliberately distort, manipulate, or experiment with that relationship in order to draw attention to the presence of the lens (the narrative artistry) through which we are peering.[33] Thus, for Hochman, Hillis Miller's main transgression is that he warps the text of *Middlemarch* because he identifies the novel with a metaphorical principle that must detract from the vision and re-emphasise the nature of the viewer. This disparity is almost made manifest in Hochman's mistrust of Hillis Miller's reading of optics themselves.

■ [In Hillis Miller's reading] . . . a constellation of mirror images is mustered to bolster a subjective reading . . . Mirrors are equated not with the traditional notion of holding a mirror up to nature but with narcissism, with the contemplation of oneself in the reflecting medium. In this perspective the distortions of vision with which the novel is concerned are taken to be at once representations of the distorting subject and validations of the notion that there is nothing out there in the world but the competing projections of self-encysted subjects.[34] □

Hochman accepts that one of the central themes of the text lies in the nature of deluded perception. It is a characteristic common to many of the protagonists and central to the relationship between Dorothea and Casaubon. What Hochman will not accept is that this delusion can be carried through to the nature of the relationship between literary representation and reality: 'Fred Vincy projects onto the world his fantasy of a providence that will help him liquidate his crippling debt through a gamble on a horse. His fantasy is real, but so is the horse that hamstrings the fantasy, and so is the debt that remains. There is, in short, a world out there . . .'[35]

In a subsequent essay, 'Teaching *Middlemarch*: Close Reading and Theory', Hillis Miller offers a direct reply to Hochman's accusations. His essay opens in the following fashion.

■ A good bit of hostility is expressed here and there these days to 'close reading' . . . there is also a lot of hostility around toward the 'abstractions of theory.' Theory is seen as words about words, more language in the void . . . [However,] though we need all the historical knowledge we can get – knowledge, for example, of the development of railroads or of the passage of the first Reform Bill or of what a tax-penny is – in order to read *Middlemarch*, it is only through the combination of close reading and the theoretical understanding that comes from it that the true (as opposed to imaginary or mystified) relations of literature to the real world can be identified.[36] □

Hillis Miller then returns us to the concept of sight and perception and reiterates the charge levied continually at realism by ideologically motivated critics: 'What is there can never be seen neutrally . . . Seeing is always interested. To see with interest is to add the plus value that makes what is seen a sign, as an innocent piece of paper or metal becomes a bill or a coin when it is stamped.'[37] By sleight of hand, then, Hillis Miller swaps his original optical metaphors for what he sees as another of the central signs in that narrative network that is *Middlemarch*: hard currency. There is, indeed, no more arbitrary metaphor than the relationship a bank-note or coin holds to the worth we give it through shared cultural means. The relationship between paper and gold is not, and never can be, metonymic; it is always metaphoric. So it is, Hillis Miller claims, with nineteenth-century realist novels such as *Middlemarch*. Returning to optics, Hillis Miller develops an analogy of his own: 'Seeing is reading, and reading means seeing one thing as another thing. To see one thing as another thing is to name it in metaphor . . . There is no language of realism, if that means naming things literally.'[38] He concludes with his own piece of close reading, based on a passage from Chapter 35.

■ And here I am naturally led to reflect on the means of elevating a low subject. Historical parallels are remarkably efficient in this way. The chief objection to them is, that the diligent narrator may lack space, or (what is often the same thing) may not be able to think of them with any degree of particularity, though he may have a philosophical confidence that if known they would be illustrative. It seems an easier and shorter way to dignity, to observe that – since there never was a true story which could not be told in parables where you might put a monkey for a margrave ['an hereditary German title equivalent to marquis'],[39] and *vice versa* – whatever has been or is to be narrated by me about low people, may be enobled by being considered a parable; so that if any bad habits and ugly consequences are brought into view, the reader may have the relief of regarding them as not more than figuratively ungenteel, and may feel himself virtually in company with persons of some style. Thus while I tell the truth about loobies ['bumpkins or louts'],[40] my reader's imagination need not be entirely excluded from an occupation with lords; and the petty sums which any bankrupt of high standing would be sorry to retire upon, may be lifted to the level of high commercial transactions by the inexpensive addition of proportional ciphers. [*M*, p. 305] □

Hillis Miller continues:

■ This passage is perhaps even richer than may at first appear. It may even be interest-bearing. It may be able to sustain the capital gains of a commentary. But does the commentary not rather tax it, deplete its value, use it up? In any case, the passage is odd, rather than even. It taxes itself, perhaps even to bankruptcy, not least in the uncertainty of its defensive irony and in the strangely multiplied negatives. Does George Eliot really mean to apologize for the 'low mimetic' mode of her realism? Surely, she does not mean the reader to take seriously the absurd invitation to think about lords while reading about loobies? Is the reader then to take seriously the alternative theory of parable that the passage proposes, even though it seems also presented ironically? . . . Does the word *true* or *truth* mean the same thing both times it appears here? What is the exact functioning of those double negatives with their qualifying adverbs?

The passage opposes two modes of elevating a low subject. One is 'objective' in the sense that it deals with external realities and external analogies. A historical parallel is presumably one that compares the low subject to some grander historical event on the basis of an analogy that is 'really there.' In the same way, both the historical event and the sociological facts imitated in the 'low subject' – for example, Peter Featherstone's funeral – are really there. The 'philosophical confidence' of which the narrator speaks is confidence in these objective realities and objective analogies. This is the mode of analogy between one event and another appropriate to realism as it is often understood. Why the lack of space and the failure to think of the historical parallels 'with any degree of particularity' are 'often the same thing' is a little puzzling. What mode of analogy makes them the same? Is this analogy to be understood parabolically or historically – that is, 'realistically'? Does the diligent narrator say she lacks space when she really means something entirely different? Does she mean that there is a blank space in her mind where the analogous particularities of history ought to be? Or does George Eliot here mean to call attention to a problem inherent in realism – namely, the superabundance of historical particularities? These inexhaustible particularities may be placed in metonymic contiguity beside any low subject. This would make a potentially endless serial work in which this is like this is like this is like this is like this and so on. It is a requirement of realism that all things be thought of with particularity. The double bind of this mode is that, if low subjects are left unadorned in their lowness, not 'illustrated,' they are merely low. If the particularities of history are adduced to 'elevate' them, there could never be enough space for the narration.

The untying of this knot is achieved by a shift to the alternative way of elevating a low subject, the 'easier and shorter way to dignity.' . . . In the parabolic mode anything can stand for anything, since the mode of equivalence is arbitrary and linguistic, rather than objective and realistic. The smallest, briefest, simplest thing can stand for the largest and most complex . . . Two models or parabolic figures are given in the passage for this parabolic mode. These are parables for parable. One is the arbitrary character of linguistic signs. The other is money.

The word *monkey* sounds like the word *margrave*, as *lord* sounds like *looby*. In historical reality a monkey is not like a margrave nor a lord like a looby, but in parable they are, by the accident of alliteration. There are, indeed, two meanings for the word *truth* in the passage – one historical or 'realistic,' the other parabolic. When the narrator says, 'I tell the truth about loobies,' she means representational, mimetic truth. When she says, 'there never was a true story which could not be told in parables where you might put a monkey for a margrave, and *vice versa*,' the truth is of a different sort. The mode of representation appropriate to parable is the substitution of one thing in emblematic shorthand for something that it 'not more than figuratively' resembles.

. . . The most literal representation – for example, George Eliot's description of Peter Featherstone's funeral – is also emblematic, which is why it is 'not more than figuratively ungenteel.' This, paradoxically, is a way of saying that figuratively it is genteel. It is figurative through and through and at the same time literal, which would also be the case of any conceivable description of a margrave or a lord. The distinction between literal and figurative breaks down in parabolic representation. It is replaced by a mode of truth generated by the relation between two interchangeable signs, each one of which is both literal and figurative, each one of which can stand for the other or be stood for by it. The relation between these signs is not that of objective similarity but a relation as arbitrary and conventional as the fact that they start with the same letter . . .

The truth value of parable is like the ascription of an arbitrary exchange value to bits of paper or metal that do not intrinsically have that worth, so that the same bit of paper or metal may, absurdly, be made more valuable by stamping more zeroes on it. The 'transactions' among parabolic signs, like the 'commercial transactions' carried on with money, are performed always with remnants left over from a prior bankruptcy or reducing to zero. The truth of a parabolic emblem is made of the ruin or emptying out of the referential truth value of the elements that enter into it. This odd fact about money and about parables – that their value is always constructed over a zero, or with what is left after a reduction to zero – is indicated by the reference to bankruptcy in the sentence that ends the paragraph: '[T]he petty sums which any bankrupt of high standing would be sorry to retire upon, may be lifted to the level of high commercial transactions by the inexpensive addition of proportional ciphers.'

If money as a parable for parable is set against the celebrated parable of the pier glass in [C]hapter 27, a difference emerges. Whereas the pier-glass parable is presented as an emblem of the universal egoism of human beings, the money parable is an emblem of the working of parable itself. Nevertheless, an element of self-analysis is intrinsic to the parabolic method as used in both cases. One passage interprets the other. The parable of the bank note indicates that the parable of the pier glass does not have to do with 'seeing,' nor does it argue that each person's perspective on the world distorts what is seen according to the needs and the desires of the ego. Nor is its 'literal' subject Rosamond's distorted vision. Both sides of the equation it makes are parables for the universal act of interpretation. Interpretation confronts things as signs to be read, not as objects to be seen correctly or incorrectly. To see something as sign is to see it as figure. To see it as figure is to see it as standing for something else with which it is not identical or that it does not literally picture. If the scenes of Dorothea looking out of a window or looking at the colossal spectacle of Rome show her spontaneously reading the world parabolically, the parable of the pier glass and the parable of the bank note show the narrator reading the world in the same way. This is true not only when she is most overtly emblematic but also when she seems most realistic.

The narration as a whole is simultaneously realistic and parabolic. It tells the truth about loobies and at the same time the sort of truth that may be told as well by means of a monkey as by a margrave. Or, rather, such truth is told by their substitution one for the other, with each as a figure for the other and neither having the priority of the literal. The relation among the various plots in *Middlemarch* is an example of this. Each repeats the others in a different mode, but none, not even the story of Dorothea, is, in the completed text, the 'original' of which the others are repetitions with a difference. George Eliot indicates this multicentered nature of *Middlemarch* when she says '[B]ut why always Dorothea? . . . Mr Casaubon [too] had an intense consciousness within him' [*M*, p. 249]. This consciousness is 'an *equivalent* centre of self' [*M*, p. 190].

Beginning with a single rather odd passage in *Middlemarch* where the activity of interpreting or modeling reality by means of metaphors and metaphors of metaphors is strikingly exhibited, I have shown that a close reading of that and other passages not only makes possible theoretical formulations about the relation of realism to parable in *Middlemarch* and perhaps in fiction in general but also leads to insights into the way *Middlemarch* is related to the real world. That way is multiple. The novel reflects social and political reality in Victorian England and gives a twentieth-century reader information about provincial Victorian culture. The novel also presents parabolic models for the way that culture worked. These models function as what may be called a critique of fundamental aspects of the ideology of that culture – for example, its dependence on money and the circulation of money as these are analogous to other features of the social system like marriage, family, and gender relations and modes of personal perception and historical understanding, as well as other class and political structures.[41] □

So Hillis Miller moves, through deconstructive textual word-play, to the political 'realities' of Victorian England. Quite rightly he asserts that complex and even playful readings neither detract from ideology, nor detract from the novel's status as realism. Developing this interest in the politics of realism, in chapter three we go on to consider Eliot's treatment of the class system in relation to ideology.

CHAPTER THREE

Eliot's Writing and the Politics of Class

ONE OF the reasons why nineteenth-century realism has been criticised by twentieth-century critics (especially those of a left-wing or
liberal political persuasion) is because of its tendency to promote bourgeois social values as if they are rightfully the only way things can be.
Because realism implies that it is simply documenting 'the way things
are' it is a perfect opportunity for duplicitous ideological stances implying
that the means of representation chosen is entirely neutral and thus
natural: it conveys not simply the obvious, but actually the *only* choice.
Realism, therefore, frequently works very hard to sew up any possible
hanging threads that might encourage us to adopt a resistant or interrogative reading strategy. Eliot's use of the pastoral tradition (which we
have seen Ian Adam locate at the centre of Eliot's realism in chapter two)
contributes to these ideological difficulties. Take, for example, the over-
weaning sentimentality expressed by David Masson in 1859.

■ [I]s it not well, is it not medicinal that . . . in the pages of our novelists . . . we should be taken away in the imagination from our common
social haunts, and placed in situations where Nature still exerts upon
Humanity the unbroken magnetism of her inanimate bulk, soothing
into peace in the quiet meadows, whispering of the unearthly in the
depths of a forest, telling tales of the past in some solitary crumbling
ruin, moaning her sorrow in the gusts of a moor at midnight, or dash-
ing the eternal monotone of her many voices against a cliff-embattled
shore?[1] □

It is worth asking ourselves, as a starting-point, what phrases such as 'the
unbroken magnetism of [Nature's] inanimate bulk' could possibly mean,
let alone why it is personified as on the one hand a whispering storyteller
and on the other a multi-voiced but monotonous moaner. But the larger

issue, of course, arises from the initial reference to the 'medicinal' qualities of such writing. To whom is it medicinal? The answer, we presume, is the reader, but only ever at the expense of the characters. In these terms a novel such as *Adam Bede* can only ever put on a sort of puppetshow, in which we delight in the spectacle and 'rural simplicity' of these poor people while they fall foul of exploitation, seduction, class inequalities, deportation, infanticide – not to mention poverty. Nevertheless, Henry Auster rather underestimates Eliot's position on class when he observes that:

■ . . . she was intent not on drawing attention to the suffering of the poor but on expressing her view of life. She was a genuinely intellectual person with a conservative bent of mind, and the problems that she thought important, the problems to which she constantly returned, were ethical and psychological – internal, permanent, and ultimate rather than external, circumstantial, and immediate.[2] □

In effect he is making a false distinction between intellectualism as a mental, internal, self-reflective preoccupation and social reform as something that is outside the realm of cognition. Both ethical *and* psychological issues impinge on class issues and Eliot's fascination with the new social science, among other things, inevitably leads her into the realm of ideology. At the same time, however, Auster is equally critical of readers who over-react to the pastoral aspects of the novel as too clearly suppressing any social critique: '[Yes,] work and the relations between landlord and tenant are idealized in the novel, purified, as it were, of all unpleasantness and oppressiveness. But toil is not the less real for being relished . . . '[3]

John Goode takes a similar line to Auster, setting out some of the hard social facts that construct the historicist background for *Adam Bede*, even though he goes on to qualify his remark:

■ The 'modernizing' influences of history are there in the novel. Arthur Donnithorne returns from Ireland full of plans for 'drainage and enclosure'. His grandfather tries to make the Poysers specialize as dairy-farmers, and, of course, Methodism is a force which sets Will Maskery against Irwine, which separates Seth Bede from his work, and which creates incipient hysteria in Hayslope. But none of these threats is realized, because George Eliot is concerned to demonstrate the intensity of tradition and the resilience of the core even in years of acute crisis.[4] □

The stasis that Goode identifies as a key element in this novel is frequently connected with Eliot's writing. But he then goes on to associate this static presence with a series of pictorial vignettes against which the social issues are played out: 'We begin with the static vision of the workshop, and when the men begin to talk it is as though a painting were to begin to move.'[5] In the first three books of the novel Goode identifies three such vignettes, all of which try to accommodate this tense relationship between stasis and social evolution: the death of Thias Bede in Book I; the church service in Book II; and Arthur's birthday feast in Book III. Though seemingly classless, organic rituals, the way in which different characters experience them is entirely determined by social status.

It is certainly true that our sympathies for Adam and Hetty in *Adam Bede* derive, in large part, not just from a genuine sense of injustice, but also because we believe them to be limited characters who know no better. Eliot's treatment of Adam, in particular, is very much that of the typical pastoral idyll, described by William Empson in *Some Versions of Pastoral*.

■ The essential trick . . . felt to imply a beautiful relation between rich and poor, was to make simple people express strong feelings . . . in learned and fashionable language . . . From seeing the two sorts of people combined like this you thought better of both; the best parts of both were used.[6] □

Eliot's approach can be more precisely illustrated using the following passage from Chapter 17 of *Adam Bede*.

■ All honour and reverence to the divine beauty of form! Let us cultivate it to the utmost in men, women and children . . . Paint us an angel, if you can, with a floating violet robe, and a face paled by the celestial light; paint us yet oftener a Madonna, turning her mild face upward and opening her arms to welcome the divine glory; but do not impose on us any aesthetic rules which shall banish from the region of Art those old women scraping carrots with their work-worn hands, those heavy clowns taking holiday in a dingy pot-house, those rounded backs and stupid weather-beaten faces that have bent over the spade and done the rough work of the world – those homes with their tin pans, their brown pitchers, their rough curs, and their clusters of onions. [*AB*, p. 170] □

The immediate context for this passage, coming as it does in the chapter in which Eliot's narrator sets out most explicitly the aesthetic manifesto for the novel, suggests that this is a narrative of social inclusivity in which all human beings (irrespective of class background) have a place in the frame and a right to dignified representation. The use of 'us' imposes a shared ideological perspective between narrator/creator and reader, and thus places 'us' in an uncomfortably unquestioning position.

But, as Simon Dentith correctly observes, this all-inclusive language conceals a far from inclusive 'realism'.

■ This [passage] has a wonderful solidity of detail, but it is little more than a rhetorical flourish in the novel as a whole, for it is certainly not to carrot-scraping women or heavy clowns that we are most drawn in *Adam Bede*, or for that matter in any of George Eliot's novels. Indeed, she finds it persistently difficult to represent such people sympathetically, finding their 'stupidity' and resistance to higher motives, however explicable, a heavy clog on the onward processes of social life. No, it is not to these people that the dominant movement of sympathy is expressed; it is to classes decidedly more respectable, in whose daily habits and values she can find evidence of the growing good of the world.[7] □

Aside from the usage of the loaded term 'respectable' as an implicit indicator of middle-class sensibilities, Dentith also identifies two elements of ambivalence in Eliot's work to which critics often allude. The first relates to an apparent paradox in her treatment of character, in that on the one hand characters are used as representatives of typicality in social/class terms, whilst also standing out against the backdrop of that class typicality as 'special' individuals (Adam and Dinah are perfect illustrations of such a paradox). The second locus of ambiguity lies in Eliot's projected readership.

■ The fact is that George Eliot's novels presuppose at least two different readerships: a naive and a sophisticated one . . . In one sense it is a *tour de force* that she can make the language of Evangelicalism, or the speech rhythms of Midlands artisans . . . sound like the advanced intellectual positions to which she subscribes. However, a contemporary reader's ability to 'translate' such language in the appropriate way is directly related to his or her class and educational position . . . George Eliot was most anxious that her novels should appeal to the 'élite', but equally desired, and rightly, that her novels should be popular. At times this dual ambition produces a kind of equivocation in her writing, so that it can be read simultaneously in two different ways. This equivocation is unavoidably élitist.[8] □

Perhaps it is this ambivalence that accounts for the ideological difficulties of the following passage, describing Adam's relation with Arthur Donnithorne in class terms.

■ Adam looked round as he heard the quickening clatter of the horse's heels, and waited for the horseman, lifting his paper cap from his head with a bright smile of recognition. Next to his own brother Seth, Adam would have done more for Arthur Donnithorne than for any other young man in the world. There was hardly anything he would not rather have lost than the two-feet ruler which he always carried in his pocket; it was Arthur's present, bought with his pocket-money when he was a fair-haired lad of eleven, and when he had profited so well by Adam's lessons in carpentering and turning, as to embarrass every female in the house with gifts of superfluous thread-reels and round boxes. Adam had quite a pride in the little squire in those early days, and the feeling had only become slightly modified as the fair-haired lad had grown into the whiskered young man. Adam, I confess, was very susceptible to the influence of rank, and quite ready to give an extra amount of respect to every one who had more advantages than himself, not being a philosopher, or a proletaire with democratic ideas, but simply a stout-limbed clever carpenter with a large fund of reverence in his nature, which inclined him to admit all established claims unless he saw very clear grounds for questioning them. He had no theories about setting the world to rights, but he saw there was a great deal of damage done by building with ill-seasoned timber – by ignorant men in fine clothes making plans for outhouses and workshops and the like, without knowing the bearings of things – by slovenly joiners' work, and by hasty contracts that could never be fulfilled without ruining somebody; and he resolved, for his part, to set his face against such doings. On these points he would have maintained his opinion against the largest landed proprietor in Loamshire or Stonyshire either; but he felt that beyond these it would be better for him to defer to people who were more knowing than himself. He saw as plainly as possible how ill the woods on the estate were managed, and the shameful state of the farm-buildings; and if old Squire Donnithorne had asked him the effect of this mismanagement, he would have spoken his opinion without flinching, but the impulse to a respectful demeanour towards a 'gentleman' would have been strong within him all the while. The word 'gentleman' had a spell for Adam, and, as he often said, he 'couldn't abide a fellow who thought he made himself fine by being coxy to's betters'. I must remind you again that Adam had the blood of the peasant in his veins, and that since he was in his prime half a century ago, you must expect some of his characteristics to be obsolete. [*A B*, pp. 152–3] □

The tone of this passage, which might well be satirical or even dismissive if used to depict a minor or peripheral character, cannot be discounted so easily when applied to 'our friend' Adam Bede. Instead it is characterised by a tone of benevolent indulgence. Adam is wronged by Arthur, but not because he is himself wrong to set him up as superior, the text infers. Rather than revealing the falsity of a class hierarchy that naively equates wealth with moral decency, Arthur falls from grace by not living up to his station in life. When we read that Adam 'had the blood of the peasant in his veins', the use of the anatomical analogy endows the class hierarchy with as much 'naturalness' and fixity as the wood with which Adam works. In addition, though the points on which he is said to feel himself well qualified to hold opinions appear, at first sight, irrelevant to issues of social justice, by further analogies, 'ill-seasoned timber' and 'hasty contracts' can also be taken as references to rising capitalism rather than landed and aged ('well-seasoned') aristocracy. The entire passage therefore becomes part of that larger 'golden age' of past idealism romanticised in part throughout the text and most directly threatened, perhaps, by the avaricious fantasies of social-climbing connected with Hetty Sorrel.

One of the ongoing cultural debates of the time, which Eliot employs to frame the relationship between Adam and Arthur, concerns the changing image of the figure of 'the gentleman'. As Daniel Cottom observes, quoting from the *Cornhill Magazine* of 1862, 'there is a constantly increasing disposition to insist more upon the moral and less upon the social element of the word . . . '[9] This leads Eliot to a more complex usage of the class hierarchy in *Adam Bede* than is often acknowledged. A similar complexity arises in *Middlemarch*, thrown into relief by the presence of Dr Lydgate. Lilian R. Furst, tackling the issue by linking the professional hierarchy of nineteenth-century medical practice directly to the class hierarchy, begins by sub-dividing the profession into three major strands, physicians, surgeons, and apothecaries: 'The prestige of the physician mandated that he use his head, not his hands, that he advise rather than do.' More importantly, in social terms, however, the physician is a 'well-bred gentlem[a]n with polished manners and a classical education'.[10] Apothecaries, on the other hand, were at the opposite extreme in class terms, operating as tradesmen, while surgeons are poised at the midway divide between the two and, therefore in class terms, the most difficult to categorise. It is to this group that Lydgate belongs:

■ . . . still smacking of trade on account of the use of hands and the dispensing of drugs . . . With the rise of the middle classes associated with the process of industrialization, surgeons were increasingly consulted because they were less expensive than physicians and more expert than apothecaries. But legally surgeons were entitled to treat only 'outward' disorders, 'internal' ones being in the physician's province.[11] □

Lydgate's social mobility is consistently equated with his literal role of incomer in the novel, but this reveals that professionally, too, there are dangers to the community's 'steadiness' in the undecidable nature of Lydgate's status.

■ From the outset [Lydgate] is immediately recognized as 'a gentleman' . . . who is 'clever' and 'talks well' [*M*, p. 82]. In short he has the style of a physician, although his qualification is that of a surgeon. His social background, too, is at least the equivalent of that of the higher type of medical man: 'he is one of the Lydgates of Northumberland, really well connected . . . ' Lady Chettam remarks . . . Even his Latinate name, Tertius, denotes a certain superiority to the more ordinary Fred, Peter, Ned, and Will of the other characters.[12] □

Speaking of the Victorian period more generally, Cottom observes:

■ [O]ne no longer deferred to the overawing person of the aristocrat. Instead, one turned to this moral figure of the gentleman, which was so troubling, which could not be fixed securely, because truth under the new dispensation of discourse was made to exist in the virtual relations among men, not in the exclusive properties of a class or a calling that could be symbolized by neat distinctions of blood, heraldry, or landownership.[13] □

Cottom's vocabulary here suggests a homosocial bond between men. But intriguingly it is with Hetty Sorrel, rather than Arthur Donnithorne, that Cottom pursues the concept of gentility in *Adam Bede*, developing it in the following terms.

■ Gentility did indeed represent to Eliot the past she believed had been outgrown through the history of England in the nineteenth century, but she also thought it represented a continuing and universal aspect of human nature. It was this that she pointed to in Hetty's vanity and more commonly referred to as egoism or egoistic desire. Ultimately, the past was interpreted by Eliot as a system of representation that objectified in the structure of society and all its associated figures an impulse to self-assertion inherent in human nature. Therefore, to evaluate her picture of the past of 'nearly sixty years ago' in *Adam Bede* and the past as it appears in her other fiction, one needs to analyze how she interpreted this past as part of the present. One must analyze how those characters most entranced by the traditional order of gentility in Eliot's novels are also those who are most egoistic. Moreover, one must ask why this is the case especially, although by no means exclusively, with women.[14] □

He continues:

■ In this portrayal society . . . is a collective representation, an ideal, suspended within the relations of a community and continuously referred to by individuals as the most meaningful standard of their lives. All of society is turned to a picture of a sun. Hetty's imaginary enshrinement of the picture of the lady from Miss Lydia's dressing room is a pathetic microcosm of this metonymic system of collective representation that provides the terms of a society based on the traditional order of gentility. Her relationship to this picture is the drama in miniature of the downfall to which this system was doomed in Eliot's fiction. To Eliot, because all the world of traditional gentility was a picture of the sun toward which all individuals were turned by egoism, these individuals were destined to be scorched by the real light of day when they found this picture no longer sustained by the united gaze of the community. And there is no question that it could be sustained forever, the way Eliot presented it. This was a world of interdependence; everyone would look to the eyes of others for his or her own definition . . .

. . . It might require only one gaze to be turned askew for the entire fabric of sociality to collapse if social institutions and life had no firmer ground than this. And this point held true for the institution of culture as well, as Eliot indicated by having Arthur hopelessly misconstrue classical literature when he kisse[s] Hetty. This world of traditional gentility could never have had more substance than the world of polite literature, which was devoted to its images; Eliot's literature appealed for its basis to the ordinary human life consumed in the manufacture of this genteel art . . .[15] □

This sense of collectively held, if only tacitly shared, social agreement links up with Raymond Williams's reading of 'Knowable Communities'.[16] It is a concept particularly useful to consider in the context of *Middlemarch*, as Eliot's remit in this novel is to transform her complex web of social fabric into such a 'knowable' concern. Williams introduces the subject as follows.

■ Most novels are in some sense knowable communities. It is part of a traditional method – an underlying stance and approach – that the novelist offers to show people and their relationships in essentially knowable and communicable ways . . . In the city kind [of fiction], experience and community would [therefore] be essentially opaque; in the country kind, essentially transparent . . . The growth of towns and especially of cities and a metropolis; the increasing division and complexity of labour; the altered and critical relations between and within social classes; in changes like these any assumption of a know-able community – a whole community, wholly knowable – became harder and harder to sustain. But this is not the full story, and once again, in realising the new fact of the city, we must be careful not to idealise the old and new facts of the country. For what is knowable is not only a function of objects – of what is there to be known. It is also a function of subjects, of observers – of what is desired and what needs to be known. And what we have then to see, as throughout, in the country writing, is not only the reality of the rural community; it is the observer's position in and towards it; a position which is part of the community being known.[17] □

In drawing attention to the role of the observer (here Eliot as implied author – the first of a series of embedded frames through which the action of the novel is related), Williams simultaneously conjures up the term 'transparent' in order to remind us that so-called realism is far from that. The frames and framing via which the narrator introduces the reader to the action of *Adam Bede* is also a key issue at times in *Middlemarch*. Take, for example, the frequently cited passage in Chapter 80 in which Dorothea, having encountered Will Ladislaw and Rosamond Vincy in a more intimate setting than she would have wished, gazes from the window of her chamber at dawn, looking out onto the world beyond while introspectively contemplating her own life.

■ [W]hat sort of crisis might not this be in three lives [Will's, Rosamond's and Lydgate's] whose contact with hers laid an obliga-tion on her . . . ?

It had taken long for her to come to that question, and there was light piercing into the room. She opened her curtains, and looked out towards the bit of road that lay in view, with fields beyond, outside the entrance-gates. On the road there was a man with a bundle on his back and a woman carrying her baby; in the field she could see figures moving – perhaps the shepherd with his dog. Far off in the bending sky was the pearly light; and she felt the large-ness of the world and the manifold wakings of men to labour and endurance. She was a part of that involuntary, palpitating life, and could neither look out on it from her luxurious shelter as a mere spectator, nor hide her eyes in selfish complaining. [*M*, p. 705] □

Framed by the window Dorothea finds herself contemplating a painterly pastoral scene suggestive of harmony in the 'natural' world. But how active a viewer is she here? The image is, of course, too perfect (and perfect-ed) to be 'credible' and too loaded down with sentimentality to be neutral. Are its consolations projected outwards by Dorothea, looking for escapism from the complexities of her own life by reading a mythic simplicity into bare-faced poverty? Dorothea is, at this point, a stand-in for the contemplative (and, in Eliot's time, privileged) reader, who feels drawn into the action but can never be part of it. In other words we are returned to Hillis Miller's reading of *Middlemarch* as a cacophony of competing and clashing reading positions (discussed in detail in chapter two) which never, fully, make up the whole picture. Dorothea looks and, in the act of looking, recognises the unfillable space between her and 'the manifold wakings of men to labour and endurance'. Yet she also feels excluded from more than this class identification. What she witnesses, across the class divide, is an equally consolationist and equally mythical image of the nuclear family unit. Dorothea, widow and orphan in one, fears she will never be part of that picture. This sense of the outsider leads Williams to make a further criticism of Eliot's ideological stance.

■ Certainly it is good to see the farmers and the craftsmen, and almost the labourers, as people present in the action in their own right. But there are difficulties here of a significant kind. It is often said about the Poysers in *Adam Bede*, as about the Gleggs and the Dodsons in *The Mill on the Floss*, that they are marvellously (or warmly, richly, charmingly) done. But what this points to is a recurring problem in the social consciousness of the writer. George Eliot's connections with the farmers and craftsmen – her connections as Mary Ann Evans – can be heard again and again in their language. Characteristically, she presents them mainly through speech. But while they are present audibly as a community, they have only to emerge in significant action to change in quality. What Adam or Dinah or Hetty say, when they are acting as individuals, is not particularly convincing . . . [T]hough George Eliot restores the real inhabitants of rural England to their places in what had been a socially selective [literary] landscape, she does not get much further than restoring them *as a landscape*. They begin to talk, as it were collectively, in what middle-class critics still foolishly call a kind of chorus, a 'ballad-element'. But as themselves they are still only socially present, and can emerge into personal consciousness only through externally formulated attitudes and ideas.[18] □

Some of the issues raised by Williams's argument are further developed by Simon Dentith, who sets up the class hierarchy of Eliot's writing through a fuller analysis of her representation of idiomatic speech.

■ A discursive hierarchy is just as much a feature of *Adam Bede* as it is of *Middlemarch* . . . Mrs Poyser's speech, which is pithy, forceful and witty, is as much to be relished as speech as Mrs Dollop's, though the relish is of a less contemptuous kind. Mrs Poyser's speech can equally be accounted for: we are to accept Mr Irwine's explanation of it as the kind of wit which originates proverbs. The hostility to Mrs Dollop's speech indicates, evidently, the distance which George Eliot has travelled from her earlier happy solidarity with many aspects of common and ordinary life. Even without this overt hostility, however, the novel would still be made up of different discourses, each with different capacities for articulating the truth, and thus each more or less opaque in the way that I have described. However, this is not just an abstract question of different ways of gaining access to the truth; these different discourses are also different class dialects. So what is at stake here is an implicit assertion of the superiority of one class dialect over another.

. . . the high proportion of commentary in *Middlemarch* is a function of the effort to locate and understand English provincial life and the movement of a society . . . the implications of such an effort are . . . perhaps not all attractive ones. If we ask how we are to understand the 'general mind' of Middlemarch, the scene at Mrs Dollop's in part affords the answer: the general mind is characterised by its failure to be scientific: 'Everybody liked better to conjecture how the thing was, than simply to know it.' The general mind is simply incapable of sustaining the sequence of inferences that Lydgate can manage; it is anyway insufficiently impressed by the intractability of facts. The conclusion to be drawn from this, indeed, is precisely not that more general enlightenment can be produced by careful education or explanation, for that too has its pitfalls. George Eliot writes: 'But let the wise be warned against too great readiness at explanation: it multiplies the sources of mistake, lengthening the sum for reckoners sure to go wrong' [*M*, p. 399]. The only guarantee for the proper operation of knowledge as a social power is when it can be enforced; it is an aspect of the incoherent social faith and order of Middlemarch that there is no conceivable agency for its enforcement.

George Eliot takes one feature of the realist text, then – the fact that it is built on a discursive hierarchy – and inflects it in a particularly authoritarian direction.[19] ☐

It is this concern with the politics of authorship and (literary) authority that leads Terry Eagleton, in his Foreword to Daniel Cottom's *Social Figures: George Eliot, Social History and Literary Representation* (1987), to pick up on what is the primary Marxist viewpoint of nineteenth-century realism in particular:

■ . . . the realist novel . . . permits a tolerant degree of dialogue with voices other than the author's own, but finally always inflects and idealizes them in that singular authorial discourse. Such a form allows maximum play to the concrete, particular, and individual, while draw-ing them covertly into a supremely well regulated whole.[20] □

In his own study, *Criticism and Ideology*, Eagleton offers a traditional, socialist account of *Adam Bede* centring on the politicisation of the work-ing-classes in the novel and their relationship with their capitalist bosses. Like other commentators, he identifies the mid-nineteenth century as a period of sudden and dramatic economic growth, the result of which he claims to have been the 'familiar political consequence of this prosperity', namely a 'marked incorporation' of the workers via small-scale but immediate rewards.[21] Even the growth of the trades union movement contributed to this progressive defeat of militancy, through the encour-agement of the workforce to join in with the spoils of capitalism. In the specific context of George Eliot's work Eagleton identifies a complex ten-sion between what he sees as two distinct ideological trajectories: the spirit of individualism within character construction and a larger frame-work of corporatism. Eliot's major flaw, for Eagleton, is her repeated decision to resolve such tension at the expense of drawing attention to the conflicts.

In the context of *Adam Bede*, for example, Eagleton follows John Goode's line in seeing the locus for the novel as a perfect framework or model for a political interrogation of such conflict.

■ As [Mary Ann Evans was] the daughter of a farm-agent . . . it is here . . . that the cluster of traditionalist practices and 'organic' affiliations imputed to the English provincial countryside is 'selected' by the national ideology as paradigmatic, at a point where that ideology demands precisely such images of social incorporation. Rural society . . . is chosen as a literary subject, not for its cloistered idiosyncratic charm but as a simplifying model of the whole social formation – a for-mation whose determining laws may by focused there in purer, more diagrammatic form.[22] □

It is, he claims, for the purposes of such social scrutiny that Eliot employs the literary modes of pastoral, myth and moral fable. Though uneasy with Eliot's capitulation in ideological terms, Eagleton is not thoroughly dismissive. Instead he sees the literary creation 'George Eliot' it/herself as a social intervention which, in its very presence, disrupts any clear-cut ideological synthesis, introducing into the literary establishment 'certain specific ideological determinations – Evangelical Christianity, rural organicism, incipient feminism, petty-bourgeois moralism – into a hege-monic ideological formation which is partly supported, partly embarrassed by their presence'.[23]

This resistance to easy bourgeois identification is further complicated by the literary techniques at work in her writing. In part these techniques are determined by the generic modes adopted. But, in addition, they signal what Eagleton identifies as an element of unease set up between implied author and implied reader.

■ [E]ach of [Eliot's] texts displays a complex amalgam of fictional devices appropriate to distinct generic modes: 'pastoral', historical realism, fable, mythopoeic and didactic discourse . . . None of these discourses can be placed in any simple expressive relation to ideological forms; on the contrary, it is the mutual articulation of these discourses within the text which *produces* those ideological forms as literary signification. Two examples of this process will have to suffice. The biographical mode of *The Mill on the Floss* encompasses at least two distinct forms of literary discourse: a kind of descriptive 'pastoral' (the Dodsons, Maggie's early life at the mill), and the complex psychological drama of Maggie's subjective development. It is the interplay of these mutually conflictual modes which produces the ideological contention between 'tradition' and 'progress' inscribed in the figures of Tom and Maggie Tulliver. But it is a contention which the novel's 'pastoral' devices simultaneously resolve. For just as the text's synthetic closure simplifies Tom to a type of eternal childhood, so the image of the river – symbol of moral drifting and wayward desire – naturalises and thus deforms the values of liberal individualism, figuring them as a mindless yielding to natural appetite rather than as positive growth. An opposition between 'natural' and 'cultural' discourses is transformed into a polarity between two modes of 'natural' signification: Nature as positive (pastoral), and Nature as negative (appetitive) . . .

That Eliot's fiction recasts historical contradictions into ideologically resolvable form is evident enough in the case of *Adam Bede*. Adam himself, with his Carlylean gospel of work and stiff-necked moralism, is an 'organic' type – a petty-bourgeois pragmatist who 'had no theories about setting the world to rights', and who thus functions as a reliable agent of the ruling class. Yet these 'organic' values are forbidden by the novel's form from entering into significant deadlock with any 'authentic' liberal individualism. Such individualism figures in the text only in the debased and trivialised form of a hedonistic egoism (the anarchic sexual appetite of Arthur Donnithorne and Hetty Sorrel), which the stable structures of rural society can expel or absorb without notable self-disruption. Hetty has unwittingly ruptured the class-collaboration between squire and artisan, turning Adam against Arthur; but once she is, so to speak, deported from the novel, that organic allegiance can be gradually reaffirmed. Moreover, the morally intransigent Adam has been humanised by his trials to the point where he is now spiritually prepared to wed the 'higher' working-class girl, Dinah Morris, whose Evangelical fervour for duteous self-sacrifice matches his own doggedly anti-intellectual conformism. Adam is thus allowed to advance into more richly individualised consciousness (he ends up owning a timber-yard) without damage to his mythological status as organic type, an admirable amalgam of naturalised culture and cultivated nature.

In choosing rural petty-bourgeois life as a 'paradigmatic' region, Eliot betrays towards it an ambiguous attitude which reveals, in turn, her problematic relationship to her readership. She extends the conventions of literary realism to a sensitive treatment of socially obscure figures; but while she insists on the latent significance of the apparently peripheral lives she presents, she also apologises, with a blend of genial patronage and tentative irony, for choosing such an un-enlightened enclave as the subject-matter of serious fiction. That hesitancy of tone focuses an ideological conflict. It exposes the contradiction between a rationalist critique of rural philistinism . . . and a deep-seated imperative to celebrate the value of such bigoted, inert traditionalism, as the humble yet nourishing soil which feeds the flower of higher individual achievement. *Adam Bede* tries for a partial solution of this dilemma by romantically idealising the common life in the figures of Adam and Dinah, fusing the intense with the ordinary. In *The Mill on the Floss*, however, such a synthesis calls for a considerably more obtrusive manipulation of literary devices.

The rural society of the *Mill* – one of struggling tenant farmers becoming enmortgaged and forced to ruin by the pressures of urban banking and agricultural industry – is less easily idealised than the society of *Adam Bede*. As urban capital penetrates into the countryside, those conflicts in rural society suggested yet suppressed in *Adam Bede* erupt to provide one of the *Mill's* central images – the financial collapse of Dorlcote Mill itself. Moreover, if Hetty Sorrel can be effectively externalised as a socially disruptive egoist, Maggie Tulliver of the *Mill* is a bearer of authentic liberal values who is by no means so easily dislodged. Whereas *Adam Bede* divided moral fervour and restless individualism between Dinah and Hetty, Maggie Tulliver combines both; and this forestalls the simple resolution available to the earlier novel. Allured by a liberal individualism which decisively breaks with the stagnant oppressiveness of the rural petty bourgeoisie, Maggie must none the less refuse that ethic in the name of a commitment to the traditionalist social milieu of her childhood. In this way, nostalgia for an idealised upbringing at the mill becomes translated into a defence of clannish, claustrophobic *mores* against the Romantic spontaneity of the self, treacherously entwined as it is with appetitive egoism. The claustrophobia, and the snare of self-sacrifice, are clearly registered by the novel; yet one reason why they cannot be decisively rejected is because the only alternative commitment which the book allows Maggie is Stephen Guest. Guest cannot represent a true fulfilment for her: his personal flaws are subtly related to his class position, as an overbred product of the predatory capitalism which is ousting the old rural world of her father. In grasping this connection, the novel at once shows a complex historical sense beyond the range of *Adam Bede*, and conveniently renders Maggie's return to St Oggs more palatable. In a parallel way, the career of Tom Tulliver strikingly renders the contradictions of rural society: Tom strives to help his ruined father by prospering within the very urban capitalism which has brought about the mill's collapse. Yet it is not this historically complex and self-divided Tom with whom Maggie finally unites. The novel's transparently engineered conclusion – Maggie's self-sacrificial drowning with her brother – suppresses ideological conflict by the magical stratagem of a literary device. Maggie's death is at once guilty expiation and affirmative self-fulfilment; in uniting with her brother, object of romantic love and bigoted type of organic community, she achieves and abnegates herself in the same act, endorsing the imperatives of 'organic' morality while attaining to a fulfilling individual transcendence of them.[24] □

With *Middlemarch*, Eagleton identifies a shift in class identification in relation to the dominant order. Here, he claims, Will Ladislaw replaces the traditional 'stock type of rural organicism' which, while still represented by the Garths, has become noticeably marginalised in comparison with its earlier centrality in *Adam Bede*. Ladislaw, then, bears a similarly destabilising relationship to the dominant order but, where the rural peasant 'forms a pocket of resistance within bourgeois society, the cosmopolitan artist inhabits such a dissentient space outside it'.[25] One of Eagleton's most perceptive remarks in this reading concerns the function played by history in the text.

■ *Middlemarch*, one might say, is an historical novel in form with little substantive historical content. The Reform Bill, the railways, cholera, machine-breaking: these 'real' historical forces do no more than impinge on the novel's margins. The mediation between the text and the 'real' history to which it alludes is notably dense; and the effect of this is to transplant the novel from the 'historical' to the 'ethical'. *Middlemarch* works in terms of egoism and sympathy, 'head' and 'heart', self-fulfilment and self-surrender; and this predominance of the ethical at once points to an historical impasse and provides the means of ideologically overcoming it. History in the novel is officially in a state of transition; yet to read the text is to conclude that 'suspension' is the more appropriate term. What is officially offered as an ambivalent, intermediate era leading eventually to the 'growing food of the world' is in fact more of an historical vacuum; the benighted, traditionalist-minded Middlemarch seems little more responsive to historical development than does the Hayslope of *Adam Bede*. There is, then, a discrepancy between what the novel claims and what it shows . . .[26] □

In summary, Eagleton concludes:

■ Eliot's fiction, then, represents an attempt to integrate liberal ideology, in both its Romantic and empiricist forms, with certain pre-industrial, idealist or positivist organic models. It is an enterprise determined in the last instance by the increasingly corporate character of nineteenth-century capitalism during the period of her literary production. Yet this is not to argue for a simple homology between literary and historical systems, or for a reductively diachronic reading of Eliot's *oeuvre*. It is not a question of Eliot's work evolving from pre-industrial 'pastoral' to fully-fledged realism in response to some linear development of bourgeois ideology. On the contrary, it is a question of grasping at once the ideological synchronies and formal discontinuities of her texts . . .[27] □

Brian Spittles[28] puts a different slant on a similar theme, taking the terminology of inter-class differentiation and demonstrating the slippage in Eliot's usage of such terms, the effect of which is to obfuscate genuine class issues, particularly in relation to the 'real history' of which Eagleton writes:

■ . . . Eliot tends to expand the meaning of [the] word ['peasant'] . . . to cover all labourers, artisans, and even small farmers such as Dagley in *Middlemarch*; and when she writes [in 'The Natural History of German Life' (1856)] of 'the peasant's inveterate habit of litigation'[29] . . . the idea immediately conjures an image of Tulliver, respectable miller and farmer, who is ruined by his predilection for litigation in *The Mill on the Floss*. Such men, in Eliot's view, are dominated by traditional attitudes, manners and behaviour . . . This creates continuity, but acts against change . . .

Change, however, is in the nature of history, and the 'peasant's' obduracy can be a limitation. When the railway agents arrive in the area of Middlemarch they are set upon by: 'six or seven men in smock-frocks with hay-forks in their hands' [*M*, p. 498]. The historical perspective indicates how small-minded this action is – for although it was not uncommon in 1831, when the railways were developing, by 1871–2, when the novel was being read, the country was covered with railways and everyone knew that 'hay-forks' could not halt the processes of science, technology, economics and history. That form of change Eliot accepted as inevitable: it could sometimes be described as progress, as improving the conditions of life, but it was not necessarily good, and could cause casualties. Her response was to look for amelioration of the harm rather than oppose the processes.[30] □

Moving on to a fuller consideration of the middle classes of the period, Spittles continues:

■ The increase in Britain's population and overall wealth that occurred in Eliot's life time meant the ranks of the middling classes, who formed the vast bulk of the readership and with which she was most directly concerned, expanded enormously. In effect this had at least two important consequences: people in those classes became much more conscious of, and anxious about, subtle demarcations between different levels of the broad social category Marx termed the bourgeoisie; and that group as a whole demanded greater political power than they had been previously granted. The expansion of industrialization, with its concomitant shift to urban living, was the mainspring of middling-class economic power – which itself created the motivation for political change.

In the 1830 parliamentary election less than 4 per cent of the population were entitled to vote. The middling classes felt that, on the whole, this caused the House of Commons to be dominated by the interests of the landed gentry, whilst the country's wealth was increasingly being generated by industrial and commercial forces which were excluded from political decision making. There was also a strong feeling amongst many of the lower, or labouring, classes that they too were producers of wealth, whilst being unrepresented politically. One aspect of the middling classes' tactics in the struggle for extension of the franchise in both the early 1830s and the mid-1860s was to mobilize the dissatisfactions of the lower classes in support of their own campaigns. In the latter period women also began to seek a vote, and the impetus of the twentieth-century suffragettes came largely from the frustrations of the 1860s pioneers.

The relationship between the classes in serious contention for political power in 1830 is graphically illustrated, in *Middlemarch*, at the burial of Peter Featherstone in Lowick churchyard. The rural characters 'watched old Featherstone's funeral from an upper window of the manor' [*M*, p. 291]. Being in 'the manor' associates them with the traditional residence of authority, and from the advantage point of 'an upper window' they naturally, and literally, look down on the mainly urban mourners. That distance, and positioning, underlines the detachment of the upper rural classes from the characters who run the town. Dorothea observes, 'It seems to me we know nothing of our neighbours' [*M*, p. 292]; and Vincy's family are not recognized by everyone, although he is the mayor of Middlemarch and therefore the most important civic figure in the town. The thematic and metaphoric value of this scene is explicated . . . [thus]: 'The country gentry of old time lived in a rarefied social air: dotted apart on their stations up the mountain they looked down with imperfect discrimination on the belts of thicker life below' [*M*, p. 292]. The conflict over parliamentary reform that provides part of the plots in *Middlemarch* . . . stemmed partially from that rarefication, and the sense of exclusion it engendered amongst some of the 'belts of thicker life'. If the upper classes could not tell the difference between one group and another 'below' them, the groups themselves could certainly discriminate, not merely between classes, but sub-sections too. The 'imperfect discrimination' offended the middling classes' sense of self-importance, and when translated into the political arena was offensive to their aspirations of power.

Walter Vincy illustrates a fundamental bourgeois attitude: 'When a man . . . is ready, in the interests of commerce, to take up a firm attitude on politics generally, he has naturally a sense of his importance to the framework of things' [*M*, p. 115]. An aspect of this is Vincy's insistence that his son Fred goes to, and remains at, the University of Oxford, despite the young man's lack of enthusiasm and aptitude for academic learning. Bulstrode is acerbic on the matter, arguing to Vincy:

> . . . you will not get any concurrence from me as to the course you have pursued with your eldest son . . . you were not warranted in devoting money to an expensive education which has succeeded in nothing but in giving him extravagant idle habits. [*M*, p. 115]

It is clear that Bulstrode sees Vincy's ambitions lying in the area of the subtleties of social class, that he is trying to buy a slight rise in status and esteem for the family through the means of 'an expensive education' for a son. This would be a movement up the sub-groups of the middling classes rather than a substantial change of actual class. Vincy's reply is also unequivocal: 'It's a good British feeling to try and raise your family a little: in my opinion, it's a father's duty to give his sons a fine chance' [*M*, p. 116]. Vincy repudiates Bulstrode's moral accusation of unnecessary extravagance with the pragmatic morality of 'a father's duty'. In any event to 'raise your family' socially is 'good'. Bulstrode, like most of the initial readers, is also middling class and so understands the argument very well. Indeed, Bulstrode and Vincy are related through marriage, as the former is married to the latter's sister, an aspect of the novel's central metaphor of the web. Although Bulstrode is speaking ostensibly in his professional capacity as a banker, there is perhaps also a suggestion of family jealousy – since Bulstrode came from humbler origins than the Vincys, and background is not something easily out-lived . . .

The Vincy family is not presented as particularly unusual, certainly not malicious or especially self-seeking within the ambitions of their class position. Yet they do appear to be obsessed with social status. The most common way for a young woman who was considered physically attractive to achieve class mobility was through marriage. Rosamond has a view of life that seems remarkably informed by the poorer kind of nineteenth-century fiction: 'a stranger was absolutely necessary to Rosamond's social romance, which had always turned on a lover and bridegroom who was not a Middlemarcher' [*M*, pp. 105–6]; but her perception of the new doctor is very much in keeping with the reality of the time and class:

> . . . here was Mr Lydgate suddenly corresponding to her ideal, being altogether foreign to Middlemarch, carrying a certain air of distinction congruous with good family, and possessing connections which offered vistas of that middle-class heaven, rank . . . [*M*, p. 106]

Lydgate is related to the aristocracy, 'good family' indeed for the daughter of a Midlands manufacturer. The word 'heaven' suggests the 'middle-class' worship 'rank', and the phrase adds up to sharp social satire of middling-class aspirations. Rank is a false idol, a graven image, that has replaced more profound values. In this context of the Vincy family it links with the disregard paid to Fred's lack of interest in a religious vocation. Bad clergymen hardly matter if heaven is conceived in terms of rank rather than soul . . .

Rosamond is representative in respect of her attitudes. Her mother's only objections to the engagement with Lydgate, as she explains to Vincy, is that Rosamond might have done better by waiting, by giving herself the chance of meeting someone else: 'She might have met somebody on a visit who would have been a far better match; I mean at her schoolfellow Miss Willoughby's. There are relations in that family quite as high as Mr Lydgate's' [*M*, p. 307]. Although Vincy himself complains, 'I don't want a son-in-law who has got nothing but his relations to recommend him' [*M*, p. 307], and sees Lydgate's comparative poverty as a disqualification – illustrating that middling-class worship of wealth at times competed with its adoration of the celestial condition of rank – he still responds to Lydgate within the limitations of his class: 'Mr Vincy was a little in awe of him, a little vain that he wanted to marry Rosamond' [*M*, p. 309]. This way of thinking comprehends nothing wrong in social mobility through marriage, it is a way of attacking class privilege on an individual basis, but does not provide, of course, a collective middling-class route to the root of political power.

The rivalry between different sub-sections of the middling classes is also depicted in the relationship of the Vincys and the Garths, two families that are eventually united through the wedding of Fred and Mary:

> Even when Caleb Garth was prosperous, the Vincys were on condescending terms with him and his wife, for there were nice distinctions of rank in Middlemarch; and though old manufacturers could not any more than dukes be connected with none but equals, they were conscious of an inherent social superiority which was defined with great nicety in practice, though hardly expressible theoretically. [*M*, p. 207]

The problem with analysing society in theoretic class terms is that the 'nicety' of 'discriminations' between sub-groups is 'hardly expressible' . . . [although] the characters themselves were fully 'conscious' of 'inherent' matters of 'rank'. Eliot observes, records and – through the implied parallel with 'dukes' – satirizes the attitudes of 'superiority'. She is able to do so with such ease partly because of the prevalence of the distinctions in the society for which she was writing, and because of that the readers may be assumed to understand the significance, and terrible importance, of those niceties. Failure on the part of the reader to appreciate the differences, and their value to the characters, will lead to a misunderstanding of both the reality of the society the fiction records, and the artistic nature of the novel itself.

On the whole, women were more central in those kind of social distinctions than men. Males met usually on some kind of formal basis, even when meeting apparently informally. The banker, the manufacturer, the vicar, etc. all had fairly defined roles, and personal background may qualify those to some extent but the basic relationships were settled. The wives of those men, however, related to one another on a more personal basis – partly because they met much more frequently, and at one another's homes rather than in the formal settings of business. The intimacy that was generated meant almost every factor in the relationship gained significance:

> Mrs Vincy had never been at her ease with Mrs Garth, and frequently spoke of her as a woman who had had to work for her bread –

> meaning that Mrs Garth had been a teacher before her marriage; in which case an intimacy with Lindley Murray and Mangnall's *Questions*[31] was something like a draper's discrimination of calico trade-marks, or a courier's acquaintance with foreign countries: no woman who was better off needed that sort of thing. [*M*, pp. 207–8]

Teaching is conceived of as a form of trade, and the popular textbooks by Murray and Mangnall as similar to 'draper's . . . calico trademarks'. It is not the kind of familiarity with the world of common trade a 'woman who was better off needed', and therefore reveals an irradicable inadequacy in the background. The perceptive initial reader would have appreciated the ironic satire in Mrs Vincy, whose own position was essentially built on trade – although at the manufacturing end – adopting a supercilious attitude to that activity. Even if Caleb were to become very prosperous his wife's acquaintances would always be conscious of her need to have 'had to work for her bread'.

Mrs Garth herself is well aware of the distinctions, and the impossibility of their being ignored:

> . . . the passage from governess into housewife had wrought itself a little too strongly into her consciousness, and she rarely forgot that while her grammar and accent were above the town standard, she wore a plain cap, cooked the family dinner, and darned all the stockings. [*M*, p. 217]

Mrs Garth really is a 'housewife', performing all the household tasks herself, rather than delegating them to servants. Even her superiority of education is unable to outweigh, in the practical niceties of social intercourse, the necessity of doing her own cooking and darning. It is an indictment of social attitudes, and female ones in particular, towards women's education. Ultimately it was not accorded a high status, which of course helped to keep it at a generally poor standard.

Middlemarch deals more perceptively, and in greater detail, than any other novel of its time with the intricacies of bourgeois intra-class relationships. In the early 1830s, when the action is set, the middling classes were relatively small and in their political conflict with the ruling classes tended to present an homogenous identity. After 1867 they had gained political ascendancy, and general prosperity had widened their ranks considerably, so that the distinctions Eliot explores were vitally topical.[32] □

John F. Hulcoop's reading of the class structure in *Middlemarch* is as specific as that of Spittles in its location of precise demarcations between various strata of the middle classes in the novel, but he relates these class nuances specifically to the 'middling' aspects of the Middlemarch community. In doing so his reading also adds a further disclaimer to the disparaging stance so many critics take on the Midlands region from which Eliot hailed. For Hulcoop, the middling aspect of *Middlemarch* relates not only to a fictitious community, but to 'that ever-expanding section of human society whose marches are contiguous, on the one hand, with the aristocracy, on the other, with the proletariat'.[33] He continues:

■ In *Middlemarch* . . . Eliot avoids social, modal and rhetorical extremes and focuses on the middle or medium. Sir James Chettam, a member of the minor aristocracy, is as high as she reaches on the social scale. Looking down, she drops in on the Dagleys, who illustrate 'the depression of the agricultural interest' and 'the sad lack of farming capital, as seen constantly in the newspapers of that time' [*M*, p. 353]. Though poor, the Dagleys are still tenant farmers, below the landed gentry and yeomanry but above the ploughman and farm-labourer: in other words, the middle of their particular class. Two relatively 'low' scenes are set in the Tankard, a pub in Slaughter Lane run by Mrs Dollop, the 'spirited' landlady 'accustomed to dominate her company' [*M*, pp. 646, 648]. But the company, which acts as a 'chorus', consists of a dyer, a glazier, and a shoemaker, all artisans and therefore in the middle of their class; in addition, a barber who feels himself above the clientele at Dollop's [*M*, p. 647], and a clerk . . .

The focus in *Middlemarch* is clearly, even relentlessly, on that vast and, in the 1830s, increasingly difficult-to-define social area loosely demarcated by the social ranks above and below, and inhabited by the middle class (middlemarchers), those 'burghers of a midland town and surrounding parishes in which "the middle-aged fellows carry the day"' . . . [*M*, p. 80][34] □

Extending the debate on class and power into the purportedly private domain of the home, Daniel Cottom identifies a class-based split between the world of work and the family unit which combines socio-economics with considerations of gender.

■ The home does not become a castle, and marriage does not become a haven of hypercathected [extraordinarily focused or targeted] senti-mentality, until the impression is fostered by the structure of society that extrafamilial relationships and the work of industry and business no longer include the family and the domestic life of the individual as their basis. This is what nurtured the sentimental values developed in the eighteenth century to their mature flowering in the Victorian period: the fact that the changing nature of society forced out the old meanings of family and marriage and left them ripe for the reception of this new influx of values, which could be taken either to complement or to transcend the values of society in its larger sense . . .

This same psychology operates in Eliot's sentimentalization of labor . . . Workers such as Adam Bede take their work personally, subjectively, as a source of pleasure and in fact as a metaphor for all behavior and order in life . . . One could instance, too, the case of Caleb Garth, whose 'prince of darkness was a slack workman' [*M*, p. 225] and who succeeds in turning Fred Vincy to the good by teaching him a sense of pride in honest labor.

This conception of work as a craft was already anachronistic even in the earlier times in which Eliot set most of her fiction – not to mention her own day. The new reality was large-scale manufacture, not guild-like control over and pride in quality. In this respect, too, one sees the purpose of her psychology to be ideological. It is directed toward the consciousness of her characters so that it may be directed away from the organization and material reality of their occupations. Like masochistic feeling and burdensome duty, craft is merely culture in a different aspect. It is the presumption of self-discovery through self-sacrifice that constitutes the running argument of all Eliot's writing.[35] □

Eve Kosofsky Sedgwick's *Between Men* further develops the relationship between class and gender relations when looking at this same interface between private and public social realms. She poses the following questions and considerations before going on to apply them to Eliot's *Adam Bede*.

■ Is it men as a group, or capitalists as a class, that chiefly benefit from the modern sexual division of labor? How close is the fit between the functions of the gendered family and the needs of capitalism? Is the gendered family necessary for capitalism? Will changes in one necessarily effect changes in the other, and if so, how?

Alternative reconstructions of the precapitalist family naturally accompany each move in this debate . . . [O]ne could say that radical feminism tends to see within history a relatively unchanging family, in which not only the fact but the basic structures of patriarchal domination have remained stable by resisting or assimilating economic difference or change; while Marxist feminism . . . tends to historicize the gendered family catastrophically, to see it as taking its present oppressive form or forms relatively late, chiefly under the pressure of capitalism, and in a fairly direct response to the needs of capital.

In the more sophisticated middle ground that is emerging between these positions, it is appearing that European capitalism was, as it were, born into, or bred in, a pre-existent language of the family.[36] □

Sedgwick applies this stance to *Adam Bede* in the following manner.

■ The explanatory power of this novel for our current theoretical crux comes from the authority and fullness with which it places its characters in relation to apparently timeless gender roles; but then from the specificity with which it anchors those roles in the productive and conservative economy of particular families at particular nodes of the social fabric; and finally from the resolute directionality with which the mythic plot pushes those families into new relations that, for some of the familial roles, mean extinction, and for others radical and alienating reorganization.

In the survey of preindustrial society at the beginning of the novel, it is of course the Poysers' farm that most strikingly represents the integrated agricultural workplace described by Marxist feminists, in which the spheres of men's work and women's work overlap substantially. Partly because commodities and services rather than cash are the main medium of exchange, the dairy and textile products over whose production Mrs Poyser reigns are never clearly differentiated as being for domestic use as against market trade. Neither is Mr Poyser's farming. Not only are the home and the workplace not physically distinct, that is, but the modes of production and consumption that characterize them are very similarly structured and, hence, similarly valued.

Demographically, as well, the Poyser family is very elastic . . . There are three direct generations of the Poyser family; then there are Dinah and Hetty, two nieces, one living there as a guest, but the other as a servant; then there are the real servants and farm-laborers. But again, in this omni-industrious household everyone not only works hard, but works relatively similarly. Surely it matters, economically, whether one is or is not in line to inherit the tenancy of the farm or ownership of the splendid linens; but in a household economy where manual and managerial labor are only barely distinguished, and more importantly where commodities, services, room and board, companionship, and training in skills are exchangeable on a complex market that does not claim to translate them all into one common rationalized measure, the different capacities in which groups of people live or work in the same household do not easily fit into the gross alternatives, 'family' and 'servant,' or again 'men's sphere' and 'women's sphere.' The family in this sense stretches along the axes of both kinship and cohabitation, apparently not reducing either to the terms of the other.

Of course, Mrs Poyser's personal authority and incisiveness make the warmest of sense in the context of this economically integrated family. She is not sparing of her words, but pointedness rather than diffuseness is their trait: they are pointed because her pointing hand is a visibly consequential one; her say in the production of family goods and power requires no dilation or mystique. In this we could compare her with Lisbeth Bede, Adam's mother, whose speech, by contrast, shows so many of the traits associated by Robin Lakoff[37] with 'female language': repetitiousness, querulousness, self-deprecation, insistence on irrelevant details, 'anxious humours and irrational persistence,' and, in addition, 'a sort of wail, the most irritating of all sounds where real sorrows are to be borne, and real work to be done.' Her speech is always vexingly beside the point of the 'real' – apologetic and defiant at the same time, 'at once patient and complaining, self-renouncing and exacting, brooding the livelong day over what happened yesterday, and what is likely to happen to-morrow, and crying very readily both at the good and the evil' [AB, p. 40]. 'But,' Eliot adds to this description, as if to contradict herself, 'a certain awe mingled itself with her idolatrous love of Adam, and when he said, "leave me alone," she was always silenced.'

When we first see Lisbeth, she is standing at the door of her house, where she lives with only her husband and sons. She is watching with practiced eyes 'the gradually enlarging speck which for the last few minutes she has been quite sure is her darling son Adam' [AB, p. 37], on his way home from the shop where he works as a carpenter. Lisbeth, we are told, is a hard worker herself – she knits 'unconsciously,' she cleans compulsively, she carries pails of water on her head in from the spring. But it is hard not to associate the fearful hemorrhage of authority and consequentiality from her language, with the physical alienation from her household of the male workers and, by the same economic process, of the emerging monetary nexus. The work she performs in the household is descriptively circumscribed as 'domestic' and conservative, *as opposed to* economically productive. Her voice, correspondingly, which presents itself as that of maternity, is really that of perceived dependence, of the talking dog: 'We are apt to be kinder to the brutes that love us than to the women that love us,' here remarks George Eliot (not then known to be a woman). 'Is it because the brutes are dumb?' [AB, p. 40] Mrs Poyser, too, is an energetic lover of her children, but the fretful category of 'the women that love us' could never be applied to her; her language is incapable of irrelevance, because she in *her* home is in a position to create relevance.

Fertile and continuous as the Poysers' arrangement originally looks, and fragile and ill-assorted as the Bedes' does, the basic historical trajectory of *Adam Bede* is to move the novel's normative vision of family from the Poysers' relatively integrated farm to the Bedes' highly specified nuclear household. *As part of this transition*, the normative female role must change from Mrs Poyser's to one like Mrs Bede's. By the Epilogue of the novel, no one is left in the Poyser household who seems likely to grow up into Mrs Poyser; Arthur Donnithorne's only child is, of course, dead; but Dinah and Adam have their baby Adam and their baby Lisbeth, whose function is to refract their parents' and namesakes' values on into the future. Of course, the degree to which the novel is not a feminist one in its *valuations* is clear from the lengths to which it goes to make this change seem palatable; but the full measure of the lengths which, as it also clearly shows, there are to go for that purpose, demonstrates the thoroughness of its feminist *analysis*.

The main vehicle for this change in the normative female role is Dinah Morris. Dinah's career in the novel has been extraordinarily full, not only in its intensity, but in its aptitude for catching up the important strands of women's fate as a gender during this period. Although she is Mrs Poyser's niece, and one of the inhabitants of the Hall Farm as the novel begins, she is also the only character in the novel who has a direct experience of the concentration of industry: she supports herself by working at a cotton mill in Snowfield. At the same time, she is visiting her aunt at the Hall Farm as part of a round of itinerant Methodist preaching. Dinah's mode of life, then, when the novel begins, seems to exemplify certain promises of individualism and autonomy held out to young working women around the time of the beginning of the industrial revolution. Her pay, for the work at the mill is, as she puts it, 'enough and to spare' [*AB*, p.83] for her individual needs; orphaned early, she lives alone by choice; and no institutional constraints, and no very potent ideological ones, seem to offer to interfere with the mobility and resoluteness with which she can publicly dedicate her talents to the cause she has chosen.[38] ☐

So it is upon Dinah that Sedgwick fastens as the most obvious illustration of the interface between gendered and class positions.

■ Although earlier in the novel, splits of signification and institutional structure between the heavenly father and the earthly male had offered Dinah the space and leverage for some real power of her own, those enabling gaps are closing up here. In fact, the regime of meaning that had empowered her forms precisely the ground for her present surrender. Dinah finds here that her heavenly Master's voice is, simply, Her Master's Voice; now voiceless herself, she can only quiver, whimper, or gaze humidly in response to it.

Importantly, too, the circumscription of Dinah's power and sphere at the end of the novel is far from taking place only in the realm of individual psychology, even though that is where the novel has most scope for making it appear voluntary and exciting. Changes in the composition of the industrial workforce, apparently enforced as much by working men as by capitalists, severely curtailed women's access to well-paid or steady industrial work as the factory system developed during this period, although the novel masks this fact by the assumption that marriage would in any case mean, for Dinah, settling down for good in her husband's village and a cessation of wage work. The novel does make explicit, however, that even had Dinah never married, she would have had to give up the preaching that had been the source of her independence and power, since in 1803 the right to preach was taken away from Methodist women. Chillingly, it is only in Adam's voice, in the Epilogue, that we hear what he claims is Dinah's defense of this rule:

> Most o' the women do more harm nor good with their preaching – they've not got Dinah's gift nor her sperrit; and she's seen that, and she thought it right to set th' example o' submitting . . . And I agree with her, and approve o' what she did. [*AB*, p. 508]

Also chillingly, the Epilogue begins with Dinah in just the same canine posture in which we first saw Lisbeth Bede: poised on the threshold of a house, straining her eyes out to catch the first possible glimpse of a returning Adam. In fact, Seth points out the continuity:

> Trust thee for catching sight of him if he's anywhere to be seen . . . Thee't like poor mother used to be. She was always on the look-out for Adam, and could see him sooner than other folks, for all her eyes got dim. [*AB*, p. 507]

If one listens to Top-40 radio, one thinks here irresistibly of Sheena Easton's hit . . . 'My baby takes the morning train/He works from nine to five and then/He takes another home again/To find me wa-a-a-a-aiting,' with its insinuating whisper between the choruses – 'Only when he's with me – I come to life!/Everything he gives me – makes me feel all right!' That nine-to-five regularization of productive work, as much as its alienation from the household, is an underpinning of the statutory tableau of sphere ideology, in which the woman who cannot venture out of 'her' sphere stands poised waiting for the man who, owning it, enters it freely but at regularly foreseeable hours specified by the needs of his own masters.

In fact, an especially incisive although tendentiously handled locus of Eliot's sociology in *Adam Bede* is the growing rationalization, the placing on a basis of measurable and interchangeable units, of male work, as it is increasingly differentiated from the increasingly feminized sphere of the household. The hours are not yet 'nine to five,' but the very first scene of the novel shows a conflict between a pre-industrial task orientation and a factorylike time discipline: as the church clock strikes six, all the carpenters in the Burge workshop throw down their tools from their unfinished tasks – all but Adam, who chides, 'I hate to see a man's arms drop down as if he was shot, before the clock's fairly struck, just as if he'd never a bit o' pride and delight in 's work' [*AB*, pp. 10–11]. Adam's ideological appeal here, as often in the novel, is to the values of an individualized, pre-industrial artisanry, in which the maker is unproblematically identified with the artifact, and extracts from it the full value of his labor in it. It is important, though, that Adam is speaking from the position of heir-apparent to Jonathan Burge who owns the workshop, and therefore as a prospective beneficiary of the alienated profits of this more collectivized labor. It makes economic sense *for him* to want to reimpose the now emptied-out values of 'pride and delight' in work; but the sharp differentiation made by Wiry Ben, his colleague and soon-to-be-employee, between the time for 'work' and the time for 'play,' corresponds more closely to the immediate, less mystified situation of the salaried workers. Outside the sphere of labor relations, the 'stiff an' masterful' [*AB*, p. 113] Adam is actually a hero of abstraction and rationalization: he 'wrote a beautiful hand that you could read off, and could do the figures in his head – a degree of accomplishment totally unknown among the richest farmers of that country-side' [*AB*, p. 91]. And what is perhaps clearest about Adam's personality is how fully it is shaped by the leverage on the world given him by rationalized work.

> There's nothing but what's bearable as long as a man can work. . . . the natur o' things doesn't change, though it seems as if one's own life was nothing but change. The square o' four is sixteen, and you must lengthen your lever in proportion to your weight, is as true when a man's miserable as when he's happy; and the best o' working is, it gives you a grip hold o' things outside your own lot. [*AB*, p. 108]

In contrast to that, the work of the (diminished) household, now become 'women's work,' remains stubbornly task-oriented and un-rationalized: care of children, the sick, or the elderly, cannot stop when the clock strikes, nor does the square root of a potroast give one a grip hold o' things outside her own lot. The result of these historical dislocations of work, as Eliot shows, is that the space and time of women's work are ideologized as not only separate but anachronistic in relation to the realm of 'real' work. In other words, the ideological soil for Dinah's relegation to the narrow sphere of 'angel in the house' had been amply prepared by her early ministry, but that ministry could have borne very different fruit, as well; it is only on the material ground of catastrophic change in the economic structure and functions

– and context – of the family, that her particular worldly relation to the transcendent becomes the engine of so narrow and specialized a fate.

Eliot's choice of the rural artisan class rather than representatives of urban industrialism as the vehicle for her genealogy of the English middle-class family was a shrewd one for her gentle defense of the status quo . . . it permits her to suggest that the values of modern industrial society are genetically – and appropriately – individualistic, couched in the mode of private property. Furthermore, the terminological slippage 'bourgeois family' – 'middle-class family' – 'working-class family,' a slippage that is both a crucial tool of capitalist ideology *and* a yet-unmet challenge to Marxist analysis, is handsomely accommodated by Adam's quiet slippage upward from worker to owner, which is much less emphatically presented than the more clearly 'historical' shift of his economic base away from personal aristocratic patronage.[39] □

Sedgwick's observations regarding the different labour patterns of working men and women take on added irony in the context of Hetty Sorrel. Several commentators have judged it to be harsh that the narrator accepts Mrs Poyser's view that Hetty is at fault in lacking love for the farm, for Totty, for her own role in the dairy. Her relationship with each of these things is different to Mrs Poyser's in important ways and of course she has no great, long-term investment in any of them. But another gendered reading of reluctant labour underlies this characterisation. Hetty desires to leave productive labour (paid work) behind, later flees from the impending threat of re-productive labour (childbirth), but learns the hard way that both fates are inescapable.

This brings us to Margaret Homans's article, 'Dinah's Blush, Maggie's Arm: Sexuality in George Eliot's Early Novels', in which she elaborates on the relationship between gender and class during the Victorian period, focusing in particular on the characters of Dinah, Hetty, Adam and Arthur.

■ Although Dinah works in a cotton-mill (probably a spinning mill) as well as preaches, it is worth noting that the narrative, which lingers at Adam's workplace and dwells lovingly, too, on the hand spinning that still goes on at the Poysers', never details that determinant of Dinah's lower and more distinct class position. Factory spinning, in contrast to the unmodernizable building trades, is part of the threatening modernity from which Eliot seeks to protect her idealized image of the middle class.[40] □

As well as blurring Dinah's class identification for the purposes of neutralising her role as she (literally and metaphorically) journeys through the text, Homans, like Sedgwick, sees gender division taking over from class division as hierarchies relating to the latter become progressively less distinct.

■ Toward the end of the novel appears a little scene between Adam and Dinah that [places] them in a hierarchy . . . of gender, not of class. By now transformed from angelic preacher to domestic woman, Dinah is a woman self-consciously in love . . . Dinah is visiting Lisbeth Bede prior to leaving Hayslope, and the narrative humiliatingly and sentimentally dwells upon Dinah's obsession with housework: '. . . if you had ever lived in Mrs Poyser's household, you would know how the duster behaved in Dinah's hand – how it went into every small corner, and on every ledge in and out of sight . . . It was painful to see how much dust there was . . .' [AB, p.465] Who could say whether her strongest emotions are for Adam or for dusting? Desire and domestic servitude are one.

Adam catches her pathetic struggle between fear of disturbing his things and eagerness to dust, and offers his help: '"Come then," said Adam . . . "I'll help you move the things, and put 'em back again . . ." But Dinah did not look at him . . . ' [AB, p.466]. For Adam, who does manly work with his head and hands, dusting is a 'playful bit o' work', but it is Dinah's vocation, at least her only remaining one. The scene exaggerates the distance between them as male and female, in contrast to earlier representations of them as more or less equals. As at Arthur's party, the carnival aspect of the scene, the temporary overturning of hierarchy, in effect confirms it, but here it is gender rather than class hierarchy. Adam's participation in cleaning, because it is only play, points up how entirely separate his sphere is now from hers.[41] □

This is Homans's reading of the novel's final consolations.

■ *Adam Bede* closes with a tableau, dated 1807, striking for its phantasmic representation of a Victorian middle-class family long before that social form became dominant and in the kind of rural location where it took root the slowest. Adam, formerly a wage-earning artisan, has taken over Jonathan Burge's carpentry business and his substantial house, and he also earns a salary managing the Donnithornes' woods. Adam and Dinah live with their two children, and Uncle Seth is a familiar visitor. Almost certainly their household includes at least one servant; in Burge's day a servant worked there, and earlier Adam has assured his mother that they can afford one . . . Entirely domesticated, Dinah has ceased preaching in public . . . She no longer works in the cotton-mill nor, it seems, does productive home agricultural work like Mrs Poyser, for Dinah's house is not a farm. We learn that Hetty, who never left the agricultural working class, has died while returning from her seven years' transportation. The family party is waiting for Adam to return from greeting Arthur Donnithorne, who has come home 'shattered' by fever [*AB*, p. 508] from his own voluntary exile. Hetty gone and Arthur diminished, this prosperous nuclear family fills the picture frame of Eliot's purportedly realist portrait of rural life, having taken up all the space previously occupied by the 'extremes' . . . of upper and lower classes.

With this sweet family picture of what Philip Fisher calls 'the new center of power',[42] the novel presents a proleptic image of the middle-class family triumphant. Although Adam's home is still, in the old way, his workplace, the narrative's focus on a moment when he returns home to his family creates the illusion of a Victorian separation of home and work. By the standards not of 1807 but of 1859, Dinah at home, straining her eyes to catch sight of her entrepreneurial husband, is the chief signifier of what will be the Victorian middle class, at least its bottom rung. Sarah Ellis defines her middle-class readership (and subject) as women in households supported by 'trade and manufactures.'[43] Adam's ambitious carpentry business, in which he invents and builds new devices to market, is a form of manufacture, even if it is not industrialized and would not be for the remainder of the nineteenth century. Joan Burstyn defines the middle class as households with over £100 of annual income,[44] and since Adam earned a guinea a week superintending the Donnithornes' woods when he started the job in 1799, he may well earn something like £100 annually now. Ellis further defines the middle-class household as 'restricted to the services of from one to four domestics',[45] very likely the case in the Bedes' household. That household, then, is a forerunner of the Victorian middle-class home, a sentimentalized image projected backward from Eliot's day onto Adam's.

After the publication of *Adam Bede* Eliot received a letter of praise from Jane Carlyle. Of this letter Eliot writes to John Blackwood that 'I reckon it among my best triumphs that she found herself "in charity with the whole human race" when she laid the book down.' She adds: 'Will you tell her that the sort of effect she declares herself to have felt from "Adam Bede" is just what I desire to produce – gentle thoughts and happy remembrances.'[46] As Mary Jean Corbett points out, citing Carlyle's letter and similar comments, this is a remarkable response to a novel that includes cross-class seduction, infanticide, and so much emotional suffering. Middle-class readers like Carlyle loved the nostalgic, pastoral mood of the novel and its workers ennobled through suffering who make the reader from another class feel 'that we are all alike – that the human heart is one'.[47] The cumulative effect of such goodwill is, I would argue, concentrated onto the final tableau and the ideological program that becomes explicit only there: the idyllic picture of Adam and Dinah's domesticity filling the frame, all disharmonious elements – that is, those who belong to other classes – expunged or pushed to the margins. For the middle-class reader and writer alike, the epilogue would represent the ascendency, not of something narrowly defined and marked as one class rather than another, but of middle-class values masquerading as universal values. Carlyle's phrase, 'in charity with the whole human race', makes this equation with particular effectiveness; the term with which she denotes the transcendence of class boundaries, 'charity', names a leisure activity of middle-class females. The middle-class family becomes the norm, and that makes the middle-class reader 'happy' . . .[48] □

On the question of Eliot's fascination with an all-inclusive middle class, Homans argues:

■ Beginning in the 1830s, it was possible for British writers to represent the middle class as the only class. Henry Brougham famously stated that 'by the people . . . I mean the middle classes, the wealth and intelligence of the country, the glory of the British name'.[49] With a deftly deployed tautology, Sarah Ellis in 1838 defends her decision to write about 'the female population of Great Britain' by writing only about the middle class:

> In order to speak with precision of the characteristics of any class of people, it is necessary to confine our attention as much as possible to that portion of the class where such characteristics are most prominent; and, avoiding the two extremes where circumstances not peculiar to that class are supposed to operate, to take the middle or intervening portion as a specimen of the whole.[50]

'Class of people' in this passage refers, ostensibly, to 'the female population', but by denominating them a 'class' Ellis implicitly equates all women with one particular social class. Moreover, in order to assert that the characteristics of the women of England are 'most prominent' among the middle classes, Ellis has already, tautologically, determined that middle-class characteristics are what is typically British.

Although at this date the middle class is not a numerical majority of Britain's population, Ellis can make it seem so:

> [W]hen we consider the number, the influence, and the respectability of that portion of the inhabitants who are, directly, or indirectly, connected with our trade and merchandise, it does indeed appear to constitute the mass of English society, and may

justly be considered as exhibiting the most striking and unequivocal proofs of what are the peculiar characteristics of the people of England.[51]

'Respectability', that prototypically middle-class virtue, is slipped in here among other more clearly objective measures of hegemony (influence and number) to suggest that her bias toward the middle class is merely a matter of numbers. She enlarges the middle class by appropriating to it a term usually reserved for the working classes, '*mass.*' Ellis goes on to explain why neither the aristocracy nor the 'indigent and most laborious' are typical of the British, because they lack what she has already decided is 'typical.' She writes that we cannot 'with propriety look for those strong features of nationality' among the poor, because 'the urgency of mere physical wants' makes England's working class much like those in other countries. Although she uses 'propriety' here to mean 'appropriateness', the word's connotations of 'properness' mean that, again, a middle-class virtue masquerades as an impartial rule of observation. Looking *with* propriety, Ellis will only *see* propriety, and from here on, she essentially erases the upper and lower classes.

Adam Bede and *The Mill on the Floss* work in much the same way. Not only generalizing mid-Victorian middle-class qualities to other classes but also projecting them backward in time, Eliot's early novels universalize the British middle class and, in so doing, align themselves with other efforts to consolidate middle-class hegemony in the nineteenth century. Eliot, having internalized middle-class norms, universalizes the middle class by making its peculiar characteristics appear natural, generically human ones, and she naturalizes those characteristics, much as Ellis does, by naturalizing Victorian middle-class womanhood as womanhood itself. When she herself wants to make more money from the publication of one of her novels, she relabels her class aspirations as the natural sympathy of a selfless Victorian woman: 'I may say without cant – since I am in a position of anxiety for others as well as myself – that it is my duty to seek not less than the highest reasonable advantage from my work'.[52] In constructing her heroines as in writing about money, Eliot represents partisanship for the middle class as supposedly classless domesticity and morality, a morality specifically identified with woman. For Eliot, whose career took her from the bottom of the middle class to the top, from estate manager's daughter to wealthy Londoner with her own carriage and pair, middle-class life encompasses all the possibilities of life itself, and her novels make class and gender work together to consolidate middle-class hegemony.[53] □

It is this connection between oppression and the politics of gender that we will now examine in further detail as we turn, in chapter four, to a sustained consideration of *The Mill on the Floss*.

CHAPTER FOUR

Sexuality, Gender and Desire in *The Mill on the Floss*

O F THE three novels addressed in this Readers' Guide, *The Mill on the Floss* has been the most critically neglected in terms of the volume of work available. Yet, ironically, the criticism of it that does exist is – by and large – of a more innovative kind than that on *Adam Bede* and, to a lesser extent, even *Middlemarch*. David Smith's article, 'Incest Patterns in Two Victorian Novels' (1965),[1] is an evident case in point. This essay looks at sexuality in two novels of the nineteenth century, Charlotte Brontë's *Jane Eyre* (1847) and Eliot's *The Mill on the Floss* (1860) and, in the context of the second of these, Smith begins by taking issue with Henry James's 1866 criticism that the ending is disturbingly and unnecessarily brutal and that it jars with what the rest of the narrative sets up as a reader expectation that all will be well in the end. James claims:

■ The chief defect – indeed, the only serious one – in *The Mill on the Floss* is its conclusion. Such a conclusion is in itself assuredly not illegitimate, and there is nothing in the fact of the flood, to my knowledge, essentially unnatural: what I object to is its relation to the preceding part of the story. The story is told as if it were destined to have, if not a strictly happy termination, at least one within ordinary probabilities. As it stands, the *denouement* shocks the reader most painfully. Nothing has prepared him for it; the story does not move towards it; it casts no shadow before it . . . But one thing is certain: a *denouement* by which Maggie should have called Stephen back would have been extremely interesting, and would have had far more in its favor than can be put in confusion by a mere exclamation of horror.[2] □

Smith disagrees: for him Tom and Maggie's death by drowning renders explicit what has been implicit throughout the novel, namely the passionately incestuous desire shared by Maggie and Tom in the text.

Smith begins his essay in a slightly apologetic tone of voice, clearly anticipating the hostility or scepticism of traditionally minded Eliot critics. In particular, he shies away from inferring any similar feelings between Mary Ann Evans and her own brother Isaac (the biographical relationship so many critics insist forms the model for the fictive one between Maggie and Tom), who imposed a hostile, even jealous, ostracism from his sister on the revelation of her relationship with George Henry Lewes. Instead Smith relies upon a psychoanalytic structure to emphasise that, both on the level of character and authorial intention, such feelings, though central to the narrative, remain only unconsciously present within it. His early caginess is characterised by the following observation: 'When it is part of the author's conscious purpose to indicate an unconscious motivation in a character, he will weave into the structure "pointers" by which the reader knows that the author knows what he is doing. Twentieth-century authors frequently are of this type. But where the depiction in a character of unconscious motivation is owing to the author's unconscious purpose, such "pointers" will be absent: Pre-twentieth-century authors frequently are of this type.'[3]

After this diffident opening, Smith follows it up with a bolder stance: 'The organizing principle of *The Mill on the Floss* is an unconscious incestuous passion between Maggie and Tom Tulliver', before retreating slightly into a further qualification: '"Unconscious incestuous passion" does not mean the commission of acts of sexual intercourse by Maggie and Tom – *at least not quite* [my emphasis] – nor does it mean an awareness on their parts of this characterization of the relationship. It does mean, however, a psychic state which is "erotic" in the fullest sense of the term: physical, sexual, and desperately intense.'[4] As my use of italics suggests, the most interesting aspect of this disclaimer is the tantalising parenthesis, 'at least not quite'. Though Smith never spells out precisely to what he refers here, he does imply, later on in the essay, that the answer lies in that final death scene to which James so vehemently objected:

■ The flood-death scene is richly suggestive. Maggie arrives at the mill in her boat with 'panting joy' [*MF*, p. 654]. Conveniently, there are no third parties to intrude. Mrs Tulliver is not at the mill ('It is I, Tom, – Maggie. Where is mother?' 'She is not here: she went to Garum, the day before yesterday') [*MF*, p. 654]. . . . As they move further on this river of impulse, they are warned by the communal observers to 'Get out of the current!' [*MF*, p. 655]. But by now it is too late. All that remains is the height of climax, then release in death: 'It is coming, Maggie!' Tom said, in a deep hoarse voice, loosing the oars and clasping her' [*MF*, p. 655]. Those who cannot unite and consummate their love in life, can do so in death . . .[5] □

Further referral to the psychoanalytic dimension renders the implicit sexual language of this passage more transparent still: 'The passionate death in this scene is structurally equivalent with the passionate "death" of the sexual orgasm . . . since the death is not single but joint, and the parties are clasped in an embrace, the posture of sexual union.'[6]

But it is not simply the final scene in which Smith locates incestuous undercurrents. For Smith, Tom's aggressive response to both Philip and Stephen is explicable most readily as that of jealous competitiveness. Furthermore, he reads both, and their contrasting roles in the novel, as foils to place Tom in clearer relief: 'Philip is a desexualized object-choice . . . Stephen a sexually-charged one. [Maggie's] ultimate abandonment of both dramatizes the intensity of her passion for Tom.'

Later on, Smith observes, despite his earlier disclaimers in relation to Eliot's lack of conscious involvement in the structures of desire, 'It was clearly Eliot's *conscious* purpose to portray [Stephen] this way, although even here she resorts to vintage Victorian circumlocution'.[7] But there are other frameworks available in the text for the expression of incestuous paradigms, not least the entire network of familial relationships, which Smith characterises as 'blood-centred eroticism'.

■ The novel develops the theme almost obsessively. Relations by blood come first, those by marriage second, and any others a poor third. It appears most blatantly among the Dodsons, for whom 'family' is a First Principle. But Mr Tulliver exhibits it as well in his fixation on the ancestral connection with the mill . . . The special feeling of Mr Tulliver for his sister Gritty, and his perception of the analogy to Tom and Maggie, appear on numerous occasions . . . The pervasiveness of this theme hardly can be exaggerated. Time and again the texture yields a variation on it. The importance for the Maggie–Tom relationship is of course obvious – an unconscious incestuous passion is the more plausible in a *milieu* where family is always first, where erotic energy takes blood relations as its objects.[8] □

In further developing the argument, however, Smith claims a wider significance than purely erotic desire in recognising this pattern as the basis of the Tom–Maggie relationship. For him, the movement from initial intensity as children to a colder, 'adult' distance (only for this trend to be reversed in the final, climactic moment), reflects a wider sense of cultural loss which Smith identifies with John Milton's *Paradise Lost*:

■ Frequently in the childhood scenes, the imagery is drawn from the Edenic myth. Then, as Maggie and Tom reach the age of sexual awareness, of loss of innocence, imagery from that myth is even more dominant. When Tom is sixteen and Maggie thirteen, the family disaster occurs;

Mr Tulliver loses his lawsuit, and thereby the mill, and is precipitated into paralysis. 'Book Third' – the section describing these events – is titled 'The Downfall,' plausible echo of *Paradise Lost*. And the paragraphs describing Maggie and Tom's sorrowful journey homeward after she has informed him of the disaster are palpably Miltonic:

> The two slight youthful figures soon grew indistinct on the distant road – were soon lost behind the projecting hedgerow.
>
> They had gone forth together into their new life of sorrow, and they would never more see the sunshine undimmed by remembered cares. They had entered the thorny wilderness, and the golden gates of their childhood had for ever closed behind them. [*MF*, p. 270]

They have been expelled from paradise; childhood is over; it is the end of innocence, the beginning of knowledge of good and evil. The change in Maggie's attitude toward erotic acts has already been shown a few pages earlier, when she is inhibited from giving Philip the charitable kiss promised in childhood. Again the Edenic imagery is patent:

> When they did meet, she remembered her promise to kiss him, but, as a young lady who had been at a boarding-school, she knew now that such a greeting was out of the question, and Philip would not expect it. The promise was void like so many other sweet, illusory promises of our childhood: void as promises made in Eden before the seasons were divided, and when the starry blossoms grew side by side with the ripening peach – impossible to be fulfilled when the golden gates had been passed. [*MF*, p. 263]

Before Mr Tulliver's 'downfall,' Maggie and Tom's world had been – at least relatively – a paradise. Family, home, and childhood had made them secure from the pain of experience and the disappointments of awareness. The disaster brings drastic changes; the splendor in the grass begins to fade. The family begins to disintegrate; the mill is about to be taken by strangers, and the shadow of erotic consciousness passes over Maggie and Tom's idyllic relationship. But although the overt manifestations of their passion, so prevalent in childhood, rapidly diminish, the passion itself does not fade. It remains, muted and masked. And as the novel continues to develop, this suppressed and submerged quality of the relationship begins to create pressure for emergence, for an eventual open and unambiguous union between Maggie and Tom. There is a feeling that the relationship must culminate.[9] □

Smith is right to draw attention to the prevalence of Edenic motifs in the novel, but one has to question the idealised way in which he depicts the Tom/Maggie partnership here. Tom is persistently cruel, denying and rejecting in his treatment of the adoring Maggie. It is, surely, partly in abject response to her rejection by Tom that she pulverises her fetish in the attic: an effigy that is simultaneously an object reflecting the self as other (and thus her self-loathing brought on by a belief in her own unworthiness of Tom's affections) and one reflecting the other – Tom – who is (at least in part) the self. This is only one of many variations on doubles and doubling in the text. Philip and Tom, for example, are repeatedly superimposed, one upon another, in the context of their relationship with Maggie, the illicit nature of this doubling culminating in Book V, Chapter 4, when Philip's secret *tête-à-tête* with Maggie leads to the following disclosure by her: 'O, it is quite impossible we can ever be more than friends – brother and sister in secret, as we have been' [*MF*, p. 437]. This revelation says as much about Maggie's desire to connect sibling affection with sexual potency as it does about her lack of desire for Philip.

Shortly afterwards, this identification between Tom, the rival and Eden shifts to Stephen Guest, firstly in the chapter title of Book VI, Chapter 1: 'A Duet in Paradise', then in the direct reference to Adam and Eve, albeit that Stephen employs this allusion in the context of his relationship with Lucy, not Maggie: 'We are Adam and Eve unfallen – in paradise' [*MF*, p. 474]. Ironically, however, in prefiguring this assertion with the observation that Philip is 'the fallen Adam with a soured temper', Stephen alludes to his own post-lapsarian, knowing stance, which he will later exploit in his ill-fated boat-trip with Maggie.

Smith ends his article with a broader sweep on paradise, seeing in the final culmination scene more than the realisation of individual desire.

■ It is as well a joint return to the mill and what the mill symbolizes – the Eden of childhood, family, and home from which this pair ha[ve] been so rudely thrust . . . The incest wish and a broader regressive wish become functions of each other. The largest structural pattern of the novel is thus one of venture and return: [p]ossession of the mill, its loss, and its repossession; Maggie and Tom's physical movement from the mill to the outside to the mill again; the movement of Maggie's erotic attachment from Tom to the outsiders Philip and Stephen back to Tom again; Maggie and Tom's union, separation and reunion; movement from incestuous eroticism to attempted normative eroticism back to incestuous eroticism; and movement from the childhood world of innocence to the adult world of experience back to the childhood world again.[10] □

Like many commentators, Smith, though perceiving this incestuous dynamic as mutually shared, allows his attentions to fall almost exclusively on Maggie, the central signifier of not just female desire, but desire *per se*. The major problem with his reading is the blame he situates upon Maggie, clearly reading the expulsion from Eden conventionally (as the fault of Eve as Adam's temptor). Smith also places upon Maggie the necessity for a moral response, one in which he identifies a tendency towards self-recrimination and guilt.

■ For a time the Maggie–Tom relationship is dormant. Then suddenly appears what must be the most bizarre section of the novel, the fourth book, 'The Valley of Humiliation' . . . This is the chapter in which Maggie, with no obvious motivation for such a radical course of action, undertakes to renounce whatever she conceives to be pleasurable.[11] □

Though Smith is far from condemnatory of Maggie's sexuality, he does seem to accept a type of 'natural' tendency for Maggie to be the one upon whom responsibility falls.

■ Maggie's 'wickedness' is liberally established in the childhood sections of the novel. There are numerous specific acts which she commits which reflect this quality, e.g., letting Tom's rabbits die, thrusting pins in her 'fetish,' cutting off her own hair, running away to the gypsy camp. There are numerous references to Maggie by other characters attributing this quality to her, e.g., naughty . . . , mischievous . . . , 'demonstrative' and 'rebellious' . . . , ugly . . . , 'culprit' . . . , 'gypsy' . . . , 'half-wild' . . . There are numerous descriptions of her appearance which confirm this quality, e.g., dirty . . . , 'brown' (i.e., her skin) . . . , 'dark-eyed' . . . , and having dark and unruly hair . . .[12] Finally, there are numerous symbolic extensions of this quality, e.g., her reading as a child Defoe's *History of the Devil* [*MF*, p.67], her 'seven small demons' [*MF*, pp.155, 161], and her trip among her 'unknown kindred,' the 'diabolical' gypsies [*MF*, p.171]. Tom is not always free from these varied associations, but their concentration is decidedly on Maggie. For her, the 'wickedness' theme is carried into adulthood as a kind of taboo associated with erotic alliances. Her friendships with Philip, Stephen, and even Dr Kenn are all 'wrong' in some way, and result in her ostracism, either from the community-at-large or – more importantly to her – from Tom. And there is of course that final alliance with Tom, the most 'wicked' of them all.

Maggie's guilt – a strictly internal matter – is suggested in some of the childhood scenes but receives its fullest development after 'the downfall' and the loss of paradise, especially in her early adolescence, when she enters 'the valley of humiliation.' The novel itself formulates

Maggie's psychic conflict not in the modern terminology of 'guilt' over an 'unconscious wish' but as an impulse toward 'renunciation' of the self-fulfillment urged by her 'passionate nature.'

It is most helpful to talk about Maggie's guilt in connection with her desire for punishment, since they relate to a single psychic process. In 'Book Fourth: The Valley of Humiliation,' Maggie is a guilt-ridden adolescent who has never really committed any crimes to justify her guilt. She is desperately in need of relief. She finds it, at least temporarily, in the writings of à Kempis, who proclaims self-denial to be the route to peace and virtue. As her internalized 'guide' he teaches her that if she punishes herself physically and mentally, either by such crude techniques as lying on a hard floor all night . . . or in the less barbaric way of deprivation of pleasures, she will find peace. The cycle of sensed transgression, guilt, punishment, and release is now complete. The relevance to the incest thesis is obvious.[13] □

For Smith, this inner guilt explains Maggie's passive acceptance of others' judgements of her and her willing submission to Tom's cruel treatment. Unlike later feminist readers, however, he does not address the extent to which this masochistic strand in Maggie's character is dictated by gender expectations. Instead he associates her, more ambivalently, with an elemental power which, while exhilarating in its strength, might again be used against her in a misogynist context: 'The river is symbolically associated with Maggie's psyche . . . [and] the movement of the river is connected with Maggie's loss of conscious control over her actions . . . If a river at normal flow is associated with Maggie's gradual loss of conscious control, a river at flood represents a kind of "inundation" of her entire being by the forces beneath consciousness.'[14]

In 1971, U. C. Knoepflmacher discusses *The Mill on the Floss* as a study in the breakdown of the Victorian family unit. Unlike Smith he directly picks up on the autobiographical comparisons between Maggie and Mary Ann and Tom and Isaac Evans in reminding us that '"George Eliot" was born in 1819, as is Maggie, her brother . . . in 1816, as is Tom'.[15] But where one might see, in this autobiographical parallel, a hoped-for happy ending (after all, brother and sister are, in both the novel and real life, finally reunited), Knoepflmacher sees the larger socio-historical shift as the key one, for which the hopefulness of the sister-brother relationship is a naive substitution.

■ The ending of *The Mill on the Floss* . . . depicts a future that has been blocked. In the novel's 'Conclusion' the wharves on the Floss are busy again 'with echoes of eager voices, with hopeful lading and unlading.' But the reader, like the small band visiting the tombs of Tom and Maggie, cannot participate in this hopefulness. The emphasis on the busy traffic on the river forces us to return in circular fashion to the book's opening paragraphs, in which the narrator who surveys the laden 'black ships' was led to recollect the tiny child who stood absorbed by the churning mill wheel, so unconscious of her future. Lost in his reverie, the narrator managed to escape the weight of time, only to discover that his transcendence was short-lived ... [T]his time-burdened narrator sadly concludes even then that he was merely 'dreaming' of an irrecoverable past.[16] □

Jules Law also picks up on the checking and blocking mechanisms Knoepflmacher identifies, but he builds an entire reading of *The Mill on the Floss* around them, using *'chiasmus,* [a] figure of syntactic reversal or symmetrical crossing'.[17] This figure, Law argues, stands at the centre of Eliot's novel and continually sets up a pattern whereby progress, flow and development are set in motion, only to be thwarted by an equally strong counter-impulse that repels, impedes, denies. On the level of plot, for example, 'The Tulliver mill changes hands and then reverts to its original owners; Maggie floats with the tide and then reverses her direction to return home; and the novel's central chapter on rhetoric underscores its radical critique of literality, metaphor, pedagogy, and misogyny precisely by way of the syntactic figure of chiasmus.' Law then proceeds by expanding upon the checking impulse that motivates so many instances of chiasmus in the text.

■ *The Mill on the Floss* begins with an action which is immediately 'checked'. The first sentence reads: 'A wide plain, where the broadening Floss hurries on between its green banks to the sea, and the loving tide, rushing to meet it, checks its passage with an impetuous embrace' [*MF*, p. 53]. In the next few lines, however, the direction pursued by the Floss is reversed, apparently anticipating the ultimate fate of both Maggie's and the father's impulsiveness. From out of the amorous embrace of river and sea, black ships laden with 'seed' and 'the dark glitter of coal' proceed upriver to St Ogg's, emblems of sexual, commercial and technological penetration which will alter forever the lives of many of the novel's central characters. This proleptic overlapping of the novel's sexual, social, and economic narratives of destruction is accomplished through the dominant, ubiquitous symbol of water.[18] □

He continues:

■ Two questions are raised by the novel's opening paragraph. First, what precisely are the 'checking' forces which oppose the seaward flow of the river and the apparently impulsive temperaments of the main characters? And second, is the reversal of direction and of impulses figured in this passage a symmetrical, containable reversal, or does it suggest a more radical disruption of equilibriums which cannot be given any simple, symmetrical characterization? We may approach these questions by looking both at the pattern of psychological 'checks' in the novel and at the struggle for legal and technological control over the narrative's principal material symbol: the river.

The 'check' of the river Floss by the ocean tide is echoed endlessly in the novel's psychological rhetoric. Maggie, in particular, is consistently 'checked' both by domestic authority and by her own sense of priorities and obligations:

> She rebelled against her lot, she fainted under its loneliness, and fits even of anger and hatred towards her father and mother who were so unlike what she would have them to be – towards Tom, who *checked her* and met her thought or feeling always by some *thwarting difference* – would flow out over her affections and conscience like a lava stream and frighten her . . . [*MF*, p. 380 – Law's emphasis]

In this passage, Maggie is identified with the river Floss, and Tom with the 'checking' or constraining tide. There is some ambiguity here, however, since the very checking of Maggie's impulses produces a new flow – in this case the lava flow of resentment – which Maggie herself evidently wishes to check. The latter dynamic is even more readily apparent in an earlier passage, when the thought of prolonged absence from her prostrate father 'checks' a 'violent' outpouring of grief: 'With these last words, Maggie's sobs burst forth with the more violence for the previous struggles against them. . . . But Maggie soon checked herself abruptly: a single thought had acted on her like a startling sound' . . .

The rhetoric of 'checking' also occurs in a less apocalyptic and more ironic register throughout the novel, as more or less prudential considerations motivate various characters to desist or pause in the pursuit of a particular course of action, or as various characters chastise and correct one another's petty foibles and behavioral tics.

One source of 'checking,' then, is *conscience*, and we would be mistaken in distinguishing categorically between authentic and inauthentic forms of social conscience in the novel (for example, Maggie's vs. Aunt Glegg's), since Eliot takes great pains to emphasize that the distinction between idealism and pragmatism in the analysis of individual motives is a highly problematic one, and that the relative proportion of the two in any one action is difficult to determine. We might also be tempted to think of 'checking' as a process which arises out of a consideration of the consequences of one's actions; but Eliot denies this too. The process of checking arises from the recognition of analogies . . . rather than from any apprehension of causes and effects, even if the characters themselves do not see it quite this way. Mr Tulliver, for instance, regresses from his determination to enforce the repayment of an onerous debt owed him by his sister, and this out of a sympathetic identification with Maggie:

> It had come across his mind that if he were hard upon his sister, it might somehow tend to make Tom hard upon Maggie, at some distant day, when her father was no longer there to take her part; for simple people, like our friend Mr Tulliver, are apt to clothe unimpeachable feelings in erroneous ideas, and this was his confused way of explaining to himself that his love and anxiety for 'the little wench' had given him a new sensibility towards his sister. [*MF*, p. 144]

Eliot's point is that Mr Tulliver misreads his own change: he has constructed a scheme of symmetrical relations in which his own sympathetic actions – his moral self-checking – can be figured as the negation of a future dynamic. The moral action of forbearing on the loan is in fact hardly a negation or reversal of any future system of relations or sequence of causes and effects, but it gives him satisfaction to imagine it in these terms. Such a conception fits perfectly with the generally chiastic logic of crossings and reversals by which he constructs his own domestic identity.[19] □

This connection, identified by Law, between 'checking' and domesticity is, as we have seen, never clearer than in the context of Maggie, for whom gothicism, surprisingly, offers a way out. Nina Auerbach's article, 'The Power of Hunger: Demonism and Maggie Tulliver', takes this gothic identification further than most in situating *The Mill on the Floss* explicitly within a vampiric tradition. For Auerbach, even Maggie's physical stature, particularly her uncontrollable hair, gives her an affinity with Medusan, witch-like figures and suggests the presence of 'destructive powers she is only half aware of and unable to control'.

The inferred connection with the vampire becomes clear in, among other things, Maggie's intensely passionate but damaging relationship with Tom, 'on whose neck she hangs "in rather a strangling fashion"'.[20] Perhaps more interestingly still, Auerbach locates within the Dodson women collectively a fascination with the deathly that is more than pure morbidity. Hence, she continues:

■ The defaced dolls, shattered card-houses, and spoiled hopes with which Maggie's life is littered suggests that in her own messy, over-heated Tulliver fashion, she inherits the Dodson penchant for death and its trappings . . . The cake she crushes and the wine she spills at Aunt Pullet's have a touch of black mass in them, for example; and her love-dismembered dolls anticipate the children from whose blood all the female vampires in *Dracula* take life instead of giving it.[21] □

Certainly a number of archetypal gothic scenarios punctuate the development of this narrative, one of the most frequently discussed being that in which Aunt Pullet displays her new hat to an assembled female audience, as if it were literally a symbol of some dark, closeted, deathly desire.

■ Mrs Pullet rose with a melancholy air and unlocked one wing of a very bright wardrobe, where you may have hastily supposed she would find the new bonnet. Not at all. Such a supposition could only have arisen from a too superficial acquaintance with the habits of the Dodson family. In this wardrobe Mrs Pullet was seeking something small enough to be hidden among layers of linen – it was a door-key.

'You must come with me into the best room,' said Mrs Pullet . . .

So they went in procession along the bright and slippery corridor, dimly lighted by the semi-lunar top of the window, which rose above the closed shutter: it was really quite solemn. Aunt Pullet paused and unlocked a door which opened on something still more solemn than the passage – a darkened room, in which the outer light, entering feebly, showed what looked like the corpses of furniture in white shrouds. Everything that was not shrouded stood with its legs upwards. Lucy laid hold of Maggie's frock, and Maggie's heart beat rapidly.

Aunt Pullet half-opened the shutter and then unlocked the wardrobe, with a melancholy deliberateness which was quite in keeping with the funereal solemnity of the scene. The delicious scent of rose-leaves that issued from the wardrobe made the process of taking out sheet after sheet of silver-paper quite pleasant to assist at, though the sight of the bonnet at last was an anticlimax to Maggie, who would have preferred something more strikingly preternatural. But few things could have been more impressive to Mrs Tulliver . . . [*MF*, pp. 149–50] □

This passage is intriguing because of the way it treats the domestic interior. We have seen, in chapter two of this Guide, that for critics interested in the novel's realist elements it is this painstaking documentation of minute domestic detail that reveals the authenticity of Eliot's stance on the interior. But for critics more interested in the gothic elements of the text, the mocking aspects of the scene only slightly undermine the disturbing nuances.

The scene is, of course, told through the mind's-eye of the two children present, a perspective that facilitates the mystery and suspense. However, it still retains many important sinister qualities that are neither annulled by the satire nor by Maggie's unanticipated final response, and that are even reinforced by the connection Aunt Pullet makes with imminent death in the family. The real significance of this scene, of course, is that the true sinister element derives from the fact that Lucy and Maggie are here being initiated, through ritual, into a form of adult womanhood that can only bring them imprisonment within a variety of sanctions. The idea that the domestic interior is the framework for this restraint is represented in the form of not just one locked door, but two. This might explain Maggie's disappointed response to the nature of the revelation in contrast to its build-up, as opposed to her mother's, which is far too complicit to fail to conform at this stage. Compare this scene with that of Mr Tulliver's chest in Book III, Chapter 4:

■ They entered very quietly, and Mrs Moss took her seat near the head of the bed, while Maggie sat in her old place on the bed, and put her hand on her father's, without causing any change in his face.

Mr Glegg and Tom had also entered, treading softly, and were busy selecting the key of the old oak chest from the bunch which Tom had brought from his father's bureau. They succeeded in opening the chest – which stood opposite the foot of Mr Tulliver's bed – and propping the lid with the iron holder, without much noise.

'There's a tin box,' whispered Mr Glegg, 'he'd most like put a small thing like a note in there. Lift it out, Tom; but I'll just lift up those deeds – they're the deeds o' the house and mill, I suppose – and see what there is under 'em.'

Mr Glegg had lifted out the parchments and had fortunately drawn back a little, when the iron holder gave way, and the heavy lid fell with a loud bang that resounded over the house.

Perhaps there was something in that sound more than the mere fact of the strong vibration that produced the instantaneous effect on the frame of the prostrate man, and for the time completely shook off the obstruction of paralysis. The chest had belonged to his father and his father's father, and it had always been rather a solemn business to visit it . . . In the same moment when all the eyes in the room were turned upon him, he stared up and looked at the chest, the parchments in Mr Glegg's hand, and Tom holding the tin box, with a glance of perfect consciousness and recognition. [*MF*, pp. 303–4] □

There is an obvious sense in which these two scenes are companion pieces. Both are set up as collective family rituals, driven by associations with the possibility of impending death, and detailing the revelation of secrets locked away in closets which require the opening of not one lock but two. Solemnity is seen as the presiding mood in both passages and the domestic interior is the location for the suspense. But gothic moments do not *just* centre on the home in this novel.

■ Maggie loved to linger in the great spaces of the mill, and often came out with her black hair powdered to a soft whiteness that made her dark eyes flash out with new fire. The resolute din, the unresting motion of the great stones giving her a dim delicious awe as at the presence of an uncontrollable force, the meal for ever pouring, pouring, the fine white powder softening all surfaces and making the very spider-nets look like faery lace-work, the sweet pure scent of the meal – all helped to make Maggie feel that the mill was a little world apart from her outside everyday life. The spiders were especially a subject of speculation with her: she wondered if they had any relations outside the mill, for in that case there must be a painful difficulty in their family intercourse: a fat and floury spider, accustomed to take his fly well dusted with meal, must suffer a little at a cousin's table where the fly was *au naturel*, and the lady spiders must be mutually shocked at each other's appearance. [*MF*, p. 80] □

For many commentators on the novel the mill is set up as a discrete world from that of the house. The mill is Tulliver territory, where the house is Dodson territory; the mill represents the outside, masculine world of business and commerce, where the house represents the feminine, internalised world of dress-codes and table-linen. The claustrophobia of the first passage is in direct contrast with 'the great spaces of the mill' and Maggie muses that 'the mill was a little world apart'. But, for Maggie, this world is not set up in competition with the domestic interior in this case, it is set up as distinct from a world in which she is punished and scorned. There is a sense of autonomy revealed in this passage that is lacking elsewhere in the early chapters of the novel and, revealingly, it is the presence of the gothic that seems to act as a reassuring continuity in all three passages. We have seen that, in the hat-revelation scene, Maggie is disappointed that what is revealed does not live up to its portentous introduction. In the second scene it is the combination of gothic secrets and family legacies that lead to Mr

Tulliver's apparent resurrection from the grave. In the third scene the spiders and their webs – key gothic images – lead to speculations in which Maggie sees them as familiar (and as witches' familiars) and fears for the nature of their familial relations – for it is in this arena that her own nightmares reside.

Returning to Auerbach's article, it can be seen to pave the way for later feminist readings of the novel. Concluding with the observation that 'The demonism of Maggie Tulliver is planted in her very woman-liness . . . [in which her] primordially feminine hunger for love is at one with her instinct to kill and to die',[22] she takes issue with those critics who have traditionally associated Eliot's work with the realm of the mas-culine intellect. In *The Mill on the Floss*, she claims, we find a very different gendering of narrative perspective and character construction. Hence, though Maggie Tulliver is fascinated with books and book-learning, what she discovers in them is very different to the type of acceptable scholarship of a Lydgate or even a stuffy Casaubon. Here, from the start, books are associated with seduction, spells, delight and witchery. Indeed, it is through Maggie's vampiric devouring of reading material as a young child that she first encounters the image of the witch that haunts her and seems to be her own alter-ego. And yet, though 'one motif shows [Maggie] avidly devouring books, another shows her oblit-erating them in dreams or flinging them aside'.[23] Such ambivalence typifies Maggie's emotions throughout the course of the book, but per-haps finds its zenith in Maggie's involvement with animals, which Auerbach expands upon in the following terms.

■ Traditional accounts of witchcraft place the witch in an intense and equivocal relationship to the animal kingdom. Animal masks are worn at the witches' Sabbath, where Satan frequently presides in the costume of a bull; animals are worshipped and used as conduits for spells, the witch's nature seeming at times interchangeable with that of her familiar. But one of the commonest manifestations of witchery is the power to blight and cause disease in the animal kingdom. Here we can see the affinity between the legends of the witch and those of the vam-pire. The vampire too has a magical sympathetic kinship with animals, being able to assume the shape of dog and wolf as well as bat. But in some legends, animals shun him: he is a scourge of cattle and sheep, and dogs howl and even die in terror at his approach. Both witch and vampire simultaneously spring from animals and are fatal to them.

Maggie too both blights animals and becomes them. The hutch of starved rabbits is presented as the first symbol of her love for Tom, suggesting a silent murderousness of which the animals are conduit and fetish. Yet much of the animal imagery in the novel clusters around Maggie. Her affinities with animals range from simple descriptive similes – she shakes the water from her hair 'like a Skye terrier escaped from his bath' [*MF*, p. 78] – to intimations of metamorphosis that carry magical suggestions, such as this image of Philip's: 'What was it, he wondered, that made Maggie's dark eyes remind him of the stories about princesses being turned into animals? . . . I think it was, that her eyes were full of unsatisfied intelligence and unsatisfied, beseeching affection' [*MF*, p. 253]. Philip's vocabulary and the narrator's reassuring explication soften the power of the picture, which is sinister. Witches in folklore are more likely to turn into animals than princesses are; and as well as expressing the rootedness of the witch in her familiar, the image evokes a string of pagan goddesses with the bodies of animals and the heads of women, of whom the lamia, the vampire's pagan ancestor, is one of the darkest.

Maggie's alliance with trees also connotes witchcraft, which is traditionally linked to tree worship: the dance around the fairy tree and invocation to it are perennial features of witches' Sabbath rituals in England. The tree appears first when little Maggie is possessed by 'small demons': 'a small Medusa with her snakes cropped,' she pushes Lucy into the mud and retreats impenitently to the roots of a tree, to glower at Tom and Lucy 'with her small Medusa face' [*MF*, p. 164]. In the sequence with Philip in the Red Deeps, the association recurs, amplified and beautified: 'With her dark colouring and jet crown surmounting her tall figure, she seems to have a sort of kinship with the grand Scotch firs, at which she is looking up as if she loved them well' [*MF*, pp. 393–4]. Philip, who seems possessed by the association of Maggie with metamorphosis, insists upon this kinship, finally painting Maggie as 'a tall Hamadryad, dark and strong and noble, just issued from one of the fir-trees' [*MF*, p. 426].[24] Philip's artist's eye continually captures Maggie in the process of equivocal transformation, which his less true language muffles by such adjectives as 'noble.' To one familiar with English witchcraft legends and rituals, these images of Maggie carry their own undercurrents, which hardly need Lucy's more explicit reinforcement later on: 'I can't think what witchery it is in you, Maggie, that makes you look best in shabby clothes' [*MF*, p. 480]. Another of Lucy's innocent remarks, about the secret liaison with Philip, carries more complex ironies: 'Ah, now I see how it is you know Shakespeare and everything, and have learned so much since you left school – which always seemed to me witchcraft before – part of your general uncanniness' [*MF*, pp. 497–8]. Lucy's initial intuition is correct, for Maggie learned about Shakespeare in the Red Deeps, which, as Philip senses, is the proper setting for and a powerful projection of her 'general uncanniness.'

But in the prophetic doppelgänger [sinister double] that arrests the young Maggie from the pages of Defoe, the witch is not lodged in an animal or a tree; she is bobbing in water, an element that follows Maggie and shapes her life. The origin of the English ducking ritual places the witch in a typically ambiguous relationship to water. In theory, a witch will not drown because the pure baptismal element must cast out the evil thing. But there is an obverse explanation of the witch's ability to float: perhaps her magical kinship with a more darkly defined water allies her with the element and prevents it from destroying her. The witch's dual relationship to nature is evident in the ducking ritual as it is in her power over animals: do they feed on or repel each other? Is the witch a growth from or an enemy of the natural world?

The vampire's relationship to water is as ambiguous as the witch's. In many versions of the legend, he is unable to cross running water on his own power. This abrupt paralysis is a suggestive dark gloss on the figure of the Virgin of the Flood, Maggie's holy analogue in *The Mill on the Floss*, whom local legends depict wailing by the river bank to be ferried across, unable to work her magical transformation until Beorl has allowed her to enter his boat. But Maggie's 'almost miraculous' flight across the river to Tom shows her powers gushing out on the water, and so, in some stories, do the vampire's. Count Dracula feasts triumphantly on the ship's crew during an ocean voyage; he is able to control storms and tides; and Mina Harker's unholy 'marriage' to him is revealed under hypnosis through a shared sense of 'the lapping of water . . . gurgling by.' The implicit question that runs through the legends of witches and vampires also runs through Maggie's voyages in *The Mill on the Floss*: is the pure baptismal element itself a conduit blending what is unholy with what is potentially divine?

. . . [T]he great crises in Maggie's life come when she abandons herself to the movement of the tides. We first see her staring intently over the gloomy water; before we hear her speak, her mother prophesies darkly about her proclivity for 'wanderin' up an' down by the water, like a wild thing' [*MF*, p. 60];[25] her father's mad fear that irrigation will drain the mill of its water deprives her of her childhood home; the flight with Stephen that uproots so many lives takes place by water; and so, of course, do Maggie's much-criticized apotheosis and death in the final flood, which raise more questions than they resolve.

These questions are the same as those raised by the childish Maggie about the witch in Defoe who is her psychic mirror: is the woman in the water a witch or not? Does she float or sink? Is water her friend or foe, condemning her to spiritual exile forever or sweeping her to final vindication and 'home'? '"O God, where am I? Which is the way home?" she crie[s] out, in the dim loneliness' of a flooded world [*MF*, p. 651], and the book's conclusion only echoes this cry.

Everything has plunged its head under water with the ducks, as the narrator had yearned to do at the beginning. The difficult ending will always be unsatisfactory for those seeking a drier world's perspective, but it is at one with the ethos of Gothic romance as Robert Kiely defines it: 'We have seen over and over again that romantic novels have troubled and unsatisfactory endings. One may say that a resistance to conclusion is one of the distinguishing characteristics of [Gothic] romantic fiction.' . . .[26]

Certainly, Maggie seems to be on the side of the flood, since it seeps into the house as an efficacious, though indirect, answer to her despairing prayer. Does she 'cause' it, as the vampire evokes storms and controls the tides? Are the waves on which she magically rides her final destructive ally against the commonality that expels and entices her? To some extent, at least, the flood is Maggie's last and strongest familiar, and it is not described through a soothing haze of death and rebirth imagery, but as a fury that crashes through houses, destroys livestock, and drowns crops. 'Nature repairs her ravages – but not all' [*MF*, p.656] is the narrator's final quiet statement about a phenomenon that uproots and scars more life than it restores.

But it preserves Maggie until she has obtained Tom. Floating toward him, she is envisioned ambiguously with 'her wet clothes [clinging] round her, and her streaming hair . . . dashed about by the wind' [*MF*, p.652]. Like the witch's watery cousin, the Lorelei or mermaid, she lures Tom out of the house where he has found temporary protection – for the waters have stopped rising – into the dangerous tides. The loosely sacramental language of the ending tells us that preternatural forces have been evoked and revealed without disclosing their source. Tom is possessed by the 'revelation to his spirit, of the depths in life, that had lain beyond his vision,' leaving him 'pale with a certain awe and humiliation' [*MF*, p.654]. At last, 'a mist gather[s] over the blue-grey eyes,' [*MF*, p.655] he falls under Maggie's spell, rows the boat into the dangerous current, clings to her, and sinks, a devotee at last . . .[27] □

It is with the psychoanalytic implications of Maggie's sexuality that Auerbach is most concerned. Hence, in Book I, Chapter 4, when Maggie plunges her head into a basin of water, Auerbach pulls back from a purely mimetic interpretation of this scene, reading it instead as a decision to 'exchange . . . a clear vision for a swimming vision, a submergence in experience at the cost of objectivity and judgment'. Later she observes, 'Burning or swimming, Maggie's eyes invoke or transmit more than they see'.[28]

In these terms all the metaphors of water, drifting and drowning are recast in terms of the unconscious and therefore reflect the larger issue of desire and sexuality at work in the text. Perhaps most surprising is Auerbach's observation that 'the unwomanly, because unnurturing, woman of whom Maggie Tulliver is a small type will come into her own in vampire literature, to be hymned most erotically in the ecstatically infertile lesbianism of [Sheridan Le Fanu's 1872 novel,] *Carmilla'*. Again, it is this powerful infertility (a concept paradoxical in itself) that aligns Maggie with the Dodsons rather than the Tullivers; for the sisters are most powerful in their collective independence from the men to whom they purportedly belong, as opposed to Mr Tulliver's sister, 'Gritty' Moss, who is isolated in her poverty, her poor choice of husband (by whom she is defined throughout), and what Auerbach refers to as her 'wearily prolific' ability to bring forth children.[29]

This theme of unsatisfactory mothering is also identified by Eva Fuchs, in her article 'The Pattern's All Missed'. She opens by drawing attention to the presiding sense of maternal loss in the novel: Philip Wakem's mother dies when he is a small child; Mr Tulliver's mother dies as a young, handsome woman; and, on a more metaphorical level, both Maggie and the toddler Laura (whom Tom minds at Mr and Mrs Stelling's house) have, she argues, 'rejecting mothers', in response to which they 'turn their unsatisfied hunger for love toward Tom'.[30]

In contrast to these hungered and deprived characters stands Bob Jakin, the peddlar, upon whom Fuchs concentrates her argument. She reminds us that he is unusual in 'liv[ing] with a mother who is hugely fat in a "queer round house" [*MF*, p. 101] which suggests a womb. Bob's enwombment within the "queer round house" of the maternal body permits him to thrive.'[31]

Unlike Maggie, and the toddler Laura, both held back by their attachment to Tom (Maggie figuratively and Laura literally by a length of ribbon tied to his wrist), Bob wanders far and wide, selling his wares – such lengths of ribbon among them. This different relation to the mother, combined with an independence and mobility denied the other characters, endows Bob with a far more healthy sexuality.

■ Bob's glee in outwitting his customers is childlike; it is akin to the triumph and delight a small boy or girl experiences when it manages to deceive the mother who is far more powerful than itself into gratifying its wishes. Bob's trickery not only amuses him but also enables him to survive. Through it, he induces the 'skinflint' women with whom he trades to surrender the payment (and symbolically the nourishment) which they wish to withhold from him. With the money which he extracts from the old women, Bob is able to get his 'dinner' [*MF*, p. 326].

George Eliot notes that the thumb which is so useful to Bob is a 'singularly broad specimen' of the 'difference between the man and the monkey' [*MF*, p. 377]. Bob's thumb is thus in several senses a mark of singularity and of 'difference.' As George Eliot reminds the reader, the apposable[32] thumb distinguishes man from the other primates. In its unusual broadness, Bob's thumb also differentiates him from less well-endowed individuals. Bob's big thumb is a mark of 'difference' in a third, implicit sense. Though George Eliot uses 'man' generically in the remark quoted above (to mean 'human'), 'man' carries with it a hint of its alternative meaning of 'male person.' The big thumb which gives Bob superiority over the women with whom he haggles (and in particular over Maggie's formidable Aunt Glegg) is phallic; it suggests his anatomical difference from them and his immunity to their power.

The comedy involving Bob and his 'skinflint' customers has misogynist overtones. George Eliot seems to take part vicariously in the peddler's victory over the 'varmint' [*MF*, p. 377] old women. The misogyny in *The Mill on the Floss* issues, I believe, out of George Eliot's unconscious fear of the female will. *The Mill on the Floss* is permeated both by intense nostalgia for early mother/infant oneness and by a dread and resentment of maternal power which date from infancy.

Like Bob's 'singularly broad' thumb, the goods in which he trades highlight his difference from his neighbors. In *The Mill on the Floss* Eliot equates separateness with deviation from pattern; the break in the pattern is both a flaw and the stamp of individual identity. Bob explains to Aunt Glegg that his lengths of net and of muslin have been cheapened because they are imperfect. Included in Bob's stock is a piece of figured muslin which has a yard at the center in which 'the pattern's all missed' [*MF*, p. 419]. The irregular yard at the center is an emblem for Bob, for he is himself an 'irregular character' and a deviation from pattern.

Bob displays his flawed goods to Aunt Glegg with a show of extreme reluctance. He voices the fear that the 'damaged' [*MF*, p. 420] bit may upset her so badly that it will nauseate her. Although Bob's unwillingness to open his pack is a mischievous pretense, designed to excite Aunt Glegg's curiosity and greed, it suggests his author's genuine dread of personal exposure. The flawed goods which Bob displays only at Aunt Glegg's repeated urging are linked with the unorthodox, sensuous, and vital self which Eliot was struggling to release as she wrote *The Mill on the Floss* and which she feared would be greeted with aversion . . .[33]

During his exchange with Aunt Glegg, Bob accomplishes a seduction. By teasing her with the goods which he in part displays and in part withholds from view, he induces a 'yearning' in her which is essentially erotic. Bob flatters Aunt Glegg, repeatedly telling her that she is a 'handsome' woman [*MF*, p. 418]. The erotic quality of their exchange is most explicit at the point at which he tempts her with a 'scarlet woollen kerchief' [*MF*, p. 418] which is flawed by a moth-hole at one end. As he displays the scarf, Bob appeals directly to appetite, observing that 'Here's a thing to make a lass's mouth water' [*MF*, p. 418]. He admiringly compares the scarf to 'a bit of a blaze' and to 'fire' [*MF*, p. 418]. 'Fire' is linked throughout *The Mill on the Floss* with the anarchic erotic and aggressive energies which George Eliot else-where calls 'the primal passionate store'.[34] The flame-colored moth-damaged cloth with which Bob tempts Aunt Glegg is emblematic of the passionate and vulnerable life of the body . . .

Though Aunt Glegg rejects the fiery scarf, Bob induces her to buy the piece of muslin with the irregularly patterned yard at its center. His triumph over Aunt Glegg is heightened by the fact that of all the Dodsons she is, at the beginning of *The Mill on the Floss*, the most rigidly intolerant of deviation from pattern. Aunt Glegg is the spokesperson for the Dodson family 'religion' which consists in 'revering' 'whatever . . . [is] customary and respectable'. As the custodian of the Dodson traditions, she scolds her sisters for daring, even in small matters, to depart from the 'ways o' the family' [*MF*, p. 109]. Aunt Glegg considers the weak Mrs. Tulliver particularly vulnerable to error and urges her to 'take pattern' [*MF*, p. 110] by her older sisters.

Throughout her history, Maggie experiences herself as an aberra-tion; the irregular yard at the center is linked symbolically with her. In her mother's eyes, Maggie is peculiar, even uncanny. Mrs Tulliver feels no kinship with the daughter who does not resemble her physically and whose turbulence and intensity she dislikes. Although her father takes pride in the gifts which he senses in Maggie, he also experiences deep uneasiness over them. In his opinion, the eager intelligence which distinguishes Maggie from more ordinary children is at best wasted in a girl, at worst unnatural and a source of 'mischief' [*MF*, p. 68]. Somberly, he remarks to his wife that 'an over 'cute woman's no better nor a long-tailed sheep – she'll fetch none the bigger price for that' [*MF*, p. 60]. Like Bob's defective goods, Maggie is, in her father's opinion, a commodity with only a dubious market value . . .

In her forgetfulness of the creatures entrusted to her care, Maggie reenacts her own abandonment. Like the mothers in *The Mill on the Floss* who have withdrawn from their children out of illness or indifference, Maggie is remote from the [rabbits] which have been relegated to a 'far toolhouse' [*MF*, p. 82] and left there to die. The animals' fierce hunger is matched by Maggie's.

At the end of his exchange with Maggie, Luke remarks that Tom will 'know better' than to 'buy such things [as the lop-eared rabbits] another time' [*MF*, p. 82]. In Luke's judgment, the rabbits, like Bob's wares, are defective goods. Early in *The Mill on the Floss* narrative, George Eliot points to Maggie's resemblance to all imperfect and strongly individual things. She comments on the distinctiveness of Maggie's features, which 'Nature seemed to have moulded and coloured with the most decided intention' [*MF*, p. 84]. On Maggie's face, the marks of individual identity are as indelible as the dyes which permeate Bob's fabrics 'till the threads melt away i' the wash-tub' [*MF*, p. 420]. In their regularity and anonymity, Tom's features contrast with Maggie's. George Eliot observes that nothing can be 'discern[ed]' in his 'physiognomy . . . but the generic character of boyhood' [*MF*, p. 84].

In the aftermath of her elopement with Stephen, Maggie's identity with Bob's flawed goods becomes explicit. Her elopement sexualizes Maggie in the minds of Tom and of the townspeople of St. Ogg's; it reveals her to the world as willful and passionate. In Tom's estimation, Maggie has 'behaved as no modest girl would have done' [*MF*, p. 613]; she has returned unmarried and unmarriageable, soiled, and (in Tom's fantasies, although not in fact) unchaste. Even Maggie's physical appearance on her return is tarnished; she has 'an expression of . . . pain . . . about her brow and eyes,' her dress is 'unchanged,' and 'her whole appearance . . . [is] worn and distressed' [*MF*, p. 612]. Like Bob's lengths of fabric, Maggie on her return is a 'damaged thing.'

From the perspective of Tom and of the citizens of St. Ogg's, Maggie's worst offense is not her elopement with Stephen but rather her solitary return. Maggie's singleness at the end of *The Mill on the Floss* evokes in Tom a repugnance so intense that he can find no words which are adequate to express it. Gathering all the force of his person-ality into his rejection of her, he tells Maggie that he finds the sight of her hateful. Even before he begins to speak, she recognizes the aver-sion in his face, which has gone 'white with disgust and indignation' [*MF*, p. 612]. In its violence, Tom's rejection of Maggie matches the nauseated response which Bob fears that his damaged goods will evoke in his customers. As though to underscore her heroine's identity with Bob's flawed fabrics, George Eliot observes that Maggie feels Tom's 'hatred . . . rushing through her fibres' [*MF*, p. 612].

In the conclusion of *The Mill on the Floss* Bob repeatedly attempts to aid and comfort Maggie. After the elopement with Stephen, when Maggie feels herself to be desperately in danger, she briefly catches sight of Bob at a steamboat landing. As though he were her guardian spirit, Bob advances 'towards' Maggie and tries 'to speak to her' [*MF*, p. 599]. Later, when Tom has cast Maggie out, she turns to Bob for shelter.

At the point at which Maggie takes lodgings with him, Bob has recently become the father of an infant girl whom he has named after her. In an attempt to comfort Maggie, Bob gives her his two-month's old baby to hold in her arms. Because she is literally distracted by grief, Maggie has difficulty concentrating her attention on the baby, whom she holds 'anxiously, as if she feared it might slip from her mind and her fingers' [*MF*, p. 616]. The baby who has her name, but whom Maggie cannot quite hold in her arms and thoughts, represents her own emergent self, but a self still too fragile and unformed to endure . . .

In the 'Conclusion' to *The Mill on the Floss*, the narrator makes reference to a 'rending' which has not been repaired, to 'new growth' which is 'not the same as the old' [*MF*, p. 656]. Maggie and Tom drown in close 'embrace' and a portion of the mill-home of their childhood is violently shattered by 'the crash of trees and stones against it' [*MF*, pp. 655, 654] so that the 'new growth' of which the narrator speaks can emerge. By imagining the death of the old Maggie who is dominated by incestuous longings and by the unsatisfied hungers of the past, George Eliot makes it possible for the new Maggie fathered by Bob Jakin to be born.[35] □

Developing this connection between the trading of ribbons and the transactions of desire, Elizabeth Weed also focuses upon the metaphor of threads and material, contrasting the control and order of well-woven fabric and its connections with 'floss' (the river's own name) with the symbolism of waves, currents and tides 'represent[ing] the flow of unleashed forces . . . [Where] the fibres represent containment . . . the currents represent the opposite, the absence of restraint.'[36] Weed continues:

■ An important locus in the novel for the conflict between [threads and currents] is the river Floss itself. On the one hand, the river means home to Maggie and Tom, the privileged place of childhood to which they are bound by the fibers of their memory. On the other hand, it remains a river, a flow of water that holds within it the ever-present danger of flood and of the unleashed forces of death and destruction. Significantly, the word 'floss' itself contains both elements of the tension. A 'floss' is a silky fiber, such as twisted embroidery thread and, at the same time, it is the preterite of the German verb *fliessen*, meaning 'to flow'. When, in the first sentence of the novel, the narrator introduces the reader to the Floss, it is described as follows: 'A wide plain, where the broadening Floss hurries on between its green banks to the sea, and the loving tide, rushing to meet it, checks its passage with an impetuous embrace' [*MF*, p. 53]. The two elements of the fiber/current tension are present in the description, but the narrator assures us that although the tide 'checks the passage' of the Floss, it is a 'loving' tide and does so with an embrace. The reader who enters the novel for the first time may be somewhat troubled by this sentence, in spite of its reassuring tone . . . [Indeed], once he has completed the novel, he finds, if he returns to the first sentence, that its unsettling elements are somewhat more problematic. The reader now knows that the loving embrace is an obvious foreshadowing of Maggie and Tom's embrace in death, and that the point at which the tide meets the Floss – a point of indetermination, where it is impossible to tell which direction the tide is flowing and which direction the Floss – can also be the point at which the destructive forces of the flood are set loose. Finally, for the reader whose interrogation of the passage extends to its etymological sources, there is the additional knowledge that just as the name 'Floss' contains both current and fiber, so, concealed beneath the image of the loving embrace of the tide, is the word 'tide' itself, which carries with it its Indo-European root, 'dā', meaning 'to divide' or 'cut up'.[37] □

This imagery of fabric and cutting is then developed more closely in the context of the gendering of economics in the novel. Despite the interchange between Bob and Aunt Glegg, Weed reminds us that women are primarily commodities rather than consumers, 'the whole story of Mr Tulliver's bankruptcy and loss of the mill, and Tom's payment of the debts and repossession of the property [being] an exclusively male one', and Mrs Tulliver's involvement in the bankruptcy taking her straight back to the terms of her own marriage: '. . . she [being] distressed chiefly at the thought that her linen with the name "Elizabeth Dodson", her "maiden mark"' [MF, p. 158], embroidered on it, will all 'be sold – and go into strange people's houses, and perhaps be cut with the knives' [MF, p. 282].[38] But Weed is unnecessarily hard on Mrs Tulliver for her response to this domestic catastrophe: 'What she is losing with her name is, in fact, nothing, for although much is made of the "Dodsons and Tullivers", there is no living Dodson in the book . . . all of the Dodson women belong to men.'

Surely this fact accounts in large part for precisely *why* household linen takes on such importance, not just in economic terms but in those of female identity. As Weed herself acknowledges, and as the passages we have analysed above confirm, 'The Mr Deans and Mr Wakems possess the keys to worldly success; the Mrs Tullivers and Mrs Pullets possess the keys to linen cabinets. The men create, control, and exploit the networks of trade; the women sew the fabrics.'

In the larger spirit of competition throughout the text, then, the 'fibers that bind men's hearts' are continually under threat from the 'instruments of penetration, tearing, cutting, and rending' that proliferate in the novel.[39] In the terms of the psychoanalytic discourses often applied to *The Mill on the Floss*, this infers a castration motif underlying any superficial Dodson subservience. In fact, despite Weed's disparaging remarks about Dodsons, this novel seems to me to offer Eliot's strongest vision of woman-centred discourse, concerning itself not just with female sexuality, witches and vampires, but also social opportunities for women. However, if Weed is hard on Mrs Tulliver she is even more so on Maggie:

■ The fabric of Maggie's fictions is weak. Not only is she forced to choose her authorities at random, but cut off as she is from a truly performative language, and unable to invent a satisfactory ending to her own story, she fabricates incomplete and fragile fictions. Her method of reading Tom's Latin grammar is illustrative: 'she delighted in new words, and quickly found that there was an English Key at the end, which would make her very wise about Latin at slight expense. She presently made up her mind to skip the rules in the Syntax, – the examples became so absorbing . . . The most fragmentary examples were her favourites.' [*MF*, p. 217][40] □

Weed continues on the subject of the role played by language.

■ An examination of the economy of values governing the formal construction of Eliot's fiction reveals a fundamental analogical relationship between the function of language on the one hand and the functioning of 'real' society on the other. Just as the language or languages of the novel are denied an absolute guarantee of significance but remain to varying degrees meaningful and potentially useful, so are societies to varying degrees meaningful and ameliorable even though they are deprived of a transcendent moral base. An illustration of this analogy may be found in the characters' relationships to language. In the first place, much of the action of the novel, much of what happens, is experienced by the characters themselves through the medium of language. The children understand the truth of Mr Tulliver's bankruptcy by confronting words and phrases from their childhood: to 'have the bailiff in the house,' 'to be sold up,' . . . 'fail[ing]' [*MF*, p. 280]. Mr Tulliver learns of his financial disaster through a letter. His curse against Wakem is inscribed in his family Bible, and this inscription becomes, for Tom, the law, and for the family, a source of much of its suffering. Tom attacks Philip with words; and Maggie is denied reentry into St. Ogg's society by the obloquy fashioned by the 'world's wife.'

Moreover, the human experience of virtually every character in the book is presented through the metaphor of language: life itself is seen as a language to which one must gain access, and success or failure in life is seen as a function of one's command of one or various languages. For Mr Tulliver, 'This [is] a puzzling world,' and all sufferings are a result of lacking the clue, the key to the enigma. From his perspective, the problem is not so much with the world of the Creator, but with the world of men: 'if the world had been left as God made it, I could ha' seen my way and held my own wi' the best of 'em; but things have got so twisted round and wrapped up i' unreasonable words, as arn't a bit like 'em, as I'm clean at fault, often an' often. Everything winds about so – the more straightforrard you are, the more you're puzzled' [*MF*, pp. 64, 69]. For the more intelligent Maggie, life begins as a joyful exploration, a delighted discovery of etymologies and of the English keys at the end of Tom's Latin books, which open up to her a whole magical world. As she gets older she searches with less joy but as much energy for the 'key that would enable her to understand and, in understanding, endure, the heavy weight that had fallen on her young heart' [*MF*, p. 379].

Once the languages of life are deciphered, they must be used in order to survive. Mr. Tulliver invests a considerable sum of money in Tom's education so that the boy can avoid the linguistic handicaps of his father and better outwit the lawyers of the world. He wants Tom to '"know what folks mean, and how to wrap things up in words as aren't actionable. It's an uncommon fine thing, that is," concluded Mr Tulliver, shaking his head, "when you can let a man know what you think of him without paying for it"' [*MF*, p. 72]. After a false start, Tom does, in fact, learn the language he needs to succeed in the world. It is not Latin, which he quickly forgets (and which Mr Dean considers to be such a luxury that it ought to be taxed), but the language of commerce that affords him an entry into the lucrative world of trade of St. Ogg's.

For Maggie the problem is not so simple. As a girl, she is unable to learn the languages that guarantee access to the larger world of men. Nor has she completely learned her 'life-lessons' in the 'very trivial language' of women [*MF*, p. 535]. Denied a coherent language of her own, Maggie is forced to search among foreign languages for one that will help her survive. And in her search she looks not only for a language, but for a full-blown narrative model that will help her to read the fiction of her own life, a fiction that will offer her control and a way of making her experience intelligible. When she is very young she is attracted to stories about witches and gypsies and women warriors.[41] As she gets older she ceases to find female models and simply adapts herself to whatever promising male authority she encounters, such as St. Thomas à Kempis, whom she looks to as the 'secret of life that would enable her to renounce all other secrets' ... [*MF*, p. 383].

Whereas Tom is rather successful in realizing the fictions he invents for his future, the unfortunate Maggie resembles her father in her inability to create the narrative of her life. For Mr Tulliver, the threads of the narrative forever form a tangled skein. For Maggie, the problem is one of becoming trapped somehow, not only in the fictions fashioned by others, such as the obloquy of the world's wife, or Philip's playful prediction as to how she will revenge the dark haired women of the novels, but in the intersection of her own narratives with the force of events.

The characters' fictions are, in fact, all tested in one way or another by the strength they show against the forces of life. To use the figures frequently used in the book, the narratives that can best withstand the onrush of life's forces are those that are strongly woven fabrics.[42] □

Returning to Law's essay on chiasmus we remember that he derives the figure from Tom's Eton Grammar. Having done so he goes on to apply it to an understanding of the representation of gender in the novel in a manner worth comparing with Weed's. Starting with Tom's emasculation through education, he bases his reading on a passage from Book II, Chapter 1:

■ [S]trange to say, under this vigorous treatment Tom became more like a girl than he had ever been in his life before. He had a large share of pride, which had hitherto found itself very comfortable in the world, despising Old Goggles, and reposing in the sense of unquestioned rights: but now this same pride met with nothing but bruises and crushings. Tom was too clear-sighted not to be aware that Mr Stelling's standard of things was quite different, was certainly something higher in the eyes of the world, than that of the people he had been living amongst, and that brought in contact with it, he, Tom Tulliver, appeared uncouth and stupid: he was by no means indifferent to this, and his pride got into an uneasy condition which quite nullified his boyish self-satisfaction, and gave him something of the girl's susceptibility. [*MF*, p. 210] □

Law continues:

■ The passage plots the decline of Tom's self-confidence in terms of an exchange of gender identities; yet as we line up the corresponding terms of the chiasmus we notice that more than syntactic order has been reversed. There is a double reversal going on here, with several of the terms from the first half of the chiasmus reappearing in negative form. The term 'different' in the first half of the passage is matched by the phrase 'not indifferent' in the second half, and the 'girl' of the first half corresponds to the 'nullified boy' of the second. Difference and femininity, by this equation, are constituted as negatives, or at best, double negatives.

Eliot is performing two distinct critiques here with one and the same device. At one level this may be read as a critique of the patriarchal gender system in which femininity is understood negatively in reference to a normative and putatively universal masculinity. This critique requires first that we pay attention to syntactic form; it is by noticing the chiastic rhythm of the chapter and by being alert for the distinctive patterns of chiasmus that we recognize the curious reversal of terms which disturbs Tom's identity in this passage. Yet once we have noticed – and thus come to expect the completion of – this syntactic pattern, we are prepared to notice the contortions (in the form of the double negative) required to fulfil it. We recognize the invidious social construction of femininity precisely by noticing a chiasmus which goes awry, by noting the discrepancy between those 'crossings' we expect and the relations we actually encounter. But this is a critique of reading as much as of social arrangements.[43] □

This brings us to Eva Fuchs's short piece in *The Explicator*, in which she argues that Maggie's struggle for an autonomous existence aside from all the male characters of the text is not as easily quashed as some might believe.[44]

■ Psychological critics of *The Mill on the Floss* have tended to emphasize Maggie's overwhelming nostalgia for childhood, home, and a psychic state in which self and others were not sharply differentiated. Marianne Hirsch interprets Maggie's 'death by drowning' in her brother's arms as the fulfillment of that nostalgia and as a return to 'pre-oedipal fusion'.[45] *The Mill on the Floss* also hints, however, at powerful impulses within Maggie of an opposing kind – impulses to individuate and to assert rather than obliterate psychic boundaries. Maggie's longing to achieve a vivid autonomous identity is encoded in an aside near the end of the novel. In this aside, Eliot imagines an alternative conclusion to her narrative – one in which Stephen marries Maggie. In that hypothetical outcome, the outrage evoked by Maggie's elopement with Stephen quickly subsides and is replaced by an attitude of benign tolerance toward the new couple. As George Eliot makes clear, the community's new charitableness toward Maggie is shallow and conventional. Because Maggie's marriage makes her respectable, her defense requires no special courage.

In the false alternative conclusion, in which Maggie marries Stephen, her individual identity is so thoroughly obliterated that she assumes his first name as well as his last, becoming 'Mrs Stephen Guest.' Although Mr and Mrs Guest are forgiven by nearly the whole of the community, a 'Miss Unit' remains unyielding in her antagonism. Because the motives for her obduracy are not stated, the reader assumes that Miss Unit represents the most inflexible and harshly judgmental elements of society. Interestingly, however, George Eliot does not suggest that 'Miss Unit' is hostile to Maggie herself; rather, Miss Unit seems only to oppose Maggie's marriage with Stephen and (by implication) the loss of name and of identity that that marriage involves for Maggie. A 'unit' is a single entity; as her odd name suggests, Miss Unit represents the part of Maggie that aspires toward autonomy and which resists submergence in another.

Miss Unit's identification with Maggie is indicated by the fact that she, too, stands alone. By speaking out boldly in opposition to public opinion, Miss Unit risks the ostracism to which Maggie herself has been subjected. The 'world's wife' (an allegorical being imagined by George Eliot as the incarnation of society) chastises Miss Unit for 'pretending to be better than other people' [*MF*, p. 620]. She hints maliciously that Miss Unit's independent moral stance is a mask for feelings of rejection. According to the 'world's wife,' Miss Unit declines to call on Mr and Mrs Stephen Guest only because she has 'had no cards sent her' [*MF*, p. 620]. Despite her ostensible prudishness, in the feelings of isolation and rejection that are imputed to her, Miss Unit is curiously allied with the solitary and fallen Maggie.

Miss Unit's strikingly unusual name is a complex play on words. *Unit* means 'one,' but in a slightly different sense a unit is an undivided whole, so that to 'miss unity' is to fail to attain union of the kind that Maggie and Tom achieve in their deaths. Miss Unit's unmarried state links her with Maggie, whom the peddler Bob invariably addresses as 'Miss.' Though Bob's use of that title is deeply respectful, it becomes a problematic one for Maggie at the end of her history. Because, as Bob recognizes, Maggie's single state is in some sense the source of her pain, he grieves over the fact that she is 'still "Miss"' [*MF*, p. 615]. While *Miss* suggests singleness, *mis* signifies wrongness or error. Because of his deformity, Philip Wakem is said to be 'mis-made' [*MF*, p. 441], as though he were a defective product. The peddler Bob deals literally in defective goods; his wares have been cheapened because they contain small irregularities. Bob persuades Maggie's Aunt Glegg to buy a length of fabric with a yard at the center in which 'the pattern's all *missed*' [*MF*, p. 419 – Fuchs's emphasis]. As a 'miss' who is (wrongly) presumed to have had sex, Maggie, on her return to St. Ogg's, is soiled and unmarriageable: figuratively, she too has become 'damaged goods.'

In her steadfast resistance to marriage (or at least to Maggie's marriage with Stephen) and in her refusal to conform, Miss Unit personifies Maggie's longings for autonomy. But rather than a realistically developed character, she is only an element in the narrator's bitterly sardonic fantasy of Maggie's assimilation in the community of St. Ogg's. The forces that prompt her to defy convention never come into sharp focus and are never articulated. Miss Unit's shadowiness suggests that the impulses for which she stands have not yet been integrated; despite their intensity, Maggie's longings for separate self-hood remain for the most part unconscious.[46] □

As we have seen, Maggie's struggle, throughout *The Mill on the Floss*, has been to try to shape and define her own place within a community that refuses to grant her full rights of citizenship. Despite Maggie's obvious intellect, she never entirely understands the workings of her own community nor why she is consistently rejected as different or 'flawed'. In the next chapter we stay with Eliot's interest in society and its methods of cohesion and expulsion, but here examine them through the filter of nineteenth-century scientific thought.

CHAPTER FIVE

Eliot and Representations of Science

THE NINETEENTH century was an era of great scientific advances, in which all highly literate and educated people felt it their business to keep abreast of new ideas. It was also the period in which what we now know as Social Science was born, deriving from a literal attempt to apply new scientific thinking from physics, chemistry, biology and botany to social problems and community structure. Eliot is particularly respected for her knowledge of science, a knowledge that found its way centrally into her work. For George Levine, Eliot's fascination with science is part of her larger approach to realism, involving in this case the exploration of those ideas that challenged long-held platitudes relating to 'the way things are'. He observes: 'Science stands to the text of *Middlemarch* as religion stands to that of *Paradise Lost*. It makes sense of an experience that threatens, to the perceptions of common sense, to disintegrate into meaninglessness.'[1]

Sally Shuttleworth[2] traces Eliot's changing usage of science in relation to social theory and narrative development, beginning with *Adam Bede*, in which she examines how Eliot's fictive organic communities follow the thoughts of Herbert Spencer, among others. Spencer takes a very different line on ideology to the type of critics whose work we addressed in chapter three – as Suzanne Graver also signals.

■ Instead of associating the emergence of an industrial system with the decline of organic community, [Spencer] observes in modern society the social organism at its highest stage of development. Though individuals pursue their own separate interests, they are knit together in voluntary associations, voicing their consent through contract, itself the rule of industry as well as the principle upon which voluntary cooperation rests. From the increasing division of labor in modern society . . . distinct spheres of interest arise, but they demand cooperation from within.[3] □

Shuttleworth develops this line of argument more fully.

■ Spencer's conception of the social organism . . . was founded on the principles of *laissez-faire* economics . . . duty lay in the exercise of one's individual faculties – a theory to which one can trace Adam's belief in the dignity and divinity of labour . . . Spencer could thus argue for the preservation of poverty rather than government interference; the 'harsh fatalities' of suffering were 'full of the highest benificence' since they would lead, by elimination, 'to a form of being capable of a happiness undiminished by these drawbacks'. Government interference he characterises as a 'dead mechanism', one which prevents vital growth . . . George Eliot similarly criticises 'the false system of enlightening the peasant' adopted by the bureaucratic government which was designed to appeal 'to a logical understanding which is not yet developed in him'.[4] In *Adam Bede* it is solely Adam who has reached the evolutionary fitness, or ripeness, for education. Of the other pupils George Eliot observes: 'It was almost as if three rough animals were making humble efforts to learn how they might become human' [*AB*, p. 222]. Significantly they are learning how to write 'The corn is ripe' – their difficulty indicates the inapplicability of the phrase to their own mental development.

Spencer's theories of organic growth were founded on ideas both of necessary passivity in relation to the development of the social organism and of economic individualism. The sole form of differentiation permitted is that of Adam's economic progress from workman to owner, a mode of transformation which merely sustains the unchanging structure of Hayslope society. Of the other individualists, Hetty is exorcised from the community, Dinah transformed into a village matron, and Arthur banished until he can truly resume his patriarchal role. Adam, who appears the sole character launched on an evolutionary path is also the figure who holds most firmly to traditional values and a static vision of the social structure . . .

. . . Adam's vision of his own connection with the [timber] yard is cast in terms of images of individual work and natural, social, and economic growth:

Adam saw here an opening into a broadening path of prosperous work, such as he had thought of with ambitious longing ever since he was a lad: he might come to build a bridge, or a town-hall, or a factory, for he had always said to himself that Jonathan Burge's building business was like an acorn, which might be the mother of a great tree. [*AB*, p. 337]

The economic differentiation of the individual creates the natural growth of the social seed . . .

Spencer's theory . . . is founded on a mathesis: in accordance with the principles of mathematical addition, the whole equals the sum of its parts. In *Adam Bede*, Adam's progress towards economic differentiation is constantly presented in terms of a mathematical calculus. Thus Bartle Massey bewails Adam's unfortunate involvement with Hetty. Adam was his only scholar who 'ever had the will or the head-piece for mathematics. If he hadn't had so much hard work to do, poor fellow, he might have gone into the higher branches' [*AB*, p.396]. Adam's social progress is synonymous with his power of mathematical addition. It is upon this power that he bases his judgements on society, judgements rarely qualified by the narrator. Adam's moral strength and correctness are shown as the product of his mathematical reasoning. At the age of 18 he had run away with his '"mensuration book" in his pocket' but had returned since 'It 'ud make a poor balance when my doings are cast up at the last, if my poor old mother stood o' the wrong side' [*AB*, pp.45–6]. Even his religion is founded on a mathematical basis. Adam's powers of addition enable him, indirectly, to offer Arthur the only sound moral warning that he receives: 'I've seen pretty clear, ever since I could cast up a sum, as you can never do what's wrong without breeding sin and trouble more than you can ever see. It's like a bit o' bad workmanship – you never see th' end o' the mischief it'll do' [*AB*, p.156]. It is Adam's solid grounding in the concrete reality of his work, a practical application of the principles of mathematics, which lends such decisive correctness to his moral judgements. He is not like Mr Ryde, whom he describes to the narrator in his old age as 'ignorant as a woman' of 'math'matics and the natur o' things' [*AB*, p.172]. Mr Ryde's religion had been like a mathematics learnt at the fireside, but never put into practice.

Whilst the concrete practice of carpentry guarantees the validity of Adam's mathematical, moral judgements it also reinforces a static vision of the world. As in natural history, the world is viewed as an aggregate of distinct parts which can be subject to quantitative addition; their sum, it is assumed, will never change. Thus Adam's deliberative judgement following his father's death:

'There's nothing but what's bearable as long as a man can work,' he said to himself: 'the natur o' things doesn't change, though it seems as if one's own life was nothing but change. The square o' four is sixteen, and you must lengthen your lever in proportion to your weight, is as true when a man's miserable as when he's happy; and the best o' working is, it gives you a grip hold o' things outside your own lot.' [*AB*, p.108]

The inner flux of experience is measured against an unchanging external state. Work is not seen as a means of transforming the external environment, but solely as an activity which can place one in contact with an unchanging external world. The model does not allow for the reciprocity of interaction between organism and medium. Change is merely a quality of subjective experience . . .

. . . Mathematical reasoning lends a rigidity to [Adam's] social judgements; he cannot accept the dissolution of traditional social categories, of the fixed social hierarchy. Thus the Epilogue finds Adam rejoicing that Arthur had smiled at him, just as he had when he was a lad . . . The view of society as the fixed sum of determinate quantities seems to remain unchallenged.[5] □

Shuttleworth summarises Spencer's work as a combination of 'history . . . drawn from organicism' and a 'theory of social interaction . . . based on a chemical or mechanical model'. Eliot's writing employs a similar combinatory strategy, but in her case drawn from 'such diverse fields as geology, physics, astronomy, and philology to sustain social arguments'. So the novelist (at least the realist novelist) shares with the scientist 'a common commitment' to 'the objective recording of external fact . . . [combined with] their shared need for imaginative construction'.[6] But it is this reference to imagination that holds the key to Eliot's work, for it enables a flexibility often lacking in the work of various scientific thinkers (including Lydgate in *Middlemarch*) to enter into the model. According to Shuttleworth, Edward Dowden, for example, took the exact principles of science and applied them to community in a manner that refused to allow for any form of social change: '[T]hese physical processes actually reveal a moral order: ". . . not only is nature everywhere constant, uniform, orderly in its operations; all its parts constitute a whole, an ensemble. Nothing is added, nothing can be lost."'[7]

Eliot's introduction of a dynamic, less predictable element to complicate the structural model of her work is best illustrated by *Adam Bede*. This novel is not, Shuttleworth argues, a static, rustic vision of unchanging pastoral idyllicism. Instead, there is a conflict at work which sets up the apparent stasis only to point towards the subversive, less predictable elements which will, ultimately, shatter the apparent harmony of the text/society. Hence her characters in the novel, though apparently stock types, will collide and interact to produce new communal shapes. Out of that re-shaped society, however, only very few individuals will emerge with genuinely new opportunities. Once again Eliot seems to reflect Spencer here.

■ The practice of generic classification is evident throughout [Eliot's early work]. In 'The Natural History of German Life' George Eliot

observes that, 'it would be possible to give a sort of topographical statistics of proper names, and distinguish a district by its rustic names as
we do by its Flora and Fauna' . . .[8] Though chronological history might
be incorporated into George Eliot's schema it is subordinated to species
identification. Thus the taxonomic practice of maintaining the same
name through generations and in collateral branches of the family . . .

Describing the villagers congregating for Dinah's address, the narrator observes: 'Villagers never swarm: a whisper is unknown among
them, and they seem almost as incapable of an undertone as a cow or
stag. Your true rustic . . .' [AB, p. 18]. 'Villagers,' despite the diversity
of life style that term includes, are a generic type like cows or stags, or,
as the verb implies, bees. The behaviour pattern of the true rustic can
therefore be unequivocally stated. The mind of the villager is also a
known quantity, requiring no qualitative assessment. The text is
sprinkled with references to 'the bucolic mind': 'in those days the
keenest of bucolic minds . . .' [AB, p. 75], 'The bucolic mind does not
readily . . .' [AB, p. 253]. The first quotation, which refers to the individualised character of Mrs Poyser, emphasises her representative
function. Yet, the facetious tone of these remarks is indicative of
George Eliot's unease within the relationship she had adopted
towards her material. It dramatises a conflict, present throughout
Adam Bede, between her desire to portray her characters as representative of fixed types, and her awareness that such typology cannot
capture the complexity of process and change.

The rural chorus is not the only subject of generic classification.
George Eliot is also anxious to portray Adam as a type. The traveller
who gazes with the eye of an external observer is introduced within
the text to enact the desired response of the reader:

> As he reached the foot of the slope, an elderly horseman, with his
> portmanteau strapped behind him, stopped his horse when Adam
> had passed him, and turned round to have another long look at the
> stalwart workman in paper cap, leather breeches, and dark-blue
> worsted stockings. [AB, p. 12]

Adam is presented as no more and no less than an admirable specimen
of the species 'stalwart workman' – a classification which later narrative emphasis on the value of labour is to endorse. George Eliot is
concerned that Adam should not be viewed as too distinct or individual to represent a type; the narrator later intervenes, therefore, to
admit that Adam is not 'an average man':

> Yet such men as he are reared here and there in every generation of
> our peasant artisans – with an inheritance of affections nurtured by

> a simple family life of common need and common industry, and an inheritance of faculties trained in skilful courageous labour: they make their way upward, rarely as geniuses, most commonly as painstaking honest men, with the skill and conscience to do well the tasks that lie before them. [*AB*, p. 202]

Though the passage refers to a process of individual growth and progress it is the historical repetition of the process which is emphasised. Upward movement occurs in every generation; individual change does not create social transformation, it is an intrinsic part of the process of cyclical repetition. Adam can thus be generalised to 'they'. The events of his life, like the villagers' habits of speech or standing, can be treated as a typical behaviour pattern conforming to a pre-established taxonomic definition. Adam's progress confirms the static, ahistoric mode of natural history.

George Eliot defines her art in *Adam Bede* in relation to the 'truthfulness' of Dutch painting:

> I turn, without shrinking, from cloud-borne angels, from prophets, sibyls, and heroic warriors, to an old woman bending over her flower-pot, or eating her solitary dinner, while the noonday light, softened perhaps by a screen of leaves, falls on her mob-cap, and just touches the rim of her spinning-wheel, and her stone jug, and all those cheap common things which are the precious necessaries of life to her . . . [*AB*, p. 169]

Significantly, George Eliot chooses the static mode of pictorial representation to illustrate the goal of her narrative. Attention is focused not on process, but on external form; the itemising of details clearly conforms to the practice of natural history . . . [John] Goode draws attention to the persistent tendency in the early parts of the narrative 'to resolve the narrative into pictures'; both Adam's workshop and the church service are fixed by sunlight.[9] Yet it is a tendency, I would argue, which is not restricted to the early sections but is indicative of the practice of natural history throughout the whole. Thus the sunlight playing on the cottage in the Epilogue effectively undermines previously constituted impressions of historical process or instability . . . The marriage [of Adam and Dinah] which marks the communal order is represented, primarily, not as an instance of individual progress but as part of the unchanging rhythms of rural life . . .

References to physiology or the social organism in [Eliot's] essay all occur in the context of arguments against social change. Government measures are criticised because they do not endeavour 'to promote to the utmost the healthy life of the Commune, as an organism the conditions of which are bound up with the historical characteristics of the peasant'.[10] History becomes the court of appeal against change . . . The analogy is drawn from vitalist biology; the idea that death would result from the slightest alteration of an organism's condition supplied a potent image for conservative social theory . . .

The theory of social growth which George Eliot proposes is one that stresses rootedness in the past, not the process of change: 'The nature of European men has its roots intertwined with the past, and can only be developed by allowing those roots to remain undisturbed while the process of development is going on, until that perfect ripeness of the seed which carries with it a life independent of the root'. . . .[11] □

By the time Eliot writes *Middlemarch*, science – most particularly medical science – stands at the centre as both theme and trope, but the organicism referred to in relation to *Adam Bede* is also in evidence here. Shuttleworth observes, 'The characters in *Middlemarch* cannot be abstracted out from the life-processes of the town . . . each part of Middlemarch life is related to every other part; individual identity is not only influenced by the larger social organism, it is actively defined by it.' Here she once again finds 'the image of the historian untangling [a] pre-existent web . . . complemented by that of the creative scientist . . .'. The town of Middlemarch is, therefore, a community 'exhibit[ing] all the characteristics of a vital organism'.[12] Robert A. Greenberg's article, 'Plexus and Ganglia: Scientific Allusion in *Middlemarch*',[13] provides us with a clear outline of the major ideas which Eliot employs to structure her narrative. It is included here with very few ellipses, being one of the most cogent explications of the subject.

■ The several notebooks that George Eliot compiled preliminary to the writing of *Middlemarch* reveal the effort she gave to researching not only the political materials that were to flesh out the activities of Brooke and Ladislaw and provide a chronological frame for the novel, but also the medical and scientific background that would contribute to the visualization and placing of Lydgate . . . Her comment to Blackwood in 1871, 'I don't see how I can leave anything out, because I hope there is nothing that will be seen to be irrelevant to my design,'[14] is especially useful because though it addresses itself to matters of abundance, it also implies the necessary process of exclusion and selectivity through whose means norms of relevance can exist . . . 'I am in danger in all my designs . . . and think of refining when novel readers only think of skipping.' The inner echoes and intricate analogical structure of *Middlemarch* are evidence enough that she persisted in her course, slighting where necessary the reader's immediate comfort . . . And as might be supposed, it was while constituting the most specialized and, for the reader, the most demanding area of *Middlemarch*, her scientific allusions – the ganglia and plexuses of the novel – that she proved most vulnerable to the dangers of too subtle 'refining.' But refine at all costs she nonetheless did, to the point that none of these allusions, however casually put, was to remain irrelevant to her design. We have but to recover their contexts to understand how delicately the mode of indirection characteristic of George Eliot's use of history and politics governed also in the selection and disposition she made of her scientific materials.

The two strains, political and scientific, that appear side by side in the Quarry are not, of course, meant to be discrete; when they most clearly converge, it is on the issue of reform. That note is sounded early in the novel, casually in the opening chapter in Dorothea's 'plans for some buildings,' and then more specifically at the start of [C]hapter 2 in a remark by Chettam:

'I am reading the Agricultural Chemistry,' said this excellent baronet, 'because I am going to take one of the farms into my own hands, and see if something cannot be done in setting a good pattern of farming among my tenants.' [*M*, pp. 15–16]

Chettam is the most conservative of men, and as a reformer the most unlikely. It is doubtless ironic that though Davy's *Elements of Agricultural Chemistry* had appeared in 1814, he is only now turning to it. His motive obviously is to accommodate himself to Dorothea ('Do you approve of that, Miss Brooke?'), but he is a forthright and literal man and we are not to doubt that he has been studying his subject. His words are indeed a direct paraphrase of certain of Davy's high-minded injunctions to landowners: 'The common labourer can never be enlightened by the general doctrines of philosophy'; it must be 'from the higher classes of the community, from the proprietors of land – those . . . fitted by their education to form enlightened plans, and, by their fortunes, to carry such plans into execution . . . that the principles of improvement must flow to the labouring classes. . . .'[15] A reformer by instinct, and with 'plans' of her own, Miss Brooke evidences her approval, while privately expecting to urge Chettam on to 'many good actions when he was her brother-in-law' – not her husband. And there is the further irony that Brooke, who campaigns later as an upper-class reformer, pronounces the application of science to agriculture a 'great mistake,' 'fancy-farming' [*M*, p. 16]. His own estates, we discover, are in a sorry way; their condition will be used against him at the hustings. . . . [*M*, p. 341]

The scene is as superbly executed as it is meaningfully conceived;

above all, it is rooted in a factual past. But there is something further. By the introduction so early of Davy, George Eliot also sets going a series of reverberations whose effects will be felt only when all of the scientific allusions are in hand. The reader of the *Elements* discovers that it constitutes the first attempt to create for agricultural chemistry 'a regular and systematic form'; that Davy, in his exposition of relationships, must account for the 'surface of the earth, the atmosphere, and the water deposited from it.' As a scientist, he recognizes in multiplicity the presence of certain elemental principles and offers us our initial metaphor for the analogical design of *Middlemarch*: '[T]here is an analogy between the forms and the functions of all the different classes of plants, and on this analogy the scientific principles relating to their organization depend.'[16] As Lydgate is devoted to anatomical structure, so Davy explores in precise detail the 'structure and constitution of plants.' As Lydgate finds in medicine the 'most direct alliance between intellectual conquest and the social good' [*M*, p. 131], so Davy also unites the theoretical and the practical, and on the highest grounds: 'Many of the sciences are ardently pursued . . . merely on account of [their] intellectual pleasure. . . . How much more, then, is this department of inquiry worthy of attention, in which . . . the love of truth and of knowledge . . . is likewise connected with much greater practical benefits . . . ?'[17] The same attitude is summarized in Lydgate's 'conviction that the medical profession as it might be was the finest in the world' [*M*, p. 131]. We are never told that Lydgate read the *Elements* . . . The point is that Davy and his work quietly evoke certain motifs that George Eliot will sustain throughout *Middlemarch*.

Chettam's resolution to establish a 'good pattern' is echoed subsequently in a less mixed context. One of the attractions to Lydgate of his profession is simply that 'it wanted reform'; his idealism engaged, he resolves in his day-to-day practice to enact 'particular reforms,' even if they are construed as 'offensive criticism by his professional brethren' [*M*, pp. 131, 133]. To act otherwise is to be a 'base truckler' [*M*, p. 395]. George Eliot informs us that this is a 'dark period' in medicine, and she draws many of her exemplary details from the reformist *Lancet* and from the writings of its editor, Thomas Wakley . . .

'Hang your reforms!' said Mr Chichely. 'There's no greater humbug in the world. . . . I hope you are not one of the "Lancet's" men, Mr Lydgate – wanting to take the coronership out of the hands of the legal profession: your words appear to point that way.'

'I disapprove of Wakley,' interposed Dr Sprague, 'no man more: he is an ill-intentioned fellow, who would sacrifice the respectability of the profession, which everybody knows depends on the London Colleges . . .' [*M*, p. 141]

143

. . . Lydgate is undoubtedly a *Lancet*-man, most of all in his awareness that professional respectability is too often the equivalent of humbug and the primary obstacle to advances in science . . . Lydgate has chosen a provincial community rather than London for the scene of his work; his hope is to contribute on both a local and an international scale as physician and discoverer – 'good small work for Middlemarch, and great work for the world' [*M*, p. 134]; his local effort is on feverous disease; he is confident that wherever they may lead, his discoveries will survive the inevitable professional objections . . .

. . . Lydgate locates his long-range ambitions in the area of anatomy. He had early been 'bitten with an interest in structure' [*M*, p. 155], his 'moment of vocation' having come suddenly in his youth when, indifferently taking down an 'old Cyclopædia,' he opened to a page 'under the head of Anatomy,' there to encounter the scientist's equivalent of a religious revelation: 'came a sudden light startling him with his first vivid notion of finely-adjusted mechanism in the human frame.' By the time of his arrival in Middlemarch, he has become 'fired with the possibility that he might work out the proof of an anatomical conception and make a link in the chain of discovery' [*AB*, pp. 130, 132]. The chain he would advance had its beginnings in the discoveries of Vesalius, yet another figure in Lydgate's ideal pantheon. Midway through the novel, he exclaims to Farebrother: 'How am I to be prudent? . . . I can't help people's ignorance and spite, any more than Vesalius could' [*M*, pp. 408–9]. Later in the same chapter, Rosamond abandons her music to interrupt her husband during one of his reveries:

'What is absorbing you?' she said. . . .

'I am thinking of a great fellow, who was about as old as I am three hundred years ago, and had already begun a new era in anatomy.'

'I can't guess,' said Rosamond. . . .

'I'll tell you. His name was Vesalius. And the only way he could get to know anatomy as he did, was by going to snatch bodies at night, from graveyards and places of execution.' [*M*, p. 410]

The true scientist is not only a reformer, but, in society's terms, inevitably a transgressor. Rosamond's rejoinder, 'I hope he is not one of your great heroes,' recalls in diction as well as sentiment Chichely's earlier response, 'I hope you are not one of the "*Lancet's*" men.' Lydgate has witnessed enough of Middlemarch and its reaction to him to make the personal application:

No wonder the medical fogies in Middlemarch are jealous, when some of the greatest doctors living were fierce upon Vesalius because they had believed in Galen, and he showed that Galen was wrong. They called him a liar and a poisonous monster. But the facts of the human frame were on his side; and so he got the better of them. [*M*, pp. 410–11]

... [S]ociety was not without its revenge on the 'great anatomist, who had nobly braved so much odium because he would not, as his predecessors had done, content himself with the dissection of animals, but suffered his scalpel to traverse the complexities of the human frame ... [Vesalius] had to appear before the Inquisition, and narrowly escaped with his life. A pilgrimage to the Holy Land was his punishment; but he never outlived the scandal.'[18] This latter material is refashioned for the novel in Lydgate's reply to Rosamond's inquiry, 'And what happened to him afterwards?'

'Oh, he had a good deal of fighting to the last. And they did exasperate him enough at one time to make him burn a good deal of his work. Then he got shipwrecked just as he was coming from Jerusalem to take a great chair at Padua. He died rather miserably.' [*M*, p. 411]

The inquisition that Lydgate himself is destined to face at the town hall is not far ahead ([C]h. 71); a little further off is its consequence, his pilgrimage, 'according to the season, between London and a Continental bathing-place' [*M*, p. 743]. In this other sense, it can be said that he too died rather miserably, 'shipwrecked' by Rosamond's 'torpedo' touch; and it can be no accident that he dies at exactly the age of Vesalius (b. 1513–14, d. 1564), 'when he was only fifty.' But in Lydgate's case, nothing remained to warrant burning, certainly not his 'treatise on Gout, a disease,' George Eliot adds, 'which has a good deal of wealth on its side' [*M*, p. 743]. The analogy that Lydgate draws and George Eliot quietly perpetuates has resonances that in his latter years he perhaps all too bitterly understood ...

Early in the novel, in a passage that begins playfully but concludes as a paradigm for the modern novelist, George Eliot demonstrates the inadequacy of telescopic sight and its necessary replacement by microscopic:

... a telescope might have swept the parishes ... without witnessing any interview that could excite suspicion, or any scene from which [Mrs Cadwallader] did not return with the same unperturbed keenness of eye. .... Even with a microscope directed on a water-drop we find ourselves making interpretations which turn out to be rather coarse; for whereas under a weak lens you may

> seem to see a creature exhibiting an active voracity into which other smaller creatures actively play . . . a stronger lens reveals to you certain tiniest hairlets which make vortices for these victims while the swallower waits passively. . . . In this way, metaphorically speaking, a strong lens applied to [her] match-making will show a play of minute causes producing what may be called thought and speech vortices to bring her the sort of food she needed. [*M*, pp. 53–4]

The more powerful the lens, the closer the observation and the greater the truth. If to see close is paradoxically to see wide, it is because the 'more intimate relations of living structure' that are uncovered are also recapitulated on a larger scale.[19] So it is that Raffles, once he is drawn into the seemingly invisible vortices of Middlemarch life, can confound the lives of creatures so dissimilar as Bulstrode, Lydgate, and Ladislaw, and in a lesser way at least complicate the lives of Rosamond and Dorothea. In his encounter with Ladislaw, Bulstrode remarks: 'Nothing, I daresay, has been farther from your thoughts than that there had been important ties in the past which could connect your history with mine' [*M*, p. 556]. Connections of this kind, everywhere present, need only be discerned – 'For there is no creature,' we are told in the 'Finale,' 'whose inward being is so strong that it is not greatly determined by what lies outside it.'

This is George Eliot's parting formulation . . . Bridging both kingdoms, man sustains at once both an integral and a relative existence. But though he does embody the organic cycle that allies him to the plant, his human definition derives from the many 'active' relations he experiences with his world. Seen from this perspective, not even Featherstone in decay – certainly not Casaubon – is purely vegetative, their human potency extending from beyond the grave. And there is an encompassing irony in Lydgate's seeking to avoid at the human level what he knows, as a student of Bichat, to be true at the scientific. His choice of a provincial town is in part to escape too active a set of relations: people there 'affect one's *amour-propre* less: one . . . can follow one's own course more quietly.' But as Farebrother so prophetically cautions: 'We have our intrigues and our parties . . . vote for me you will offend Bulstrode' [*M*, p. 158]. Lydgate would resist the commitment of a vote, just as he would the prospect of marriage; but none of us, as George Eliot prophesies more generally for the reader, is merely organic. To imagine otherwise implies a failure of observation:

> Certainly nothing at present could seem much less important to Lydgate than the turn of Miss Brooke's mind, or to Miss Brooke than the qualities of the woman who had attracted this young

surgeon. But any one watching keenly the stealthy convergence of human lots, sees a slow preparation of effects from one life on another, which tells like a calculated irony on the indifference or the frozen stare with which we look at our unintroduced neighbour. [*M*, p. 85]

Her procedure in *Middlemarch*, she tells Blackwood several months later . . . is 'to show the gradual action of ordinary causes rather than exceptional.' One observes a 'slow preparation of effects,' the 'gradual action of ordinary causes,' best of all through the concentrative powers of the microscope. The telescope, being mainly panoramic, is limited by comparison, even when administered by a genius . . . 'I at least have so much to do in unravelling certain human lots, and seeing how they were woven and interwoven, that all the light I can command must be concentrated on this particular web, and not dispersed over that tempting range of relevancies called the universe.' [*M*, p. 128]

But we must return to Lydgate, who in 1829 is dedicated, by use of the scalpel but especially the microscope, to extending the work cut short by Bichat's premature death. Though the fact of a common tissue was now known, it remained to others to inquire whether 'these structures [have] some common basis from which they have all started' [*M*, p. 134]. Lydgate is not alone, however, in pursuing the 'primitive tissue,' and an ominous note is introduced twice in conversation with Farebrother. Assuring the latter that the question of 'homogeneous origin' will one day be resolved, Lydgate adds: 'Raspail and others are on the same track, and I have been losing time' [*M*, p. 408]. Earlier, during his engagement to Rosamond, he had complained that his 'unsettled state of affairs uses up the time, and when one has notions in science, every moment is an opportunity' [*M*, pp. 312–13]. But the time that has been lost is beyond recovery. Lydgate has slowly undergone numbing from Rosamond's 'torpedo contact,' and when he searches for the 'impulse needed to draw him out of himself,' that is, to counteract her numbing shocks, it is to his daily practice that he turns rather than to 'spontaneous research and speculative thinking' [*M*, p. 599]. His hopes having been shattered well before his public disgrace, the field is left to his competitor, Raspail, who in 1833 is to announce his success in accounting for the 'substance membraneuse' that both have sought . . . Committed to the cause of mankind, Raspail had participated in the revolution of 1830 (the time roughly of Lydgate's marriage), had suffered confinement, and had been obliged to complete his work in prison. Buttressed, however, by his political hopes, he can look ahead . . . in a way that his English counterpart, by 1833, no longer can. But none of this makes its appearance formally in the novel, whose action proper ends in 1832; it is left rather to the reader to recover the ironies implicit in the one passing reference to Raspail.[20]

The burden falls similarly with respect to other aspects of Lydgate's Paris studies. It was at this time presumably that his interest in Bichat took form: the clue comes early but is all the vaguer for issuing from Mr. Brooke, who is recommending the new surgeon to Middlemarch society: 'likely to be first-rate – has studied in Paris, knew Broussais; has ideas, you know' [*M*, p. 83]. Broussais' success had been in both fever and anatomy – the latter especially – and along lines that we have already encountered. He was, in fact, an heir to Bichat . . . [But] Broussais was also interested in the application of electrical shocks and the evidences of interconnection it afforded: 'Hence the first vital law observed in relation to the effect of electricity, is a very manifest increase of contractility . . . its transmission from one part to another; or, in other words, an increase of the sensibility of relation and of sympathies.'[21] It was perhaps at the older man's urging that Lydgate undertook the one experiment that we hear of during his Paris time, his 'galvanic experiments.' Their having proved unfruitful, he one night abandons 'his frogs and rabbits to some repose under their trying and mysterious dispensation of unexplained shocks'; goes to the theatre; and on seeing Madame Laure suffers in his own person a decided increase of contractility, of the 'sensibility of relation and of sympathies.' The subsequent shock, his discovery of Laure's complex nature, drives him back to the relative security of his laboratory galvanism [*M*, pp. 136–9].

But though slower in effect, the deadlier shocks come from the torpedo sting of Rosamond – a metaphor so brilliantly orchestrated that we are prone to forget its scientific base. Its locus is set early in the novel when Lydgate announces proudly to Farebrother that having his profession, he has no need of hobbies – 'I have the sea to swim in there' [*M*, p. 155]. But it is in these waters especially that he is to be most susceptible to Rosamond, whose desire 'looked through watchful blue eyes, whereas Lydgate's lay blind and unconcerned as a jelly-fish which gets melted without knowing it' [*M*, p. 243]. The melting continues after marriage and despite, by then, Lydgate's awareness: 'and again, she had touched him,' causing his 'resolution . . . to relax under her torpedo contact' [*M*, p. 592]. Later still, we hear that 'poor Lydgate had a throbbing pain within him, and his energy had fallen short of its task'; that he 'felt miserably jarred' [*M*, p. 679]. The effects on his professional hopes, culminating in Raspail's triumph, we have already seen.

It was Galvani who first insisted on the characteristics shared by animal and torpedo electricity. His analysis of the operational mode of the torpedo has much to offer on the destructive charms of Rosamond Vincy:

[The] peculiarity of the torpedo in particular, and other related animals, [is] that they can arbitrarily and at their pleasure discharge and eject electricity from their skin in such a way that it completes its circuit outside the body. . . . This produces a strong reaction and concussion, which occasionally assaults little animals coming in the path of this circuit so that they are either killed or are rendered stunned or dazed.[22]

But it is Broussais who formulates the long-range symptoms that characterize Lydgate's affliction: 'The excitement . . . produced by galvanism and electricity, does not fail, when intense and often repeated, to exhaust . . . the body is languid – the power of attraction predominates over that of vitality, and, in general, nearly overpowers the vital chemistry . . .'[23] Officially, Lydgate dies at the age of fifty, but his vital chemistry, worn down by successive assaults, has subsided long before.

The references to Laennec and Ware, though efficiently managed in the novel, are more local in impact. They reveal of Lydgate not only his substantial talents, but his effort even in adversity to attend to the most recent scientific advances. The volume containing 'Dr. Ware's abundant experience in America' had appeared in 1831; Lydgate treats Raffles for alcoholism in 1832. Moreover, Ware's findings confirm his own innovative methods of treatment: '[H]e had repeatedly acted on this conviction with a favourable result' [*M*, p. 627]. Were it not for Lydgate's moral and emotional numbness, his repeated experiences would have raised stronger doubts about the nature of Raffles's death than he is capable of feeling.[24] While of another order, the irony is no less telling in Lydgate's diagnosis of Casaubon's 'heart' complaint: '[W]hat is called fatty degeneration of the heart, a disease . . . first divined and explored by Laennec, the man who gave us the stethoscope, not so very many years ago' [*M*, p. 379]. His diagnosis would probably have been similar had Lydgate applied the stethoscope to Rosamond's heart, though, as he informs Casaubon, his conclusions in this area must be 'uncertain not only because of my fallibility, but because diseases of the heart are eminently difficult to found predictions on' [*M*, p. 379].

A final instance, seemingly detached and insignificant, offers perhaps the best testimony to George Eliot's purposefulness in selecting and disposing of her scientific allusions. Lydgate is examining Farebrother's collection of natural specimens and is attracted to one in particular, a 'lovely anencephalous monster' (whose human analogue may well be Rosamond Vincy).[25] He offers in exchange 'some sea-mice. . . . And I will throw in Robert Brown's new thing – "Microscopic Observations on the Pollen of Plants" if you don't happen to have it already' [*M*, p. 156]. The time is 1829 or early 1830; Brown's new thing had appeared in 1828. Its two-part title is all that is recorded in the *Quarry*, but it explains the reasons for Lydgate's and George Eliot's interest: *Microscopic Observations on the Particles Contained in the Pollen of Plants; and On the General Existence of Active Molecules in Organic and Inorganic Bodies.*[26] As in the treatises of Louis and Raspail, observation through the microscope provides the basis for general theory. Brown begins by noting that his 'observations . . . have all been made with a simple microscope,' and we follow him from experiment to experiment, supposition to supposition: 'led me to attend more *minutely* than I had done before to the *structure* of the Pollen' . . .[27] That Lydgate should be offering up his Brown for the lovely monster as early as [C]hapter 17 is a sad foreboding of all that is to come . . .

To ask why George Eliot refined so narrowly, compressing so much into an incidental remark, is to return to the larger question of her expectations of the common reader . . . The significance of certain of the allusions – Ware, Wakley, the *Lancet* – is inferable more or less from the contexts in which they appear. Vesalius and Bichat are the source of essential tropes and so receive something more than casual mention. But it would have required the patience and resources of large and learned families to have made clear the relationship of each of the foregoing to Broussais, Brown, Davy, Louis, and Raspail, and of one and all to the 'vital structure' and thousand minute 'processes' that make up the texture of *Middlemarch*. The more characteristic response, as she must certainly have known, was likely to have been of the same order of incomprehension that greeted Mr. Brooke's remark, 'studied in Paris, knew Broussais.' □

The detailed information provided by Greenberg enables us to look with greater insight at the arguments developed by Gillian Beer in her highly influential book, *Darwin's Plots*.[28] Beer begins by reminding us of the manner in which contemporary reviewers of the period would have differed in the allusions to science that they recognise in Eliot's fiction, many of which would be lost on us today because scientific language has already passed into a figurative application that has lost its original sense of specificity.

■ George Eliot was often taken to task by contemporary reviewers for the persistent scientific allusions in her works. Henry James, indeed, complained that '*Middlemarch* is too often an echo of Messrs. Darwin and Huxley'. And R.H. Hutton objected to her use of the word 'dynamic' in the opening sentences of *Daniel Deronda* as being pedantically over-scientific: 'Was she beautiful or not beautiful? and what was the secret of form or expression which gave the dynamic quality to her glance?'[29] The surprise that any modern reader is likely to feel at Hutton's particular objection should alert us to the degree to which language that has now lost its scientific bearing still bore a freight of controversy and assertion for George Eliot and her first readers. If, in the light of James's remark, one turns to the Prelude to *Middlemarch* words that may now read as flat generality renew their powers of controversy. The concluding paragraph asserts ironically the problems of treating the social lot of women:

> . . . if there were one level of feminine incompetence as strict as the ability to count three and no more, the social lot of women might be treated with scientific certitude. Meanwhile the indefiniteness remains, and the limits of variation are really much wider than any one would imagine from the sameness of women's coiffure and the favourite love-stories in prose and verse. [*M*, p. 4]

To take up only one of several possible words from that passage: 'variation'. The limits of variation are part of the controversy about species and about how far it is possible to describe species through their characteristics. They are part also of that argument about whether resemblances of appearance and use could count as 'real affinities' or as 'analogical or adaptive resemblances' – resemblances brought about, that is, by a common response to the pressures of environment. Although the example that Darwin uses is remote from George Eliot's, the argument follows the same course: 'The resemblance, in the shape of the body and in the fin-like anterior limbs, between the dugong, which is a pachydermatous animal, and the whale, and between both these mammals and fishes, is analogical.'[30] Response to environment can make very diverse creatures look and behave alike: '[T]he limits of variation are really much wider than any one would imagine from the sameness of women's coiffure.'

Within each species, in Darwin's argument, *variation* is the key to evolutionary development. Diversification, not truth to type, is the creative principle, as he emphasises throughout the first chapter of *The Origin of Species* whose title is 'Variation Under Domestication'. George Eliot takes the word 'variation', in which so much current controversy is moving and applies it to 'the social lot of women': 'variation under domestication' is for them a difficult endeavour. So her use of the phrase 'limits of variation' is a polemical signal which harbinges much for the 'domestic epic' she is about to present.

Some of her critics appreciated this weighting of words with the fullest concerns of the time – those concerns in which emotion and intellect are not kept apart but most completely imply each other. Colvin commented in these terms on her use of medical knowledge and imagery in *Middlemarch*, and Edward Dowden, in particular, seized upon the implications for language of the turmoil of scientific ideas and hypotheses current in the period:

> She has actually employed in a work of fiction such words as 'dynamic' and 'natural selection', at which the critic picks up his delicate ears and shies. . . . Language, the instrument of literary art, is an instrument of ever-extending range, and the truest pedantry, in an age when the air is saturated with scientific thought, would be to reject those accessions to language which are the special gain of the time. Insensibility to the contemporary movement in science is itself essentially unliterary. . . . The cultured imagination is affected by it, as the imagination of Spenser's time was affected by his use of the neo-classical mythology of the Renaissance.[31]

The comparison with Spenser is particularly just and telling. The acquired cultural language of science, like that of neo-classical allusion, offers a controlled range of imaginative consequences shared by writer and first readers. It offers an imaginative shift in the valency of words, new spaces for experience to occupy in language, confirmation of some kinds of vocabulary, increased prowess of punning, in which diverse senses are held in equipoise within the surveillance of consciousness. These effects register a moment when a particular discourse has reached its fullest range. It can then suggest new bearings for experiences which had earlier seemed quite separate from each other. At such moments of transposition emotion can find its full extent in language.[32] □

Picking up on Darwin's theories of variation as the creative element of Evolution in *The Origin of Species*, Beer turns to a reading of not just the themes but also the structural organisation of *Middlemarch* as an exemplum of Darwinian theory in fictional practice. That science, theology, and the reassuring role of the authoritative narrator are connected is made clear in her observation that '[f]iction in the second half of the nineteenth century was particularly seeking sources of authoritative organisation which could substitute for the god-like omnipotence and omniscience open to the theistic narrator.'

She also draws attention to the consolations of narrative form when, in relation to plot, she reminds us that, for the reader, a response to plot is in part governed by the relationship that plot structure holds to the social patterning it mimics: 'Plot must appear to have an equivalence with ulterior organisation beyond the control, and to some extent the knowledge, of the single psyche. It can never be generated solely out of the subjective individual.'[33] In other words, just as we live out a plot which we can only ever partially control, so the plot acted out by an individual character must always seem partially beyond his/her control, or we will lose interest in the narrative as incredible.

Like Shuttleworth, in her reading of *Adam Bede*, Beer sets up a distinction, in *Middlemarch*, between the pattern of movement (which she sees as futile and ensnaring) and development, which is far more in line with Darwinian Evolution. Historical events may move on, but may impede rather than facilitate character development. On the one hand, Lydgate is a core illustration of the novel's overall concern with social organicism, being fascinated by the role played by the organism within systems. On the other hand, Beer draws attention to the tensions existing within that organic unity and draws specifically upon Lydgate as the character who best illustrates the failings of such a model, his main weakness (as true of his observations of women as of his medical aspirations) being that 'he seeks the underlying unity beneath the diversity of matter'.[34] It is this tension, rather than any cohesion, which makes the web image of *Middlemarch* so successful, because though instantly generic in type, webs are unique and, within themselves, 'a product as much of strain and conflict as of supple interconnection'. Hence, she reminds us, though 'George Eliot's intellectual characters are preoccupied with sources: "the primitive tissue", "the key to all mythologies" . . . the text is organised in terms of variability . . . [The novel's] "provisional framing" . . . draws the focus ever more sharply, shifting and refocusing where necessary, testing situations through diverse consciousnesses, repudiating the subjectivity of the single point of view . . . In a world which no longer consisted of fixed species a struggle had begun to be manifest between external form and potential meaning . . .'[35]

As Beer reminds us, the image of the web, so consistently applied to the structure of Eliot's novel, is Darwin's own analogy:

■ The two major and interconnected problems on which Darwin wrote which fascinated George Eliot were those of *relations* and of *origins*. These preoccupations control her late novels both as theme and structure. The interdependence of the two ideas is expressed in *The Origin of Species* in the metaphor of 'the inextricable web of affinities'. In his discussion of descent and morphology Darwin writes:

We can clearly see how it is that all living and extinct forms can be grouped together in one great system; and how the several members of each class are connected together by the most complex and radiating lines of affinities. We shall never, probably, disentangle the inextricable web of affinities between the members of any one class; but when we have a distinct object in view, and do not look to some unknown plan of creation, we may hope to make sure but slow progress.[36]

Darwin's metaphor is striking, not for its novelty, but because it combines in a peculiarly Victorian manner two models of 'the web' and adds a third, which further complicates the explanatory and imaginative possibilities of the image. 'The several members of each class are connected together by the most complex and radiating lines of affinities' – the spatial pattern suggests a spider's web. 'We shall never, probably, disentangle the inextricable web of affinities between the members of any one class' – the suggestion is now of woven fabric. There is also the further space-free suggestion of chemical affinities, unsettling the space-bound order of the web. But the degrees of relatedness suggest, further, the 'table of affinities' by which sexual relations between kin are tabooed and this introduction of the family connections needs further discussion.

For us now, the spider's web is probably the predominant association of the word 'web'. But for Victorian people, woven fabric seems to have been the predominant reference. Web imagery is to be found everywhere in Victorian writing. It is as common among scientists and philosophers as it is among poets and novelists. Mill wrote in the *System of Logic* that 'the regularity which exists in nature is a web composed of distinct threads', and G. H. Lewes in *Foundations of a Creed*:

> Out of the general web of Existence certain threads may be detached and rewoven into a special group – the Subject – and this sentient group *will* in so far be different from the larger group, the Object; but whatever different arrangement the threads may take on, they are always threads of the original web, they are not different threads.[37]

The absence of transformation is important in both these citations. Threads remain themselves, though part of a total fabric. When Tyndall seeks expression for endless movement he achieves it through an implicit metaphor which draws simultaneously on the concepts of wave and web – the process of weaving is foregrounded here, rather than the achieved fabric.

> Darkness might then be defined as ether at rest; light as ether in motion. But in reality the ether is never at rest, for in the absence of light-waves we have heat waves always speeding through it. In the spaces of the universe both classes of undulations incessantly commingle. Here the waves issuing from uncounted centres cross, coincide, oppose and pass through each other, without confusion or ultimate extinction. The waves from the zenith do not jostle out of existence those from the horizon, and every star is seen across the entanglement of wave motions produced by all other stars. [The

waves of interstellar ether] mingle in space without disorder, each being endowed with an individuality as indestructible as if it alone had disturbed the universal repose.[38]

Spider, fabric, human tissue: Alexander Bain in *Mind and Body* describes the nerves thus: 'They are a set of silvery threads, or cords of various sizes, ramifying from centres to all parts of the body, including both sense surfaces and muscles.'[39] The webs of bodily order – veins, nerves, tissues – allow the metaphor of the web to move into the intimate ordering of life. Tissue and cloth are contiguous images. So are web and tree: 'threads . . . ramifying'. The web could intimate the '*milieu intérieur*' – the relations within bodily and mental experience as much as the interconnections of society . . .

The web as woven cloth expressed also the process of coming to knowledge . . . Tennyson's Lady of Shalott works on the reverse side of her weaving and sees the pattern gradually emerging only through the mirror, through which she also sees the world beyond. This narrative element in the image had a particular usefulness for George Eliot. The web exists not only as interconnection in space but as succession in time. This was the aspect of the image emphasised by Darwin in his genealogical ordering.

Several connections implicit in the Victorian apprehension of the image do not seem self-evident to us now. One is family and kin; the other is the idea of origins . . .

The web is a different shape from the chain, and this formal property of the image has great importance for Darwin: 'The several subordinate groups in any class *cannot be ranked in a single file*, but seem rather to be clustered round points.'[40] Sequence is so ramified and diversified, so devious, that it presents itself in the form of web or cycle rather than pure onward procedure . . .

The cluster of common contiguous metaphors (tree, family, web, labyrinth) was given a new meaning by his theory. No single one of the metaphors was peculiar to Darwin. But in his argument the gap between metaphor and actuality was closed up, the fictive became substantive. Fictional insights were confirmed as physical event. The web is not a hierarchical model. It can express horizontality and extension, but it does not fix places, as on the rungs of a ladder or 'in single file'. Yet an important emphasis in the idea of the web is fixed patterns and achieved limits. That tendency of the image is taken up by Darwin immediately after his description of 'the inextricable web of affinities' in his discussion of morphology:

What can be more curious than that the hand of a man, formed for grasping, that of a mole for digging, the leg of the horse, the paddle of the porpoise, and the wing of the bat, should all be constructed on the same pattern, and should include the same bones, in the same relative positions?[41]

Undeviating patterns and their diverse uses raise problems which are the novelist's province. George Eliot's awareness of the varying powers of the web image are expressed in the successive, and very diverse, references in [C]hapter [15] of *Middlemarch*. In the well-known passage that opens the chapter she compares her own practice with that of Fielding, the 'great historian, as he insisted on calling himself':

> We belated historians must not linger after his example . . . I at least have so much to do in unravelling certain human lots, and seeing how they were woven and interwoven, that all the light I can command must be concentrated on this particular web, and not dispersed over that tempting range of relevancies called the universe. [*M*, p. 128]

The web is not co-extensive with the universe. The weaver poring over the fabric needs a concentrated light. Indeed (as in the round eye of the microscope), it is the light which concentrates and which creates an effect of wholeness.

Next the narrative alludes to the web of the human body and its contiguous image, the labyrinth, which will become of such importance later in *Middlemarch*. The connection of evolutionary theory and labyrinth was already established for example, in an article by Julia Wedgwood (Darwin's niece) in *Macmillan's Magazine* in 1861. We read:

> The infinitude of small deviations from the parent type . . . may be regarded as a labyrinth laid out by the hands of the Creator, through which he furnishes a clue to a higher state of being, in the principle which rewards every step in the right direction.[42]

The *Middlemarch* passage describes the awakening of Lydgate's scientific interests:

> The page he opened on was under the head of Anatomy, and the first passage that drew his eyes was on the valves of the heart. He was not much acquainted with valves of any sort, but he knew that *valvæ* were folding-doors, and through this crevice came a sudden light startling him with his first vivid notion of finely-adjusted mechanism in the human frame. A liberal education had of course left him free to read the indecent passages in the school classics, but beyond a general sense of secrecy and obscenity in connection

with his internal structure, had left his imagination quite unbiassed, so that for anything he knew his brains lay in small bags at his temples, and he had no more thought of representing to himself how his blood circulated than how paper served instead of gold. But the moment of vocation had come, and before he got down from his chair, the world was made new to him by a presentiment of endless processes filling the vast spaces planked out of his sight by that wordy ignorance which he had supposed to be knowledge. From that hour Lydgate felt the growth of an intellectual passion. [*M*, p. 130]

The 'presentiment of endless processes filling the vast spaces' the circulation of the blood, the *valvæ* through which 'a sudden light comes', all these interpenetrating metaphors express the process of coming to knowledge. And the imagery reaches its issue in the concept of 'primary webs or tissues' which Bichat has established [*M*, p. 133]. Lydgate's speculation adds to the consideration of tissues the question, again, of origins: 'some common basis' of 'the raw cocoon'.

Of this sequence to Bichat's work, already vibrating along many currents of the European mind, Lydgate was enamoured; he longed to demonstrate the more intimate relations of living structure, and help to define men's thought more accurately after the true order. . . . What was the primitive tissue? In that way Lydgate put the question – not quite in the way required by the awaiting answer; but such missing of the right word befalls many seekers. [*M*, p. 134]

The various threads from which are woven 'sarsnet, gauze, net, satin, and velvet' have one basis. The image of the spider's web stirs again in 'the vibration along many currents'. Lydgate's work is to demonstrate 'the more intimate relations of living structure'. Relations, and origins, are both implicit in the one metaphor. This organisation is taken over into that of the book itself, so that its enterprise is preoccupied both with morphological [organic] likeness and with variation.[43] □

Continuing to explore the web imagery of *Middlemarch*, Beer also cites the famous pier-glass passage from Chapter 27 of the novel, already quoted in full in chapter two of this book. In response to the passage, Beer observes:

■ The labyrinth, the web, the tree, the microscope: the contiguity of these concepts is significant for *Middlemarch*. But George Eliot needs also a sense of disparity and unrelatedness which cannot be expressed by any of these means. Much earlier, in a letter, she had used the web as an image of impassive uniformity and unvarying process from which she needed to escape: 'If one is to have the freedom to write out of one's own varying unfolding self, and not to be a machine always grinding out the same material or spinning the same sort of web, one cannot always write for the same public' . . .[44]

The web is not co-terminous with life: it is not, either, identical with organicism. The shears as well as the spinning haunt the metaphor from its oldest use. In this final section of her book the imagery of the web is hauntingly suggested but never reconstituted. At the beginning of the final paragraph its powers are fugitively recollected and then given up:

> Her finely-touched spirit had still its fine issues, though they were not widely visible. Her full nature, like that river of which Cyrus broke the strength, spent itself in channels which had no great name on the earth. [*M*, p. 747][45]

'Finely-touched' suggests the tremor of a spider's web as well as of musical instrument, and that parallelism of 'finely-touched', 'fine issues', with the four insistent preceding 't's just stirs the suggestion of 'tissues' to extend the parallelism. Then the image changes to that of the nameless river, spent in many channels: the irrigating version of the labyrinth.[46] □

Tess Cosslett points to a shift in scientific preoccupation, midway through the nineteenth century, coinciding once again with Darwin's *The Origin of Species*. The shift, she notes, is away from the more Promethean models found in Mary Shelley's *Frankenstein* (1818), in which humanity employs science as a means to control nature, to later models (including those employed by George Eliot) in which the scientific truths of Nature are shown to be controlling humanity. This, Cosslett argues, explains the otherwise seemingly negative ending of *Middlemarch* in relation to the prospects of Dorothea: 'Here the widely spreading effect of Dorothea's character is imaged not as a web, but as a river broken into many small channels. Though the apparent force of the river is thus reduced, its effect is more widely distributed . . . So instead of a Promethean victory of force against external obstacle we are given an image of human power restricted and broken by external conditions . . .'[47]

Looking at Darwin's metaphor of the Tree of Life, however, Cosslett reminds us that this image 'is a living organism, not a dead machine'. As in Shuttleworth's study, once we consider the metaphorical possibilities open to the novelist, organic theory provides a new way of mapping society as an endlessly-changing phenomenon: 'The unity, interconnection and livingness of the Universe imply that it functions as an organism, rather than as a machine . . .'[48] By extension, Cosslett combines 'the mechanistic "chain" image and the organic "tree" image' inherent in Beer's reading of Darwin, but returns us to *The Mill on the Floss* by way of a comparison:

■ . . . The interweaving of 'human lots' in [*Middlemarch*] creates a cumulative picture of society as organism, as one 'involuntary, palpitating life'. But the 'web' image has a deeper interest, a more complex function. Without the Bichat parallel, it appears at first as an *in*organic image – an artificial tapestry woven from dead pieces of thread. However, the actual word 'web' suggests the organic image of the spider's web; and when the same word is used to describe Bichat's conception of the human organism, it suggests a structure of filaments and fibres within a living body . . .

The richly ambiguous use of words such as 'bind', 'tie', 'thread', and 'fibre' occurs in George Eliot's other novels too, most noticeably in *The Mill on the Floss* . . . When Maggie runs off with Stephen Guest, the action is seen by Stephen as an escape from the 'unnatural bonds' of their other relationships, but by Maggie as a rending of the ties that had given meaning to duty. 'If the past is not to bind us, where can duty lie? We should have no law but the inclination of the moment', she says, when she has resolved to return. She is helped by Philip's letter, which 'had stirred all the fibres that bound her to the calmer past'. This recalls the narrator's earlier nostalgia for the scenes of childhood: '[W]hat grove of tropic palms, what strange ferns or splendid broad-petalled blossoms, could ever thrill such deep and delicate fibres within me as this home-scene?' Maggie's causal connection to her own past is a bond that restricts her, a tie that provides guiding laws, and a living fibre that connects her to her roots. In the language of the scientific writers, the restricting 'chain' of causation also provides us with the coherence and unity of 'law' and the kinship and livingness of 'organism'.[49] □

As far as plot development is concerned, Cosslett reminds us that Darwin 'drew attention to the cumulative importance of numerous small, insignificant events in bringing about vast changes over a huge time-span . . . humanity is being seen as one perpetual, self-renewing organism'.[50] This is very much the pattern of plot in all three novels discussed in this volume, where incidents (often insignificant individually) mesh together to construct a plot based on causality with more telling effects on the community as a whole. For Cosslett, this is where Rosamond is at fault, for she is 'unscientific' in her means of thought: 'Her conception of the world is constructed on arbitrary associations, not on a coherent, ordered vision of natural causation.'

A similar charge is levelled at Casaubon: 'Mr Casaubon's research . . . remains on the surface, where everything seems fragmentary, and arbitrarily constructs apparent "correspondence", instead of finding the deeper causal connections . . .'[51]

Clearly this reading harks back again to Darwin, who connects organisms both synchronically and diachronically through his evolutionary methodology. Like Rosamond, Casaubon falls foul of the egotistical (Promethean?) belief 'that all events are providentially arranged for his exclusive benefit'. Unlike Casaubon, however, is the function of the narrator (a presence Cosslett genders as feminine and hence as a direct stand-in for the author). This figure, she claims, 'always draws a strong distinction between misleading surface appearances and subtle inward processes',[52] a power of discernment Cosslett also attributes to Lydgate in his fascination with systems rather than symptoms.

So far we have primarily considered the role played by biology, botany and medicine in *Middlemarch*, but Selma B. Brody also emphasises the role played by physics in Eliot's fictive vision.[53] It, too, she claims, takes on a materiality in conjunction with the human form that enables it to operate as a metaphor for systems and networks – human and communicational. Her article concentrates on the disciplines of thermodynamics and the Kinetic Theory of Gases, applying both to the novel with regard to the nature of the interrelationships between characters. In doing so she considers the forces of action and reaction, collision and force, chance and intention, that direct their behaviour and its consequences. As in the famous 'pier-glass' image, pattern may only seem to be born out of reason. But then, Brody reminds us, in molecular physics '[t]he great success of the Kinetic Theory of Gases was its ability to deal with random assemblages as organized entities governed by statistical laws'.[54] If we pause to think this through in a more internally literary context, we see that this pattern does indeed mimic that of the author's task. She must produce a work in which pattern is sufficiently evident for readerly affects such as suspense, inevitability, coincidence and chance to be conveyed, while refraining from turning pattern into the type of predictability that leads to our frustration and rejection of the text. Again, this paradox meets its equivalent within this theoretical physics.

Brody observes that 'Eliot's scientific metaphors are like the models – what Lewes termed "fictions" – which were gaining recognition as important in the formation of scientific hypotheses. A model . . . is a hypothesized fiction which helps in understanding real relations.'[55] In other words there is (as in nineteenth-century realism) a simultaneous and paradoxical contiguity between the signifier (here the novel) and the signified (nineteenth-century urban communities and their ongoing evolution) and a space of fictiveness – a gap or slippage within which the true creativity takes place and in which the dangers of false creativity lurk. Chapter six explores further this relationship between models and fictions, centring upon Eliot's use of metaphors of circulation in relation to her construction of fictive community.

CHAPTER SIX

Eliot's Metaphors of Circulation

L EADING ON from issues of science and, in particular, social science, the theme of circulation, most fully explored in *Middlemarch* through Dr Lydgate and his interest in the blood, connects up with information currents of other kinds. These include not only the presiding analogy of the web, but also networks relating to gossip, blackmail and monetary circulation (gossip being 'currency' of another kind, of course). Perhaps the most literal connection with the previous chapter lies in the circulation of disease and its social implications. As Jan B. Gordon reminds us:

■ By the 1870s, cholera had already been medically recognized as the result of water-borne bacteria . . . Although initially regarded as a 'lifestyle' illness, exclusively prevalent in impoverished societies, it became a demographic example of the potential of the socially inferior to infect the civilized . . .

. . . cholera is like gossip in [*Middlemarch*] insofar as it requires 'carriers', agents who may or may not evidence symptoms of the disease . . . [T]he various 'strains' of the *E. coli* bacteria can become endemic, comfortably at home in the intestinal tract, awaiting the chance to spread and change environments. The most effective treatments depend not upon finding any source, almost impossible given its permutations, but upon socio-political interventions (rather than therapy) which quarantine the carrier/agent and mobilize the public to change habits of sanitation and personal hygiene. In other words, the illness is at least partially a political illness. As Lydgate's energies are being consumed defending himself from gossip, his research into the structure and origin of tissues and the effect of galvanic lesions is being over-shadowed by an illness which induces fears because it spreads as does information in the novel. Both gossip and cholera democratically level previously invulnerable populations in whom are engendered fears of the loss of control.[1] □

Gordon's observations build on Lilian Furst's more solidly historical account of the disease in relation to Eliot's novel, which introduces a further theme of circulation, namely that of the foreigner or incomer as the primary threat to the stability and 'greater good' of the body politic. Drawing out the full implications of her observation, cholera can be personified as a circulating threat from outside and interpreted figuratively as a foreigner within our midst.

■ A rudimentary Health Act was passed in England in 1848 and a further Health Act in 1875, which laid the foundations for an efficient national sanitary administration. Meanwhile cholera, which had never been endemic in Britain, was advancing rapidly from China and Japan through Eastern and Central Europe . . . The first English cases, probably carried by ship, occurred in the harbor town of Sunderland in 1829, but it was only in 1831, when the disease hit Hamburg, a port of regular communication with Great Britain, that the danger was seen to be acute. A Central Board was set up that encouraged the formation of Local Boards and the organization of isolation hospitals for the sick.[2] □

Gillian Beer expands upon the main relevance of these key interrelated themes to *Middlemarch*.

■ The body is itself a circulatory system; so is money, so is gossip. Apart from Lydgate, the other characters in the book are not much interested in the activity of their own bodies – though fever and the recurrent return of typhoid and typhus are made part of the plot. Lydgate's research is on fever; he first visits the Vincys' to treat Fred when he has typhus; the hospital which Bulstrode helps to fund will advance Lydgate's research; and it is at a meeting to discuss the funding of a graveyard outside the town for the latest victims of a new typhoid epidemic that Bulstrode is denounced and his and Lydgate's fortunes reach their nadir. Lydgate dies prematurely of diphtheria. This emphasis on epidemics may have called to mind another circulatory system to the first 1870s readers: that of the drainage system which Chadwick's work had managed to establish between the setting and the writing of the book. But that system is not, so far as I have traced, remarked on in *Middlemarch*.

There is, however, a further circulatory system, much connected both with money and with gossip, which does mark the historical moment of the work. That is the coming of the railways. That development is always on the periphery of the characters' concerns, demonstrating how little we understand in the moment the crucial forces of change in a community and in its relations with other communities. The Liverpool and Manchester Railway opened in 1830. In the twenty years after that, 6,000 miles of track carrying about 1 million passengers was laid. In 1750 the journey from London to Edinburgh took as much as ten days; by train in 1830 it took 50 hours; by 1850, 17½ hours; by 1855, 13¾ hours. This change in ease of interconnection would, of course, have been vivid to George Eliot's first readers. In *Middlemarch* we are reading of the last period in which it would be possible for a man like Bulstrode confidently to bury his past, or for a community like Middlemarch quite so confidently to believe itself the middle of the world – the heart of England. Middlemarch as a community behaves as if it were a closed system; but reading opens it.[3] □

Picking up this invitation for an opening, U.C. Knoepflmacher asks the rhetorical question 'What is *Middlemarch* about?', identifying within it, by way of his own answer, a presiding dynamic rather than a theme.

■ One of the principal word clusters . . . is centered around the idea of motion and exploration: the progress of the individual characters, their strides forward, their halts, indecisions, and detours . . . assessed against the larger movements of historical change. The novel's own shuttlelike motions encourage this continuous process of contrast and assessment by weaving separate strands into an evergrowing tissue of relations and connections.[4] □

So we once again lay the foundations for a larger and ever more encompassing exploration of the web-like imagery of *Middlemarch*. Knoepflmacher continues:

■ In *Middlemarch* each individual strand intersects with four larger circles or orbits of experience. These four concentric circles are graduated in proportion to their comprehensiveness and universality. Thus, the outermost circle consists of general allusions: to history, science, literature, and myth; the second circle is made up of more specific references to the events of the 1830s: the death of George IV, the threat of a cholera epidemic, the state of law and medicine, the initial rejection and final passage of the Reform Bill. The third circle incorporates the attitudes and manners of the Middlemarch community; and the innermost circle focuses on the particular events that make up the stories of Dorothea's two marriages, of Lydgate's defeat, of Bulstrode's crime and exile, and of Fred Vincy's regeneration by the Garths . . . [T]hese four circles frame the experiences or motivations of each individual character.[5] □

Later he develops this reading of the narrative structure further.

■ The connections afforded by the novel's plot lines are infinite. By gratefully accepting Bulstrode's financial aid, Lydgate invites comparison to both Will Ladislaw and Caleb Garth, who, for different reasons, have refused to be dependent on the banker. Mr Brooke's unsuccessful attempts to address the unruly crowd [which] mocks his reformist speech is complemented by Caleb's success in calming the mob of laborers who threaten to destroy the railroad . . . Dorothea has given her mother's amethyst to Celia; Rosamond is reluctant to give up her 'purple amethyst' necklace to Lydgate.[6] □

It is precisely such connections, linking apparently unrelated characters, events and reputations, which are drawn out in Alexander Welsh's discussion of *Middlemarch* in *George Eliot and Blackmail*.[7] However, if we digress momentarily from *Middlemarch* itself, it is useful first to recall the significance of reputation to George Eliot's career, before coming on to re-examine it in her fiction. Mary Ann/Marian Evans was no stranger to the evils of gossip. Her life with George Henry Lewes, along with the controversy surrounding the anonymous publication of *Adam Bede*, could well have destroyed her writing career. However, as Welsh explains, though George Eliot exploited the possibilities of blackmail fully in her novels, Evans was careful to evade its potency in real life.

■ [She] chose, in effect, to live with Lewes in a manner not open to blackmail. The concealments they permitted themselves were only petty ones, the kinds necessary to prevent the eruption of landladies. With persons whose opinion mattered to them, they were frank and assertive. In September 1855, six months after returning from Germany with Lewes and before settling in Richmond, Marian Lewes – as she now determined to call herself – wrote these well-known words to Caroline Bray:

If we differ on the subject of the marriage laws, I at least can believe of you that you cleave to what you believe to be good, and I don't know of anything in the nature of your views that should prevent you from believing the same of me. . . . We cannot set each other quite right on this matter in letters, but one thing I can tell you in a few words. Light and easily broken ties are what I neither desire theoretically nor could live for practically. Women who are satisfied with such ties do not act as I have done – they obtain what they desire and are still invited to dinner.

Women who care to be invited to dinner and conceal their affairs would be subject to blackmail; but Marian Lewes has braced herself for a scandal and actually prefers it to concealment. To her mind the private morality of the step she has taken shall weigh against public infamy, as her ensuing paragraph makes clear:

> That any unworldly, unsuperstitious person . . . who is sufficiently acquainted with the realities of life can pronounce my relation to Mr Lewes immoral I can only understand by remembering how subtle and complex are the influences that mould opinion. . . . From the majority of persons, of course, we never looked for anything but condemnation. We are leading no life of self-indulgence, except indeed, that being happy in each other, we find everything easy. We are working hard to provide for others better than we provide for ourselves, and to fulfil every responsibility that lies upon us. Levity and pride would not be a sufficient basis for that.[8]

As she frequently does later as George Eliot, Marian remarks the limited capacity of letters to convey feelings safely, but she also takes advantage of writing, even to her friend. Her feelings have been armored in the kind of argument one can only construct in writing, and the defense of her actions is predicated on distance and the withholding of personal confrontation. Her irregular marriage is predicated on these conditions, as is her profession, and these are very literate cross-purposes, which we are privileged to examine years later, in an equally literate way, because of their preservation in writing and print.[9] □

In the context of *Middlemarch*, Welsh uses the relationship between letters, writing, secrecy and the type of jealous protection so typical of the blackmailer to connect the fearful possessiveness of Casaubon with the archetypal fears of the scientific innovator. This linkage is also returned to later on in his book when he looks at the concept of professional reputation as an enhancing phenomenon for both the writer and the scientist, as opposed to more limiting notions of reputation, which usually derive from a sense of dishonour and/or transgression.

■ *Middlemarch* is not only concerned with the limitations of knowledge but with the close bearing of motives of reputation on knowledge . . . [Hence] the extreme case of blackmailing Bulstrode is but one of four relevant actions. Casaubon, Lydgate, Brooke, and Bulstrode are every one susceptible to threatening publicity . . .

George Eliot makes abundantly clear that virtually the sole motive of Casaubon's scholarship is fame, and that this relation between his knowledge and his being known runs far deeper than mere vanity, his pleasure in sitting for the portrait of St. Thomas Aquinas and the like. Casaubon is both vain and 'resolute in being a man of honour,' a person 'unimpeachable by any recognized opinion'; but he is subject to the deepest terror by authorship. He will be judged in absentia from his writings, and already is so judged, as he fears. Authorship entails risks that are less within his control than his personal conduct.

> In conduct these ends [of honour] had been attained; but the difficulty of making his Key to all Mythologies unimpeachable weighed like lead upon his mind; and the pamphlets – or 'Parerga' as he called them – by which he tested his public and deposited small monumental records of his march, were far from having been seen in all their significance. He suspected the Archdeacon of not having read them; he was in painful doubt as to what was really thought of them by the leading minds of Brasenose, and bitterly convinced that his old acquaintance Carp had been the writer of that depreciatory recension which was kept locked in a small drawer of Mr Casaubon's desk, and also in a dark closet of his verbal memory. These were heavy impressions to struggle against, and brought that melancholy embitterment which is the consequence of all excessive claim: even his religious faith wavered with his wavering trust in his own authorship, and the consolations of the Christian hope in immortality seemed to lean on the immortality of the still unwritten Key to all Mythologies. [M, pp. 250–1]

The independent life of writing, divorced from its author, becomes a strong reason for not writing at all, lest some terrible failure in the Key – like a previous mistake in a dedication of a Parergon to Carp – open the author 'to ridicule in the next age' or to 'be chuckled over by Pike and Trench in the present' [M, p. 252]. George Eliot knew of the terror herself, as the recension put away in the locked drawer may suggest by resemblance to the drawer to which Lewes consigned even those writings about the novelist that he approved. Scholarship has its good days, and Dr. Spanning's praise of 'my late tractate on the Egyptian Mysteries' puts Casaubon in a rare good humor [M, p. 331], but on the whole the perils outweigh the pleasures. When Will Ladislaw, 'not at all deep himself in German writers,' criticizes Casaubon's failure to consult the Germans who 'have taken the lead in historical inquiries,' the narrator comments wryly that 'Mortals are easily tempted to pinch the life out of their neighbour's buzzing glory, and think that such killing is no murder' [M, pp. 186–7]. The equation of this diminishment of reputation with murder, however lightheartedly represented as insecticide, connects with the one murder case in *Middlemarch*, which is in response to blackmail, and may recall that at the beginning of this century blackmail was popularly referred to as 'moral murder.'[10]

The importance of Lydgate's relation to his public is more evident because he is a doctor. In the nature of such a career, he must not only know what he is doing but be perceived as knowing. His success is bound to depend on public relations that ostensibly have little to do with medical science. Lydgate's particular failure, therefore, follows from his neglect and scorn for this aspect of the practitioner's life, just as his ironic success in later years depends more on being fashionable than on scientific achievement. But Lydgate is more than just a doctor, and is far closer than Casaubon to George Eliot's idea of an intellectual. His troubles both personal and professional conflict with an ideal. 'Only those who know the supremacy of the intellectual life – the life which has a seed of ennobling thought and purpose within it – can understand the grief of one who falls from that serene activity into the absorbing soul-wasting struggle with worldly annoyances.' [M, p.661]

Some of Lydgate's troubles result from his finely described 'commonness,' or unconscious snobbery – a taking for granted of status that fatally ignores opinion. He does begin to understand, what had not occurred to him, that even popularity may interfere with a career, as when his talent attracts Rosamond 'because it gives him prestige, and is like an order in his button-hole or an Honourable before his name' [M, p.521]. Lydgate's is the most sharply differentiated talent in *Middlemarch*: in his intellectual aim and in his specialization he is the most modern hero of the novel, and the constraint that his marriage places upon him is partly due to what Georg Simmel analyzed as the typically differentiated relations of modern men, which prompt concealment in several directions at once.

> These differentiated friendships which connect us with one individual in terms of affection, with another, in terms of common intellectual aspects, with a third, in terms of religious impulses, and with a fourth, in terms of common experiences – all these friendships present a very peculiar synthesis in regard to the question of discretion, of reciprocal revelation and concealment. They require that the friends do not look into those mutual spheres of interest and feeling which, after all, are not included in the relation and which, if touched upon, would make them feel painfully the limits of their mutual understanding.[11]

The analysis is extremely suggestive of Lydgate's partial relations with his fellow doctors, with Bulstrode, with Farebrother, with Ladislaw, with his family, and with his own wife, no one of which relations admits of frank intimacy. Without question Rosamond's concealments from her husband are stunning, but as perceptive students of that marriage have begun to comment, he is not open with her.[12] Nor can Lydgate, the most promising and undoubtedly talented seeker of knowledge, be open with any of the Middlemarchers: it is this isolation that makes Dorothea's befriending of him so touching. George Eliot hints at some tragic flaw in the 'commonness' of Lydgate [M, p.136], but succeeds brilliantly in portraying the common relations of a modern person with his fellows. This intellectual's embroilment with Bulstrode and his recognition that even 'valid evidence' will not clear him [M, p.663] dramatize his position beyond a doubt. It is the nature of his position in society that it will not support him by close friendships, and it is the nature of opinion and circumstances to indict.[13] □

Welsh's reading of the relationship between writing and exposure (including exposure to ridicule) reveals further connections between Casaubon, Ladislaw, Raffles and Bulstrode.

■ The course of action adopted by Bulstrode is murder, but the roles of the several characters are blurred. The chapter in which the banker, against the doctor's orders, makes brandy available to Raffles is headed by an epigraph of George Eliot's own composition: 'Our deeds still travel with us from afar,/And what we have been makes us what we are.' The application is obviously to Bulstrode, but no doubt also to Lydgate, and most immediately to the sick man. 'Bulstrode's first object after Lydgate had left Stone Court,' the chapter begins, 'was to examine Raffles's pockets, which he imagined were sure to carry signs in the shape of hotel-bills of the places he had stopped in, if he had not told the truth in saying that he had come straight from Liverpool . . .' [M, pp.629–30]. Curious transpositions occur here: Bulstrode is the hunted victim, but he goes through the blackmailer's pockets in search of evidence; Lydgate is the doctor in charge, but his prescription for the treatment of alcoholism is so advanced, and so contrary to received opinion, that the banker can easily risk altering it. Bulstrode's being, his 'what we are,' is uppermost in the text, but Lydgate we care more about, and Raffles is the one who has most recently traveled 'from afar' – as if to embody the transience of the other two. Bulstrode prays for his blackmailer's death, and his prayer – assisted by the brandy – is answered. 'As he sat there and beheld the enemy of his peace going irrevocably into silence, he felt more at rest than he had done for many months. His conscience was soothed by the enfolding wing of secrecy, which seemed just then like an angel sent down for his relief' [M, p.637]. Of the three strangers to Middlemarch in the chapter, one has been sacrificed, the second experiences some temporary relief from the information that threatens to ruin him, and the third has become still more enmeshed in circumstances that tell against him.

... Next to Bulstrode or Lydgate [Raffles] weighs almost nothing at all, and he must clearly count for what rather than who he is in the novel. His role in the fine story of Bulstrode is obviously essential, and he is thus important to the story of Lydgate as well. If it will help to make his presence felt, he ought to be compared with Will Ladislaw – a much more substantial character, but one whom readers have also judged too lightweight for the part.[14] It is astonishing how often Ladislaw, the only other stranger of note, is perceived by other characters as threatening, and precisely because he bears information of some kind. When he appears in Middlemarch as editor of the *Pioneer*, Mr Hawley claims to recognize the foreign type – 'some emissary,' as he says [*M*, p. 321]. Bulstrode unhappily is forced to associate Ladislaw directly with Raffles's presence in the town and tries to buy him off, as if in danger of blackmail from this quarter also. 'It was the first time he had encountered an open expression of scorn from any man higher than Raffles'; but after talking with Ladislaw the banker comforts himself with the reflection that he, at least, is not likely to 'publish' their conversation [*M*, p. 559]. Later Ladislaw remarks to Lydgate that he is surprised gossip has not accused him of plotting 'with Raffles to murder Bulstrode' [*M*, p. 700]. There is no getting around the fact that this stranger poses a certain threat from the past to Casaubon, also, and that he is the first to inform Dorothea of her husband's inadequate scholarship [*M*, pp. 186–7].[15] □

In relation to Eliot's work itself, Welsh reminds us that here, too, there are connections with the Bulstrode affair and Casaubon's paranoia: 'As opposed to gossip then or now, writing may occur at one time and be read at another, and as evidence may therefore both conceal secrets and reveal them. With her fine metaphysical image of the whispering gallery George Eliot elaborates this difference: one can actually construct a reliable means to deliver gossip across a large space, as in a whispering gallery; paradoxically, the more permanent record of writing is subject over time to greater effect of chance.'[16]

He continues: 'George Eliot is [by the time she writes *Middlemarch*] now working at a great distance from the initial experience of her own secret, the affair with Lewes and pseudonymous authorship; yet both kinds of secret are present when Raffles appears on the scene . . . "Who shall tell what may be the effect of writing?" is her introduction of Raffles and his low relations.'[17] This remark can also be applied, of course, to the connection with 'W/will'-making within the text: 'In an extended soliloquy, uncharacteristic of *Middlemarch*, [Casaubon] foresees Dorothea's marriage to Ladislaw . . . [T]he background for these dramatic moments is authorship; and the cause of alienation is authorship, for it is Dorothea's opinion of him as a scholar rather than her possible unfaithfulness that Casaubon has come to fear . . .' It is against such paranoia that authorship provides most protection: 'For a man so utterly given to the distances of reading and writing, the intimacy of two persons is tantamount to public exposure.'

Though the following passage from Welsh most obviously relates to Bulstrode and Raffles, there is a sense in which it might also be said, once again, to relate to Casaubon: 'Killing the blackmailer is like expunging information, undoing the past, reversing wrongdoing . . . [It also] has the practical motive . . . of stopping payment and also the social motive . . . of attacking someone who professes neither private nor public loyalty to anyone.'[18]

Relating this theme to urban expansion, Welsh finds in the presiding nineteenth-century movement to the town a matching increase in the nature of suspicion, fear and secrecy in the community at large: 'In closer proximity with one another individuals knew both more and less about their neighbours . . . Thus a common fascination of urban life, frequently remarked by novelists, was the sense of being surrounded by other people's secrets.'[19] A similar point is made by Ruth apRoberts, in her essay 'Middlemarch and the New Humanity'.

■ Middlemarch may be the best illustration of the Victorianism of the Victorian novel. In its panorama of society we see man functioning and interacting in his conventions or institutions – church (and chapel), land-holding and inheritance, marriage, medicine, scholarship, politics, and labour. Provincial society exhibits the linkages better because there *are* more linkages there than in the more separate multitudinous lives in great cities. All the people of the town are aware of each other: Bulstrode's downfall *matters* here, where it would not so much in London. The coincidences in Middlemarch – Ladislaw happens to be connected both with Casaubon and with Bulstrode, and Dorothea happens on Ladislaw just when he is holding Rosamond's hands – these mar the art of the novel, but they bear out George Eliot's concern with linkages, 'the steady convergence of human lots', as she puts it, or the 'weavings and interweavings' of 'this particular web' [M, p. 128].[20] □

It is in such terms as these that Suzanne Graver's reading of community once again demonstrates the aptness of Eliot's use of the web analogy. She identifies a shift in the make-up of social cohesion during the Victorian period which derived directly from improved transportation links:

■ The traditional community, because it consisted of a group of people living for generations in a given place and regulating their lives according to set customs and beliefs, could be described by a constellation of shared, concrete realities. But when individuals became more mobile, these constellations of patterns fragment and disintegrate. Newer definitions of community place less emphasis on concrete attributes . . . and more emphasis on . . . affective ties, or the feelings, ideas, and interests that exist apart from fixity of place and social role. As a result, these modern definitions lack solidity.[21] □

Like a web, then, the strands of society are fragile and elastic, shifting with the elements or expanding to take in additional strands. Seen in different lights they offer up different shapes, resisting fixture, definition, and especially permanence. This takes us on to gossip, of course. For Welsh this is a cohesive as much as a divisive social concern, helping to 'acquaint' neighbours as well as set up factions.

■ The importance of the past to a person's identity is firmly asserted in [Eliot's] first two novels but not finally tested. In *Adam Bede* the past is said to inhere in all our feelings and also to be secret, something that divides us from each other: 'The secret of our emotions never lies in the bare object, but in its subtle relations to our own past: no wonder the secret escapes the unsympathizing observer, who might as well put on spectacles to discern odours.' The reference, oddly, is to Adam's churchgoing, which has been continuous and, as part of the community life, not particularly secret. George Eliot is thinking of her own situation and counting on the pastoral narrative, including an allusion to 'early Christians who had worshipped from their childhood upwards in catacombs,' to reflect the difference [*AB*, p. 189] . . . The very moral of *The Mill on the Floss* – 'If the past is not to bind us, where can duty lie?' – insists on the continuity of personal identity over time, and there are several passages discoursing on the subject:

> There is no sense of ease like the ease we felt in those scenes where we were born, where objects became dear to us before we had known the labour of choice, and where the outer world seemed only an extension of our own personality: we accepted and loved it as we accepted our own sense of existence and our own limbs. Very commonplace, even ugly, that furniture of our early home might look if it were put up to auction: an improved taste in upholstery scorns it; and is not the striving after something better and better in our surroundings, the grand characteristic that distinguishes man from the brute – or, to satisfy a scrupulous accuracy of definition, that distinguishes the British man from the foreign brute? But

heaven knows where that striving might lead us, if our affections had not a trick of twining round those old inferior things, if the loves and sanctities of our life had no deep immovable roots in memory. [*MF*, p. 222]

Again pastoralism, already projected into a satire of 'British man' and enhanced in a sentence to follow by a contrast between 'the finest cistus or fuschia' and a humble 'elderberry,' pulls away from the represented object. It is wonderful writing, with the undercutting of upholstery and all the rest; but the immediate reference is to Tom Tulliver's homecoming from school, and Tom's later material striving is tightly rooted in his upbringing. Usually, of course, it is Maggie's past that matters – but actually, throughout the novel, the heroine seldom recalls her childhood. The narrator recalls it for her . . .

Each of George Eliot's novels after *The Mill on the Floss* explores some life history that is discontinuous yet surreptitiously connected with a past. The discontinuity is social, and nothing strange to the history of the author's own times; but its replication in narrative begins to resemble, through the importance bestowed on the past, the tracing of distortions and finally a transference, the conditions that have come to be known as 'the analytic situation.' As Paul Ricoeur has written of psychoanalysis and its pursuit of continuous narratives, 'the patient is both the actor and the critic of a history which he is at first unable to recount. The problem of recognizing oneself is the problem of recovering the ability to recount one's own history, to endlessly continue to give the form of a story to reflections on oneself.'[22] These words will serve to characterize George Eliot's personal commitment to the art of the novel, a commitment that evinces many of the historical conditions for psychoanalysis. She was not prepared to cede the priority of moral demands, but she gradually enlarged her study of consciousness, told of unconscious thoughts and mental suffering inflicted upon the self as well as upon others, and experimented with narrative reconstructions of both shame and guilt.

A comparison of the project of George Eliot with the project of Freud may need to be qualified in one respect, since the latter almost never treats shame directly as an object of his inquiries. George Eliot and other nineteenth-century novelists, in their creative work, were seldom unconcerned with shame in one way or another. The culture of information and publicity disarmed honor, so to speak, and diffused the possibility of shame in all directions. Avoidance of shame becomes the passive strategem of private life, while threatening shame is the implicit means of control in the rise of public opinion. The novelists of the century repeatedly explore situations conducive to shame, the defenses against it available to protagonists, and the salutary effects on the community when wrongdoing coincides with shame. Guilt and shame are often hard to distinguish, whether as community judgments or as internalized feelings. As the latter, they appeal to the great novelists of character, but because both feelings originate in social life (including the family), it is not difficult for a lesser novelist to imply their existence. The internalizations of guilt and shame are important, and not merely to the psychologist, since these feelings help to enforce peaceful social existence. But whereas guilt can be characterized as internalized punishment, shame is an internalized sense of the self's appearance to others; the one sensation reflects the subordination of the self to more powerful figures, as of the child to a parent, and the other, coordination of the self with fellow beings in the formation of personal identity. Even this definition has to struggle against a Judeo-Christian tradition that conceives of morality and guilt as essentially inward, pride and shame as outward considerations. For this tradition, any regard for shame is less worthy than obedience to conscience . . .

Shame and guilt may finally be impossible to distinguish clearly, since shaming is often threatened as a punishment and guilt may be a cause of shame. What seems to happen, in the course of psychotherapy as well as in novels, is that certain negotiations take place between shame and guilt.[23] There may be a trade-off, say, in which shame becomes less excruciating because of a strengthened sense of responsibility, or guilt becomes less oppressive through private or public confession. The shifting of a burden from one side to the other is not the same as laying it down altogether, but it brings substantial relief. Psychoanalysis seems to take for granted that shame is constitutive in repression and then quite commonly assists the patient in arriving at an understanding of his or her feelings of guilt – as if one always started with shame, apparent in the resistance to psychoanalysis itself, and converted it to guilt, which is assuaged by speaking of it with the analyst. This pattern is something like the progress of George Eliot's motives as a writer of fiction . . .

Negotiations with a blackmailer tend to take an opposite tack. Yet by threatening guilt with shame, the blackmailer may do his clients and the public some good. The novels of George Eliot and her contemporaries were first of all great social novels. By beginning with social relations, these novels may end by demonstrating that shame is as basic to Freud's project as it is to their own.[24] □

What we are dealing with, then, is the *manner* in which seemingly separate phenomena connect up. This takes us back to the metaphor of the web.

■ [L]et me posit that the single most inclusive theme of *Middlemarch* is knowledge, and that the theme keeps resolving, in one way or another, into statements of the limitation of knowledge. This is not a new position to take: readers from the first have noted how much knowledge is contained and expressed in *Middlemarch*. Academic reviewers like Sidney Colvin responded with enthusiasm, found the novel 'all saturated with modern ideas, and poured into a language of which every word bites home with peculiar sharpness to the contemporary consciousness.' Henry James judged the 'philosophic' George Eliot superior to the 'didactic' Fielding, but complained that the discursive portions of the novel were 'too clever by half.' He seemed to find the burden of learning unliterary: '. . . *Middlemarch* is too often an echo of Messrs. Darwin and Huxley' . . . But it was not until the mid-twentieth century, after the publication by Anna T. Kitchel of the notebook called the 'Quarry for *Middlemarch*,' that students of George Eliot began to have a practical idea of how some of the knowledge found its way into the novel.[25] In the same decade techniques of the New Criticism were brought to bear, and critics were able to demonstrate that the interconnectedness of things, such as the novelist frequently urged, was imaged forth in her text. Reva Stump expounded in detail what she believed to be 'the governing image' of *Middlemarch*, the web; Quentin Anderson, selecting the same image, suggested that it might be thought of as 'a vast switchboard in which every signal is interpreted differently by each receiver, and each receiver is in its turn capable of propagating in response a signal of its own with equally dissonant consequences.'[26] Anderson's slightly anachronistic translation of the image is worth pausing over, because it intuits the degree to which the famous 'web' of the novel is an information network and at the same time indicates that the network is imperfect. For all the vast knowledge that George Eliot incorporated in her work, by *Middlemarch* she had arrived at a position somewhat critical of her own and her age's faith in knowledge, and her wariness extended both to the grounds for knowing anything and to the social implications of the theme.

Our understanding of sources and our appreciation of the integument of imagery and analogy in *Middlemarch* has tended to supplant the older estimation of George Eliot as the brilliant exponent of character and morality. There have, of course, always been studies of the ideation in the novels, but now a shift has become discernible in the general critical assessment of her achievement. Once the form of her novels was defended against the strictures of Henry James; now, the echoes of Darwin and Huxley are defended and frequently celebrated . . . [U. C.] Knoepflmacher wrote of *Middlemarch* as essentially an inquiry into truth; later he began to stress that 'rationalizations abound' among the characters of the novel, and still more recently he has observed that the novelist 'turns her knowledge of science against the presumption of those scientists who fail to admit that they, too, are allegorists, makers of fictive models of reality.[27] □

Gillian Beer, in *Arguing With the Past* (1989), opens her consideration of the workings of circulation metaphors in *Middlemarch* by connecting up the act of narration and fictive 'real time' in the text.

■ The writing is not simply mirroring society, as a 'classic realist text'. Rather its discursive twists and turns set up turbulences which unsteady these reflections. This effect is intensified . . . by the ironic abrasions produced by the double time of the novel. The referential circle between the time of production and first reading – the 1870s – and the time of enactment, forty years earlier, is never quite a closed system. The unwritten time between the two, which is the time of George Eliot's own life and of all her emotional, political, and intellectual involvement, disturbs the apparently reflective surface of the work. As later readers we may too placidly level the text and miss the circulating energies within it, which declare themselves both temporally and discursively.[28] □

From this point Beer goes on specifically to consider the relationship between the discourse of economics and that of narration in relation to images of circulation.

■ Even 'utterance' had a trading meaning in the Middle Ages (and still does in specialized City and legal circles): utterance is bringing goods for sale; it requires a buyer as well as seller for its meaning, an addressee as well as an addresser. 'Telling' likewise moves freely to and fro across counting and retailing, and retailing means both selling in small lots and retelling a story. The same slippage occurs in 'an account'. *Credit* and *crediting* is the tightest of significations. We are allowed credit if our standing is good; we credit a story if we believe in its consistency or inconclusiveness; we behave creditably; we perform discreditable acts and find ourselves out of credit.[29] □

This brings Beer on to the manner in which economics most obviously impinges on circulatory issues, namely in relation to hard currency. Again, Bulstrode's shady past forms the key connection in these terms and takes us back to the relationship between credit and trust(s).

■ Bulstrode is the town's banker . . . At the end of the 1820s the West Midlands, as it happened, had more banks per head of population than any other area: one bank for 12,000 people as against 17,000 in

London. The Bank of England and the London City banks were supplemented by the country banks, of which there were only a handful in 1750 but around 800 in 1810 and a good many more by the peak of 1825. The capitalization of such banks was surprisingly low, an average of £10,000 – the same sum, we recall, as Fred was likely to inherit from Featherstone. Moreover, they were unit banks, without branches, lodged close within the single community. Not only industrialists but shopkeepers, lawyers, and other relatively small capitalists could set up as bankers. In 1825–6 sixty country banks failed. . . .

. . . [W]e are in the period where the transfer from metal [gold currency] to paper [bank-notes] is taking place, where the promissory or symbolic character of money has come to the fore, and where the community is very much at the mercy of one banker . . . We see now, I think, more clearly why in the passage [concerning Lydgate's attraction to anatomy] . . . George Eliot sets 'paper and gold' alongside the action of the heart and the valves ['. . . he had no more thought of representing to himself how his blood circulated than how paper served instead of gold' [*M*, p.130]].[30] □

Beer's larger argument is therefore that at this specific historical period, the newly circulating bank-notes would make money seem sufficiently interchangeable with private letters to render the relationship between reputation and finance more apparent to Eliot's nineteenth-century readers than it is to us today.

Such issues of economics, speculation, circulation and rumour are also the concerns of Jeffrey Franklin, in his article on the subject of gambling in *Middlemarch*.[31] For Franklin money can be equated with desire, and in his opinion it is money rather than any other system of circulation that enables the plot structure of *Middlemarch* to cohere: 'Fred Vincy is connected to his miserly uncle Featherstone by inheritance; Rosamond Vincy's marriage to Dr Lydgate comes to be dominated by the issue of debt; Dorothea Brooke's relation to Lydgate, as to Reverend Farebrother, is one of charity; the banker Bulstrode is bound to the disreputable character Raffles (and his own past deeds) by ill-gotten money and blackmail . . .'

Franklin continues: 'Money, then, is the public yardstick of private relationship . . . The danger of gambling, whether with money or relationships, is that it can transpose private loss or gain into the public domain of scandal . . .'

So gambling (and the risk involved) is the most desirous of all social transactions, as is shown in Lydgate turning to it as compensation for his disappointment in marriage. However, as Franklin succinctly observes, 'One cannot take the gamble out of marriage through either the romance of gambling or the gamble of romance . . .'[32]

Daniel Cottom, whose work we looked at in detail in chapter three, also picks up on the circulatory theme of gambling in Eliot's work, but reads it in a more specifically socio-historical manner. For him Eliot uses gambling as a type of shorthand communicating 'moral surrender to wayward opinion, desire, and action'.[33] In that context it also becomes a metaphor for social change, particularly in relation to the security of previous class-based hierarchies:

■ [A]s the genteel status of . . . Fred . . . [and] Lydgate indicates . . . [gambling] marks Eliot's recognition that the law embodied in the traditional system of deference has fallen. One cannot trust individuals solely on account of their rank in society any more than these individuals can trust their position to confer on them an innate guidance in moral and social affairs. This is the most conventional aspect of Eliot's imagery, as gambling had long been represented in her culture as the characteristic vice of the upper classes . . .

. . . What one [therefore] sees in Eliot's image of gambling . . . is the nightmare underside of the *laissez-faire* doctrine that was still dominant in her time, despite increasing instances of state intervention and regulation. In this nightmare, the pursuit of individual self-aggrandizement does not prove to serve the best ends of society as a whole. It results only in a chaotic mass of people having no common law. In other words, it results in a completely fragmented society . . . In this respect one might compare Eliot's writing to Burke's description of postrevolutionary France as 'a common-wealth founded upon Gambling'[34] – a description directly referring to the freeing of the French economy at this time but more generally conveying Burke's sense of the import of all the changes brought by the Revolution. True, Eliot's own writing to a certain extent represents an adoption of *laissez-faire* doctrine . . . However, this imagery of gambling in her writing also shows how tenuous such a casual belief in this doctrine may prove when one descends from generalities to a representation of social life . . . Caleb Garth, [for example,] suffers his one great failure when he extends his business operation to a large, speculative scale – that is, when he gambles in commerce.[35] □

The most sustained discussion of the theme of gambling, however, can be found in Gordon's book on gossip in the nineteenth century. He, too, sees gambling as an important aspect of the text, but goes on to relate it to issues of property and propriety in general:

■ If gambling is a game in which what is not owned is put into the 'play' of the prospect(ive) in George Eliot's novel, the auction of household properties might be a domestic corollary . . . As Fred Vincy makes Fate rather than Featherstone his authority by allowing one horse to become collateral for his speculation upon another and Lydgate uses that which he does not own – a successful medical practice – as the basis for borrowing against the future, so Casaubon does the same *negatively*: he speculates on Dorothea's character by putting his money on her future marital status at the very moment when he becomes aware that his (physiological) future and that of his project is limited. In each instance the person or scheme which *grounds* the speculation as a kind of surety is revealed to be dependent upon a prior surety. As Lydgate explains to a naive Rosamond Vincy, as their household furnishings disappear one by one, 'That was only a security and behind that security there is a debt' [*M*, p. 583]. Behind the presumed Origin, there is always another claim . . .

Rather than being dependent upon some originary pedigree or line of explanatory descent, intentionality becomes a function of an *economy* where exchange occurs virtually *ad hoc*. Trumbull, the licensed auctioneer who also serves as a notary for last wills and testaments (suggesting that he 'guarantees' the last narratives of both individuals and their possessions, a typical conflict-of-interest in *Middlemarch*), can alter the intention of any object, merely by imbedding it within another narrative of dubious authenticity. Possessions, like their owners, can be bent to a narrator's will:

> 'Now, ladies,' said Mr Trumbull, taking up one of the articles, 'this tray contains a very recherchy lot – *a collection* [ital. added] of trifles for the drawing-room table – and trifles make the sum of human things – nothing more important than trifles – (yes, Mr Ladislaw, yes, by-and-by) – but pass the tray round, Joseph – these bijoux must be examined, ladies. This I have in my hand is an ingenious contrivance – a sort of practical rebus, I may call it: here, you see, it looks like an elegant heart-shaped box, portable – for the pocket; there, again, it becomes like a splendid double flower – an ornament for the table; and now' – Mr Trumbull allowed the flower to fall alarmingly into strings of heart-shaped leaves – 'a book of riddles! No less than five hundred printed in a beautiful red.' [*M*, p. 542]

Rather than someone who 'banks' ideas or desires within a respository of dependencies as did Casaubon with his pigeon-holes of accumulated notes and a long bachelorhood wherein was 'stored up . . . a compound interest of enjoyment' [*M*, p. 76], the auctioneer releases private histories to retail consumption. As we might expect, his 'riff' is the precise opposite of Casaubon's measured, cautious utterance: long, run-on sentences in which those in attendance (and their life-styles) are quickly incorporated into the narrative. Like the information narrated by gossips, the prospective uses to which objects may be put by the intending consumer are suggested, but, finally, left open to the imagination.

As Trumbull amuses himself and any attendant audience by oral recitations from Scott's *Anne of Geierstein,* aware of rough vulgarities in his pronunciation, so his performances as auctioneer invariably 'drew all classes' [*M,* p. 539] under one tent, no mean achievement in the stratified society of Middlemarch. His fêtes are attended by the suitably anonymous 'everybody' [*M,* p. 539] who will eventually come to comprise both the dangers and the political possibilities of public opinion in George Eliot's novel. The auctioneer retains the interest of diverse classes and occupations by a unique turn of speech. Obscuring the distinction between declarative and interrogative modes, he quickly incorporates potentially disturbing queries into his own narrative continuity:

> 'Anybody may interrogate. Any one may give their remarks an interrogative turn,' he continued, his sonorousness rising with his style. 'This is constantly done by good speakers, even when they anticipate no answer. It is what we call a figure of speech – speech at a high figure as one may say.' The eloquent auctioneer smiled at his own ingenuity. [*M,* p. 278]

Turning both figures of speech and the 'practical rebus' upside down to suit his needs, Trumbull's monologues create the illusion of participation within the dialogic register, one of the characteristics of gossip. Rhetorically, all potential queries thereby become part of an object's (or character's) provenance; gossip 'encloses' its own potential negations.

Dorothea Brooke's resistance to the life of 'small talk' is . . . early on threatened by the spread of gossip, another name for the miniature made larger than life. But the release of the 'trifle' to a public consumption at auction may in fact be symbolic of this larger threat to both private life and great plans. And the first stage of this dissemination occurs when the 'trifle' is made part of an *aggregate* which supplies the wholeness, unity and internal consistency to which so many models of intentionality are dedicated. The fragmentary and incomplete is given 'coherent meaning' through the illusion of participation within a larger entity, the ubiquitous *collection.* In certain ways the purposes of the auction resemble the activities common to dissenting sects like those of Bulstrode. No wonder George Eliot, in describing the banker's evolution from lay preacher, through pawnbroker, to banker and attendant (by proxy) at Trumbull's auctions, sees them as allied activities, characterized as profiting from the reclamation of the lost. Gossip, discursively and politically, has similar objectives:

> The profits made out of lost souls – where can the line be drawn at which they begin in human transactions? Was it not even God's way of saving His chosen? 'Thou knowest,' – the young Bulstrode had said then, as the older Bulstrode was saying now – 'Thou knowest how loose my soul sits from these things – how I view them all as implements for tilling Thy garden rescued here and there from the wilderness.' [*M*, pp. 551–2]

. . . But what makes both objects at auction and newcomers to Middlemarch equally unreliable as 'fine subject[s] for betting' [*M*, p. 135] at the putative beginning of a new career, is that this beginning is never really an Origin. At auction, all lots are surrounded by, if not inseparable from, a *narrative*, in this case one enhanced by Trumbull's imported vocabulary and a tendency to induce scarcity. The winning bidder buys both the object and its narrative, the way in which it enters historical or economic discourse. Those in attendance are prone to forget what George Eliot's omniscient narrator tells us, even as they bid on the future of objects, careers or socially meliorative plans. For example, a lavish portrait of Wellington comes under the hammer only to arouse a round of speculation about the scandals which dogged the late stages of a hero's career and which must be discounted by any intending bidder. Everything *is always-already* enmeshed in discourse which prevents it from ever being perceived, much less evaluated, from any starting-point which, as at auctions, is fixed arbitrarily.

The conventional wisdom would have it that *Middlemarch* is a novel in which a number of youthful, naive newcomers committed to reforming the attitudes and institutions of a provincial community find themselves hindered by narrow, local recalcitrance. Yet such an interpretation, crucial to the history of critical responses *to* George Eliot's novel, may in fact share the defects of certain characters' strategic misreadings of circumstances *within* Middlemarch. Lydgate, for example, is already known, enmeshed within Farebrother's narrative by the time he arrives. His reputation precedes him, just as it does material goods put up for auction, and is part of his public reception:

> 'I have not yet told you that I have the advantage of you, Mr Lydgate, and know you better than you know me. You remember Trawley who shared your apartment at Paris for some time? I was a correspondent of his, and he told me a good deal about you. I was not quite sure when you first came that you were the same man. I

was very glad when I found that you were. Only I don't forget that you have not had the like prologue about me.' [*M*, p. 156]

And even when people and material goods are not shadowed by a 'prologue', a narrative which precedes or accompanies the ostensible beginning of a transactive career or an economic transaction, there is often an echoing 'epilogue', the philosophically contaminating supplement, which threatens to infect other goods on offer unless they are removed:

'Come, Trumbull, this is too bad – you've been putting some old maid's rubbish into the sale,' murmured Mr Toller, getting close to the auctioneer. 'I want to see how the prints go, and I must be off soon.'
'*Imm*ediately, Mr Toller. It was only an act of benevolence which your noble heart would approve. Joseph! quick with the prints – Lot 235.' [*M*, p. 543]

'Old maid's rubbish' could be one euphemism for gossip, converting as it does the merely abandoned to a surplus within a specific sexual or material economy. And, though technically by no means an old maid, the Rector's wife, Mrs Cadwallader, appears entirely at home in a world where leftovers are subjected to barter. In many ways, she represents the negation of any attempt to recover an antecedent ground which serves the need for logocentric order in *Middlemarch*. The dowager accommodates rather than petitions any source as a matter of personal convenience. She recognizes that the origin (and hence the ground of intention) is never sacred, but rather constructed arbitrarily and *a posteriori*:

Oh, my dear, when you have a clergyman in your family you must accommodate your tastes: I did that very early. When I married Humphrey I made up my mind to like sermons, and I set out by liking the end very much. That soon spread to the middle and the beginning, because I couldn't have the end without them. [*M*, p. 291]

When we first encounter Mrs Cadwallader in the sixth chapter of *Middlemarch*, she is attempting to obtain a lower price in the name of the Rector's Sunday dinner for a pair of fowl from a tradesman. The *ad hoc* negotiations through which she obtains daily provisions is in marked contrast to the dependency upon momentous plans which subsidizes the energies of so many of the characters in the novel. For Mrs Cadwallader, there are no fixed sources of value, which exists, rather, entirely in exchange. The buyer never obtains without yielding to the spirit of compromise over price; barter necessitates her *presence* in the vendor's narrative. In a novel where so many people are paralyzed by either threats to their personal reputation or the public reception of their work, the Rector's wife remains unconcerned about her 'share' in the narrative of others. She gives body to the gossip of those who 'would have felt a sad lack of conversation but for the stories about what Mrs Cadwallader said and did' [*M*, p. 47]. As both a facile narrator and a lively presence in the narrative of others, she gives the quality of 'neighbourliness to both rank and religion' [*M.* p. 47], which is what Dorothea Brooke is somewhat more idealistically striving for in her utilitarian schemes for tenants' housing which would create a more interdependent community. It is precisely Mrs Cadwallader's lack of dignity which gives her easy access, like the auctioneer, Borthrop Trumbull, to both 'farmers and labourers in the parishes' [*M*, p. 47] as well as the well-bred, like Sir James Chettam. She has surrendered the *exemplary* for the dialogic:

> A much more exemplary character with an infusion of sour dignity would not have furthered their comprehension of the Thirty-nine Articles, and would have been less socially uniting. [*M*, p. 47]

Like so many social or biological parasites, Mrs Cadwallader is simultaneously present (as a communicative channel, a tongue) and absent (as an individuated presence, a dignity) in *Middlemarch*. And yet, her presence in one register appears as a compensation for her absence in the other.

Gossip exhibits a similar dynamic insofar as it most often appears not as 'authored' speech, but rather as the 'general knowledge' which an anonymous 'everyone' *already* knows. This characteristic of gossip is surely enhanced by Mrs Cadwallader's easy access to privileged information as the wife of a Rector. Part of the religious establishment and yet separable from it when deniability is needed, she has a kind of freedom from being held responsible for what she says, and it is that freedom which enables her to gain additional information . . .[36] □

Mrs Cadwallader holds a particular fascination for Gordon, who rereads the 'whispering gallery' that is, for him, the discursive centre of *Middlemarch*, as a 'spider's-web converted to the space of the ear' in the centre of which Mrs Cadwallader is poised, 'recycl[ing] what she consumes . . . The devourer is the creator of a curious *text*-ile of presence and absence, which, like that of Penelope, she weaves, reads, and responds to as a play of miniscule pressures. Any design is surely purposive, but intentionality would be revealed only under powerful magnification, is determinable only after the fact, and is always recognized too late by any (intended?) victim.'[37]

Gordon continues: 'In *Middlemarch*, gossip, like that practised by Mrs Cadwallader along her informational web, will exhibit many of the characteristic operational features of the parasite: easy adaptation to a variety of environments; the ability to dwell both in and as an ontic [living/organic] miniature . . . and a voracious appetite which reduces all input to the same relational context in such a way as to create the appearance of a "consequential plot". Like novelists, the gossip makes patterns of meaning where only "thought and speech vortices" exist.'[38]

This leads Gordon to a further observation on social and textual parasitism, this time relating to a minor character, Mrs Taft's, 'reading' of Lydgate's presence in the community of Middlemarch. First Gordon quotes directly from the text: 'Many people believed that Lydgate's coming to the town at all was really due to Bulstrode; and Mrs Taft, who was always counting stitches and gathered her information in misleading fragments caught between the rows of her knitting, had got it into her head that Mr Lydgate was a natural son of Bulstrode's, a fact which seemed to justify her suspicions of evangelical laymen.' [*M*, pp. 235–6] Then, Gordon observes, 'Even if one does not knit . . . there would appear to be always "another story", a competing narrative, literally between the "lines" of the inscripted one. Her interpretation is like that of the best literary criticism insofar as it opens a channel in another, too consequential plot which it pretends to supplement, but finally, supplants.'

He then returns this discussion to one analogous with parasitism: 'The two alternative narratives of personal, intellectual and social development – the linear, consequential (textual) and the fragmentary, interstitial (sub-text) – appear in a shadow or parasitical relationship. The former occupies the originating, inscripted, productive and monumentalizing registers; the latter is deployed along the axis which would be described as consuming, the oral/aural, reproductive and miniaturizing. But, if the narrative of gossip is capable of displacing, miming, subverting or reproducing the "host" on which it feeds, then it could conceivably become a substitute for it . . .'[39]

This returns him to Mrs Cadwallader: 'Equipped with an open mouth, a flexible purse, and the vehicularity of a speedy phaeton, she has considerable advantage over the confined, painfully slow *writers* in *Middlemarch* who must always refer to a prior correspondence, secure irrefutable "documents" as support, or pay social or academic patronage to antecedents.' In this sense one might argue that her companion character is Raffles, whose endless mobility makes him the embodiment par excellence of gossip itself. Indeed, like gossip, he is dangerous 'only as long as he circulates'.[40] This brings us back to the competing authenticity of oral and written forms.

■ Even the one advantage which writing has over speech, the susceptibility to an easy closure which assures both addressivity and privacy,
would appear particularly compromised in George Eliot's novel. For
not only is writing especially inefficient insofar as, at least in the case
of Casaubon's marriage proposal to Dorothea, it is incredibly convoluted and syntactically composed of layers of the parenthetical, it
often exists as *always-already* enclosed within other writing. In this
way the (epistolary) letter assumes a resemblance to academic 'letters'.
As Casaubon's marginal publications are always contained *within* or
are an intended response *to* another scholar's manuscript, so Will
Ladislaw sends his early letters to Dorothea Brooke 'under cover', that
is to say, as enclosure, within his more formal correspondence to
Casaubon, his patron. And, though these enclosures remain sealed,
Casaubon is threatened by what he assumes to be their affectionate
contents . . .

. . . Perhaps the first instance in which the reader becomes aware
of an alternative informational network in competition with those
of writing and the research into inscripted 'resources', occurs in
Chapter 4 when Celia informs her sister that she has heard that Sir
James Chettam is about to propose marriage:

> 'Pray do not make that mistake any longer, Dodo. When Tantripp
> was brushing my hair the other day, she said that Sir James's man
> knew from Mrs Cadwallader's maid that Sir James was to marry
> the eldest Miss Brooke.'
>
> 'How can you let Tantripp talk such gossip to you, Celia?' said
> Dorothea, indignantly, not the less angry because details asleep in
> her memory were now awakened to confirm the unwelcome reve-
> lation. 'You must have asked her questions. It is degrading.'
>
> 'I see no harm at all in Tantripp's talking to me. It is better to
> hear what people say. You see what mistakes you make by taking
> up notions. I am quite sure that Sir James means to make you an
> offer. . . . Every one can see that Sir James is very much in love with
> you.' [*M*, pp. 32–3]

Whereas those with grand projects in *Middlemarch* attempt to repetition
[*sic*] some originary moment, gossip in practice is always mediated
through a number of (verbally) invisible hands which add to communicational 'value' in the same gesture by which original intention is
obscured. In this instance, gossip has coursed through the mouths of
three servants prior to reaching Celia Brooke. The gentry, engaged in
research designed to improve the status of the disadvantaged, is
opposed by another community comprised of those 'in service' whose
narrations are both horizontal (linking each other) and vertical, insofar

as it, if not they, can climb the social ladder easily. Thus, gossip appears initially as a conspiracy to gain access to a social space denied the servants, but is quickly perceived as simultaneously 'new(s)' and 'old' (what 'every one sees'). Not for the last time will *hearing* become a contraceptive to (notational) 'notions', 'taken up', as in woven material of the novel's various textual projects.

Although Dorothea (abstractly) works at improving the quality of life for tenants, when her own life is orally consumed by those socially beneath her, she must see it as a *degradation*, rather than any application of knowledge. Allied as it is with transcendent belief in her mind, she cannot countenance a knowledge originating from below. As with the [*sic*] Lydgate for whom any knowledge must have a starting point, 'through [whose] crevice came a sudden light startling him with his first vivid notion of finely-adjusted mechanism' [*M*, p.130], Dorothea is duty-bound to locate knowledge within some starting point from which intention might be traced.

If narrative intention has a specific trajectory as an extension from some 'beginning' (Dorothea's habit of 'taking up notions'), gossip, for Celia, is enmeshed within an alternative economy which is partially dependent upon 'hearing', and thus the *dialogic*. Unable to imagine meaning as the product of dialogue, Dorothea Brooke must regard the unwelcome news of Chettam's expected proposal as authored, instantiated by some question from Celia that plants one of many metaphoric 'seeds' to be found in the rhetoric of *Middlemarch*. Similarly, gossip, as it comes to dominate the politics of the novel, exists as a reminder of what Dorothea *should have known* and maybe does know, but has repressed, obscuring the distinction between a dialogic economy and some secret, interior monologue. No wonder gossips often appear parasitical, since their interventions create of repressed self-sameness (what one 'knows' as part of oneself) a potentially subverting 'otherness' which masquerades as common knowledge: what an anonymous 'every one can see'. One of the remarkable features of gossip in this discussion between the two Brooke sisters is the way in which what had been evidently both known and repressed in Dodo's mind comes to constitute 'public opinion', an invisible unanimity . . .[41] □

* * *

In this Readers' Guide we began and have ended with circulatory systems of communication. In a nineteenth-century context we have considered the role played by periodicals, railways, libraries and disease. In a late-twentieth-century context it is television and the media in general which have added new impetus to Eliot's popularity. But that we end with gossip is particularly significant, not jusı because Eliot was the victim of rumour, speculation and ostracism in her personal life, but because the endurance of her reputation underlines the attraction of her work, beyond historical limits and across class divides. In that regard it is just like gossip: always going on at a distance from the action, but increasingly appealing as the web of associations spreads and thickens in the mind of the recipient/reader. I began by observing that Eliot has had a chequered career: nevertheless this volume has demonstrated how far her own literary reputation has outgrown the limitations of negative criticism. In consistently comparing nineteenth- and twentieth-century connections I have tried to demonstrate her relevance to the present as much as the past: George Eliot is very much a writer for our own time.

NOTES

1 Readers interested in following up their work on Eliot are referred to the following: Gordon S. Haight *George Eliot: A Biography* (Oxford: Clarendon Press, 1968); Gordon S. Haight (ed.), *A Century of George Eliot Criticism* (Boston: Houghton Mifflin, 1966); Barbara Hardy, *The Novels of George Eliot: A Study in Form* (London: Athlone Press, 1959); Barbara Hardy, *Particularities: Readings in George Eliot* (London: Peter Owen, 1982); Barbara Hardy (ed.), *Critical Essays on George Eliot* (London: Routledge and Kegan Paul, 1970); Barbara Hardy (ed.), *Middlemarch: Critical Approaches to the Novel* (New York: Oxford University Press, 1967); Barbara Hardy, *Forms of Feeling in the Victorian Novel* (London: Methuen, 1985).

2 See, for example, David Carroll (ed.), *George Eliot: The Critical Heritage* (London: Routledge and Kegan Paul, 1971); Gordon S. Haight (ed.), *A Century of George Eliot Criticism* (Boston: Houghton Mifflin, 1965); John Holmstrom and Laurence Lerner (eds.), *George Eliot and Her Readers: A Selection of Contemporary Reviews* (London: The Bodley Head, 1966); Karen L. Pangallo (ed.), *The Critical Response to George Eliot* (Westport: Greenwood Press, 1994).

CHAPTER ONE

1 Charles Dickens, *Letter to George Eliot*, 10 July 1859. Reprinted in David Carroll (ed.), *George Eliot: The Critical Heritage* (London: Routledge and Kegan Paul, 1971), p.85.

2 Mathilde Blind, *George Eliot* (London: W.H. Allen, 1883), p.175.

3 Leslie Stephen, *George Eliot* (London: Macmillan and Co. Ltd., 1902), pp.86, 97, 104.

4 Edith Wharton, 'George Eliot', *Bookman*, no. 15, May 1902, pp.249, 247.

5 Virginia Woolf, 'George Eliot', *The Times Literary Supplement*, 20 November 1919; reprinted in *Women and Writing*

(London: The Women's Press, 1979), [pp.150–60], pp. 155–6.

6 Ibid., p.156.

7 David Gervais, 'Televising "Middlemarch"', *English*, vol. 43, 1994, pp.59–64.

8 Ibid., p.59.

9 Anonymous review, *The Spectator*, 7 December 1872; cited in Carol A. Martin, *George Eliot's Serial Fiction* (Columbus: Ohio State University Press, 1994), p. 242.

10 Brian Spittles, *George Eliot: Godless Woman* (London: Macmillan, 1993).

11 J.H. Clapham, *An Economic History of Modern Britain 1820–1850* (Cambridge: Cambridge University Press, 1950), p.460.

12 Frank L. Huggett, *Life Below Stairs* (London: Book Club Associates, 1977), p.72.

13 Spittles, *George Eliot*, p.39.

14 A.S. Byatt, 'Introduction', *The Mill on the Floss* (Harmondsworth: Penguin Classics, 1985), p.7.

15 Alan W. Bellringer, *George Eliot* (London: Macmillan, 1993), pp.45–6.

16 Gervais, 'Televising "Middlemarch"', p.64.

17 Ibid., pp.59–61.

18 Spittles, *George Eliot*, p.18.

19 Ibid., pp.38–41.

20 Bernard O'Keefe, 'The "Soaping" of *Middlemarch*', *The English Review*, vol. 5, 1994, [pp.7–12], p.8.

21 Carol A. Martin, *George Eliot's Serial Fiction* (Columbus: Ohio State University Press, 1994), p.11.

22 Ibid., p.247.

23 Ibid., pp.94–5, 99.

24 Alexander Welsh, *George Eliot and Blackmail* (Cambridge, Mass.: Harvard University Press, 1985).

25 Welsh notes, in an aside: 'Redinger ... does not fully believe the daring of Liggins either and suggests that enemies of Lewes may have put him up to it [Ruby Redinger, *George Eliot: The Emergent Self* (London: The Bodley Head, 1975), p.393]. For a sample of contemporary confusion about the man, see a letter of Elizabeth Gaskell to Harriet Martineau, October 1859, in *The Letters of Mrs Gaskell*,

ed. J.A.V. Chapple and Arthur Pollard (Cambridge: Harvard University Press, 1967), pp. 583–6.' Welsh, *George Eliot and Blackmail*, p. 128n.

26 George Henry Lewes to the Editor of the *Times*, 15 April 1859. Gordon S. Haight (ed.), *The George Eliot Letters*, 9 vols. (New Haven: Yale University Press, 1954–5), III, p. 50.

27 Welsh notes, in an aside: 'Blackwood also persuaded himself that the moral contribution of the fiction could compensate for the irregularity of the author's private life. He wrote to George Eliot on 28 November 1859: "As to the withdrawal of the incognito, you know how much I have been opposed to it all along. It may prove a disadvantage and in the eyes of many it will, but my opinion of your genius and confidence in the truly good, honest, religious, and moral tone of all you have written or will write [an implied contract, perhaps, as to the tone of her future writing] is such that I think you will overcome any possible detriment from the withdrawal of the mystery which has so far taken place."' Haight (ed.), *The George Eliot Letters*, III, p. 297.

28 *The Saturday Review*, no. 59, 1885. See David Carroll (ed.), *George Eliot: The Critical Heritage*, p. 129n. The passage as a whole is taken from Welsh, pp. 124–30.

29 Martin, *George Eliot's Serial Fiction*, pp. 118–19.

30 Robert B. Heilman, '"Stealthy Convergence" in *Middlemarch*', in Gordon S. Haight and Rosemary T. Van Arsdel (eds.), *George Eliot: A Centenary Tribute* (London: Macmillan, 1982), [pp. 47–54], p. 49. A 'polyptych' is defined as 'an altarpiece consisting of more than three panels set with paintings or carvings, and usually hinged for folding' (*Collins English Dictionary*).

31 Sandra Gilbert and Susan Gubar, *The Madwoman in the Attic: The Woman Writer and the Nineteenth-Century Literary Imagination* (New Haven: Yale University Press, 1984), p. 48.

32 Hester Prynne is a character shunned by a North American Puritanical community for giving birth to a child out of wedlock. Her punishment is to wear a scarlet 'A', like a brand, on her clothing for all to see. In his own novel Hawthorne, like Eliot, emphasises the double standard that castigates Hester while letting her male lover go officially unpunished. One significant difference between the two characters, however, is the love Hester Prynne has for her cherished daughter, whom she names Pearl as a recognition of her treasured status. That Eliot is encouraging both contrasts and comparisons between the two protagonists may be inferred from the fact that Hetty is an abbreviated form of the name Hester.

33 Dorothea Barrett, *Vocation and Desire: George Eliot's Heroines* (London: Routledge, 1989), p. 31.

34 U.C. Knoepflmacher, *Laughter and Despair: Readings in Ten Novels of the Victorian Era* (Berkeley: University of California Press, 1971), p. 180.

35 'Prolepsis' (from which this adjective derives) is defined by the *Collins English Dictionary* as 'a rhetorical device by which objections are anticipated and answered in advance'.

36 Bellringer, *George Eliot*, pp. 39–40.

37 Jane Austen, *Emma* (Harmondsworth: Penguin, 1966), p. 37.

38 J. Hillis Miller, 'Narrative and History', *ELH*, vol. 41, 1972, [pp. 455–73], p. 463.

39 Hilary Fraser, 'St. Theresa, St. Dorothea, and Miss Brooke in *Middlemarch*', *Nineteenth Century Fiction*, vol. 40, no. 4, March 1986, [pp. 400–11], pp. 400–1.

40 U.C. Knoepflmacher, *Laughter and Despair*, pp. 181–4 *passim*.

41 Elizabeth Weed, 'The Mill on the Floss or the Liquidation of Maggie Tulliver', *Genre*, vol. 11, 1978, pp. 427–44.

42 Lynne Roberts, 'Perfect Pyramids: *The Mill on the Floss*', *Texas Studies in Literature and Language*, vol. 13, 1971, pp. 112–14.

43 Weed, 'The Mill on the Floss', pp. 437–8.

44 Ibid., p. 438n.

45 George Eliot, 'Silly Novels by Lady Novelists', in Thomas Pinney (ed.), *Essays of George Eliot* (London: Routledge and Kegan Paul, 1963), pp. 300–24.

46 Ibid., p. 316.

47 Ibid., p. 322.

48 Gilbert and Gubar, *The Madwoman in the Attic*, p. 17.

49 Weed, *'The Mill on the Floss'*, pp. 443–4.

50 Barrett, *Vocation and Desire*, pp. 25–6.

51 Haight (ed.), *The George Eliot Letters*, II, p. 503; III, p. 175.

52 Kristin Brady, *George Eliot* (London: Macmillan, 1992), pp. 85–93 *passim*.

53 Ibid., p. 95.

54 Ibid., p. 106.

55 Ibid., pp. 166–8.

56 Eliot, 'Silly Novels by Lady Novelists', pp. 302–3.

57 William Baker (ed.), *Some George Eliot Notebooks* (Salzburg, 1976–85), pp. 161, 274n.

58 Haight (ed.), *The George Eliot Letters*, V, 330. The whole passage is taken from Brady, *George Eliot*, pp. 168–73.

CHAPTER TWO

1 Henry Auster, *Local Habitations: Regionalism in the Early Novels of George Eliot* (Cambridge, Mass.: Harvard University Press, 1970), p. 122.

2 Alison Booth, *Greatness Engendered: George Eliot and Virginia Woolf* (Ithaca: Cornell University Press, 1992), p. 68.

3 Eve Kosofsky Sedgwick, *Between Men: English Literature and Male Homosocial Desire* (New York: Columbia University Press, 1985), p. 140.

4 Q. D. Leavis, 'Regional Novels', *Scrutiny*, vol. 4, 1935–36, p. 440; cited in Auster, *Local Habitations*, p. 19.

5 Leslie Stephen, *George Eliot* (London: Macmillan and Co. Ltd., 1902); Virginia Woolf, 'George Eliot', *The Times Literary Supplement*, 20 November 1919; cited in Graham Handley, *State of the Art: George Eliot* (Bristol: The Bristol Press, 1990), pp. 27–8, p. 36; Gillian Beer, *Darwin's Plots: Evolutionary Narrative in Darwin, George Eliot and Nineteenth-Century Fiction*

(London: Routledge and Kegan Paul, 1983), p. 173 – my emphasis.

6 Nina Auerbach, *Woman and the Demon: The Life of a Victorian Myth* (Cambridge, Mass.: Harvard University Press, 1982), pp. 174–6 *passim*.

7 Ian Adam, 'The Structure of Realisms in *Adam Bede*', *Nineteenth Century Fiction*, vol. 30, no. 2, September 1975, pp. 127–49.

8 Ian Watt, *The Rise of the Novel: Studies in Defoe, Richardson and Fielding* (Berkeley: University of California Press, 1957), p. 12.

9 Adam adds a note at this point: 'For some detailed parallels between *Adam Bede* and *Paradise Lost*, see U. C. Knoepflmacher's *George Eliot's Early Novels: The Limits of Realism* (Berkeley: University of California Press, 1968), pp. 89–127. In the course of this essay [Adam] . . . demonstrat[es] similarities between the two works, but they [are] broader than [Knoepflmacher's], and used for different purposes.'

10 Adam, 'Structure of Realisms', pp. 127–48 *passim*.

11 Jerome Thale, *The Novels of George Eliot* (New York: Columbia University Press, 1959).

12 Ibid., pp. 40–5.

13 Ian Adam, 'The Ambivalence of *The Mill on the Floss*' in Gordon S. Haight and Rosemary T. Van Arsdel (eds.), *George Eliot: A Centenary Tribute* (London: Macmillan, 1982), pp. 126–7.

14 Auster, *Local Habitations*, p. 113.

15 Joseph Wiesenfarth, 'Antique Gems from *Romola* to *Daniel Deronda*', in Gordon S. Haight and Rosemary T. Van Arsdel (eds.), *George Eliot: A Centenary Tribute*, [55–63], p. 55.

16 U. C. Knoepflmacher, *Laughter and Despair: Readings in Ten Novels of the Victorian Era* (Berkeley: University of California Press, 1971), p. 192.

17 Ibid., p. 193.

18 Quentin Anderson, 'George Eliot in *Middlemarch*', in Boris Ford (ed.), *From Dickens to Hardy* (Baltimore: Pelican Books, 1958), [pp. 274–94], p. 280; cited

in Auster, *Local Habitations*, p. 56.

19 Suzanne Graver, *George Eliot and Community: A Study in Social Theory and Fictional Form* (Berkeley: University of California Press, 1984), pp. 203–4.

20 Carol A. Martin, *George Eliot's Serial Fiction* (Columbus: Ohio State University Press, 1994), pp. 205–6.

21 Dorothy Van Ghent, '*Adam Bede*', in Harold Bloom (ed.), *George Eliot* (New York: Chelsea House, 1986), pp. 1–36.

22 Ibid., pp. 27–9.

23 J. Hillis Miller, 'Optic and Semiotic in *Middlemarch*', in Harold Bloom (ed.), *George Eliot* (New York: Chelsea House, 1986).

24 Ibid., p. 104.

25 Ibid., p. 105.

26 Ibid., pp. 109–10.

27 Baruch Hochman, 'Recon/Decon/ Structing *Middlemarch*', in Kathleen Blake (ed.), *Approaches to Teaching Eliot's Middlemarch* (New York: The Modern Language Association of America, 1990), pp. 39–50.

28 Ibid., p. 39.

29 Ibid., p. 41.

30 Ibid., p. 46.

31 Ibid., p. 47.

32 Ibid., p. 42.

33 For a fuller explication of the arguments surrounding this issue see David Lodge 'The Language of Modernist Fiction: Metaphor and Metonymy', in Malcolm Bradbury and James McFarlane (eds.), *Modernism* (Harmondsworth: Penguin, 1976), pp. 481–96.

34 Hochman, 'Recon/Decon/Structing *Middlemarch*', pp. 43–4.

35 Ibid., p. 44.

36 J. Hillis Miller, 'Teaching *Middlemarch*: Close Reading and Theory', in Kathleen Blake (ed.), *Approaches to Teaching Eliot's Middlemarch* (New York: The Modern Language Association of America, 1990), pp. 51–63.

37 Ibid., p. 52.

38 Ibid., p. 55.

39 Margaret Harris and Judith Johnston, editors of the 1997 Everyman edition of *Middlemarch* (p. 773n).

40 Ibid., p. 773n.

41 Hillis Miller, 'Teaching *Middlemarch*', pp. 60–3.

CHAPTER THREE

1 David Masson, *British Novelists and their Styles* (Cambridge, 1859); cited in Henry Auster, *Local Habitations: Regionalism in the Early Novels of George Eliot* (Cambridge, Mass.: Harvard University Press, 1970), p. 28.

2 Henry Auster, *Local Habitations*, p. 34.

3 Ibid., p. 111.

4 John Goode, '*Adam Bede*', in Barbara Hardy (ed.), *Critical Essays on George Eliot* (London: Routledge and Kegan Paul, 1970), [pp. 19–41], p. 21.

5 Ibid., p. 22.

6 William Empson, *Some Versions of Pastoral* (Harmondsworth: Penguin, 1995), p. 17.

7 Simon Dentith, *George Eliot* (Brighton: Harvester Press, 1986), pp. 35–6.

8 Ibid., p. 54.

9 Daniel Cottom, *Social Figures: George Eliot, Social History and Literary Representation* (Minneapolis: University of Minnesota Press, 1987), p. 37.

10 Lilian R. Furst, 'Struggling for Medical Reform in *Middlemarch*', *Nineteenth Century Literature*, vol. 48, no. 3, 1993, [pp. 341–61], p. 343.

11 Ibid., pp. 343–4.

12 Ibid., pp. 346–7.

13 Cottom, *Social Figures*, p. 40.

14 Ibid., pp. 89–90.

15 Ibid., pp. 91–2.

16 Raymond Williams, 'Knowable Communities', in Harold Bloom (ed.), *George Eliot* (New York: Chelsea House, 1986), pp. 81–97.

17 Ibid., pp. 81–2.

18 Ibid., pp. 84–5.

19 Dentith, *George Eliot*, pp. 99–100.

20 Cottom, *Social Figures*, p. xv.

21 Terry Eagleton, *Criticism and Ideology* (London: New Left Books, 1976), p. 110.

22 Ibid., p. 112.

23 Ibid., p. 113.

24 Ibid., pp. 113–16.

25 Ibid., p. 118.

26 Ibid., pp.120–1.

27 Ibid., p.124.

28 Brian Spittles, *George Eliot: Godless Woman* (London: Macmillan, 1993).

29 George Eliot, 'The Natural History of German Life', *The Westminster Review*, 1856; reprinted in A.S. Byatt and Nicholas Warren (eds.), *George Eliot: Selected Essays, Poems and Other Writings* (Harmondsworth: Penguin, 1990), p.118.

30 Spittles, *George Eliot*, pp.33–4.

31 Margaret Harris and Judith Johnston note that these were 'standard school textbooks in the early nineteenth century: Lindley Murray's *English Grammar* (1795) and Mrs Richmal Mangnall's *Historical and Miscellaneous Questions* (1800)'. [*M*, p.768n.]

32 Spittles, *George Eliot*, pp.142–8.

33 John F. Hulcoop, '"This Petty Medium": In the Middle of *Middlemarch*' in Gordon S. Haight and Rosemary T. Van Arsdel (eds.), *George Eliot: A Centenary Tribute* (London: Macmillan, 1982), [pp.153–66], p.154.

34 Ibid., pp.155–6.

35 Cottom, *Social Figures*, pp.157–8.

36 Eve Kosofsky Sedgwick, *Between Men: English Literature and Male Homosocial Desire* (New York: Columbia University Press, 1985), p.136.

37 Robin Lakoff, *Language and Woman's Place* (London: Harper and Row, 1975).

38 Sedgwick, *Between Men*, pp.138–40.

39 Ibid., pp.143–5.

40 Margaret Homans, 'Dinah's Blush, Maggie's Arm: Sexuality in George Eliot's Early Novels', *Victorian Studies*, 36, no. 2, 1993, [pp.155–78], p.163.

41 Ibid., pp.164–5.

42 Philip Fisher, *Making Up Society: The Novels of George Eliot* (Pittsburgh: Pittsburg University Press, 1981), p.65.

43 Sarah Ellis, *The Women of England: Their Social Duties, and Domestic Habits* (Philadelphia, 1839).

44 Joan N. Burstyn, *Victorian Education and the Ideal of Womanhood* (New Brunswick: Rutgers University Press, 1984).

45 Ellis, *Women of England*, p.24.

46 Letter to John Blackwood, 24 February 1859. Gordon S. Haight (ed.), *The George Eliot Letters*, 9 vols (New Haven: Yale University Press, 1954), III, pp.23–4.

47 Cited in Mary Jean Corbett, 'Representing the Rural: The Critique of Loamshire in *Adam Bede*', *Studies in the Novel*, vol. 20, 1988, [pp.288–301], p.292.

48 Homans, 'Dinah's Blush', pp.158–9.

49 Cited in Asa Briggs, 'The Language of "Class" in Early Nineteenth-Century England', *The Collected Essays of Asa Briggs*, 2 vols (Brighton: Harvester, 1985), I, [pp.3–33], p.11.

50 Ellis, *Women of England*, pp.16, 18.

51 Ibid., p.18.

52 30 November, 1859. Haight (ed.), *The George Eliot Letters*, III, p.219.

53 Homans, 'Dinah's Blush', pp.155–6.

CHAPTER FOUR

1 David Smith, 'Incest Patterns in Two Victorian Novels', *Literature and Psychology*, vol. 15, no. 3, Summer 1965, pp.135–62.

2 Henry James, 'The Novels of George Eliot', *Atlantic Monthly*, vol. 18, 1866, p.490; cited in Smith, 'Incest Patterns', pp.144–5.

3 Smith, 'Incest Patterns', p.147.

4 Ibid., pp.147–8.

5 Ibid., p.160.

6 Ibid., p.161.

7 Ibid., pp,149, 155 – my emphasis.

8 Ibid., p.150.

9 Ibid., p.152.

10 Ibid., pp.161–2.

11 Ibid., p.153.

12 Smith provides the following note here: 'Maggie's hair is the subject of a sustained synecdoche which is a minor *tour de force* of the novel's texture, whether the symbolic association was conscious or unconscious on Eliot's part. Time after time Maggie's psychic state is correlated with and indicated by the condition or behavior of her hair. For example, she tosses it to show spirit, it refuses to curl when she is being rebel-

lious, and it is behind her ears or plaited when she is being ascetic and submissive . . .' Ibid., p. 156n.

13 Ibid., pp. 156–7.

14 Ibid., p. 159.

15 U.C. Knoepflmacher, *Laughter and Despair: Readings in Ten Novels of the Victorian Era* (Berkeley: University of California Press, 1971), p. 111.

16 Ibid., p. 116.

17 Jules Law, 'Water Rights and the "crossing o' breeds"', in Linda M. Shires (ed.), *Rewriting the Victorians: Theory, History and the Politics of Gender* (New York: Routledge, 1992), [pp. 52–69], p. 55.

18 Ibid., p. 55.

19 Ibid., pp. 56–7.

20 Nina Auerbach, 'The Power of Hunger: Demonism and Maggie Tulliver', *Nineteenth Century Fiction*, vol. 30, no. 2, September 1975, [pp. 150–7], pp. 156, 157.

21 Ibid., pp. 158–9.

22 Ibid., p. 172.

23 Ibid., pp. 167–8.

24 Auerbach notes that 'In discussing a novel which contains two definite allusions to Dante's *Inferno* and many atmospheric and emotional suggestions of it, it might be revealing to remember that in Canto 13 of the *Inferno*, Dante transforms his suicides into wailing, bleeding trees. Suicide is a frequent cause of vampirism in legend, though not in vampire literature.' Ibid., p. 162n.

25 Auerbach notes, by way of elaboration: 'In her next speech, Mrs. Tulliver brings in the motif of Maggie as "a Bedlam creatur", which recurs throughout the novel. Uncle Pullet relates her brown skin to her possible craziness . . . [*MF*, p. 493]. Demonism and psychosis have worn similar faces throughout history, legend, and literature, as we can see in *Jane Eyre* when the raging Bertha Mason appears to Jane as "the foul German spectre – the Vampyre." This "crazy" motif colors our last image of Maggie, riding through the flood with wild eyes and streaming hair, a weird mélange of Beorl's Virgin of the Flood, Defoe's witch in the water, and Millais' *Ophelia*.' Ibid., p. 164n.

26 Robert Kiely, *The Romantic Novel in England* (Cambridge, Mass.: Harvard University Press, 1972), p. 252.

27 Auerbach, 'The Power of Hunger', pp. 161–6.

28 Ibid., pp. 151, 166.

29 Ibid., p. 159.

30 Eva Fuchs, 'The Pattern's All Missed: Separation/Individuation in *The Mill on the Floss*', *Studies in the Novel*, vol. 19, Winter 1987, [pp. 422–34], pp. 425, 426.

31 Ibid., p. 426.

32 'Capable of being moved into a position facing the other digits so as to be able to touch the ends of each' (*Collins English Dictionary*).

33 Fuchs notes: 'As she was writing *The Mill on the Floss*, Eliot was moving toward the decision to loosen her hold on her incognito; the imagery of concealment and disclosure in the scenes between Bob Jakin and Aunt Glegg seems, therefore, to reflect her deepest personal preoccupations. In revealing her actual identity, Eliot knew that she would inevitably bring her irregular union with George Henry Lewes to the world's disapproving attention . . .'; Fuchs, 'The Pattern's All Missed', pp. 433–4n.

34 George Eliot, 'Brother and Sister', *Poems, Essays, and Leaves from a Notebook* (New York: Doubleday, Page and Co., 1901–1904), Sonnet 5, p. 321.

35 Fuchs, 'The Pattern's All Missed', pp. 428–32.

36 Elizabeth Weed, '*The Mill on the Floss* or the Liquidation of Maggie Tulliver', *Genre*, vol. 11, Fall 1978, [pp. 427–44], p. 432.

37 *American Heritage Dictionary of the English Language*. The whole passage is taken from Weed, '*The Mill on the Floss*', pp. 433–4.

38 Weed, '*The Mill on the Floss*', pp. 439, 440.

39 Ibid., pp. 440, 441.

40 Ibid., p. 431.

41 Weed notes: 'When Maggie first

pounds nails into her doll, for example, "that luxury of vengeance" is "suggested to her by the picture of Jael destroying Sisera in the Old Bible" [*MF*, p.79]. See Judges 4 for that story of a woman killing the (male) enemy.' Ibid., p.431n.

42 Ibid., pp.429–31.

43 Law, 'Water Rights', p.62.

44 Eva Fuchs, 'Eliot's *The Mill on the Floss*', *The Explicator*, vol. 52, no. 1, pp.79–80.

45 Marianne Hirsch, 'Spiritual Bildung: The Beautiful Soul as Paradigm' in Elizabeth Abel, Marianne Hirsch and Elizabeth Langland (eds.), *The Voyage In: Fictions of Female Development* (Hanover: University Press of New England, 1983), [pp.23–48], pp.36–7.

46 Fuchs, 'Eliot's *The Mill on the Floss*', pp.79–80.

CHAPTER FIVE

1 George Levine, *The Realistic Imagination: English Fiction from Frankenstein to Lady Chatterley* (Chicago: University of Chicago Press, 1981), p.256.

2 Sally Shuttleworth, *George Eliot and Nineteenth-Century Science: The Make-Believe of a Beginning* (New York: Cambridge University Press, 1984).

3 Suzanne Graver, *George Eliot and Community: A Study in Social Theory and Fictional Form* (Berkeley: University of California Press, 1984), p.163.

4 George Eliot, 'The Natural History of German Life', *The Westminster Review*, 1856; reprinted in Thomas Pinney (ed.), *The Essays of George Eliot* (London: Routledge and Kegan Paul, 1963), [pp.266–99], p.282.

5 Shuttleworth, *George Eliot and Nineteenth-Century Science*, pp.35–9.

6 Ibid., pp.10, 14, 1.

7 Edward Dowden, *Studies in Literature: 1789–1877* (London: 1878), p.100; cited in Shuttleworth, *George Eliot and Nineteenth-Century Science*, p.7.

8 George Eliot, 'The Natural History of German Life', p.276.

9 John Goode, '*Adam Bede*', in Barbara

Hardy (ed.), *Critical Essays on George Eliot* (London: Routledge and Kegan Paul, 1970), [pp.19–41], p.22.

10 George Eliot, 'The Natural History of German Life', p.282.

11 Ibid., p.288. The passage as a whole is taken from Shuttleworth, *George Eliot and Nineteenth-Century Science*, pp.29–35 *passim*.

12 Shuttleworth, *George Eliot and Nineteenth-Century Science*, pp.143, 144, 152.

13 Robert A. Greenberg, 'Plexus and Ganglia: Scientific Allusion in *Middlemarch*', *Nineteenth Century Fiction*, vol. 30, no. 1, 1975, pp.33–52.

14 Gordon S. Haight (ed.), *The George Eliot Letters*, 9 vols. (New Haven: Yale University Press, 1954–5), V, p.168.

15 John Davy (ed.), *Elements of Agricultural Chemistry, in Collected Works of Sir Humphrey Davy* (London: Smith, Elder, 1840), VII, pp.196–7.

16 Ibid., pp.177, 181, 222.

17 Ibid., pp.182, 199.

18 G.H. Lewes, *The Physiology of Common Life*, 2 vols. (Edinburgh: Blackwood, 1859–60), I, pp.336–7. Greenberg notes: 'Lydgate suffers the same odium: cf. Mrs Dollop's conviction, endorsed by her audience at the Tankard, that he "meant to let the people die in the Hospital . . . for the sake of cutting them up"' . . . Greenberg, 'Plexus and Ganglia', p.39n.

19 Greenberg notes: 'Cf. Eliot's parallel but loosely generalized remark in *The Mill on the Floss*, offered to justify the "comparison of small things with great; for does not science tell us that its highest striving is after the ascertainment of a unity which shall bind the smallest things with the greatest? In natural science, I have understood, there is nothing petty to the mind that has a large vision of relations, and to which every single object suggests a vast sum of conditions"' [*MF*, p.363]. Greenberg, 'Plexus and Ganglia', p.44n.

20 Greenberg notes: 'The convergence in Raspail of political and scientific idealism comments forcefully on Lydgate's

separation of the two – his smugness, for example, on hearing that his Paris room-mate Trawley, once "hot on the French social systems", has since chosen to practice "at a German bath, and has married a rich patient" [*M*, p. 156]. Lydgate's own comfortable practice is to take him to "a Continental bathing-place" [*M*, p. 743]. Raspail, who was to become known as the "Poor Man's Doctor" beginning in the 1840s (Dora B. Weiner, *Raspail* (New York: Columbia Univ. Press, 1968), Chs. 6, 7), is also the one scientist alluded to in the novel who was still alive at the time of its composition; he may have come to George Eliot's attention as one of the old-time Republicans active during the Paris uprising of late 1870 (Edward S. Mason, *The Paris Commune: An Episode in the History of the Socialist Movement* (New York: Macmillan, 1930), p. 73)'. Greenberg, 'Plexus and Ganglia', p. 47n.

21 François Joseph Broussais, *Treatise on Physiology Applied to Pathology*, trans. John Bell and R. La Roche (Philadelphia: Carey and Lea, 1828), p. 58; cited in Greenberg, 'Plexus and Ganglia', p. 50.

22 Luigi Galvani, *Commentary on the Effects of Electricity on Muscular Motion*, trans. Margaret G. Foley (Norwalk, Conn.: Burndy Library, 1953), pp. 77, 78.

23 Broussais, *Treatise on Physiology*, p. 58; cited in Greenberg, 'Plexus and Ganglia', p. 50.

24 Kitchel, *Quarry*, pp. 21, 22, 35–6. Greenberg cites Kitchel as noting, 'as a further nicety, that the treatment Raffles actually received accorded with current practice; if brought to trial, Lydgate would have been exonerated'; Kitchel, *Quarry*, p. 10; Greenberg, 'Plexus and Ganglia', p. 50n.

25 Greenberg attributes this to: 'David R. Carroll in his perceptive essay, "Unity Through Analogy: An Interpretation of *Middlemarch*", *Victorian Studies*, vol. 2, 1959, p. 311. Carroll also notices that Lydgate has in progress an experiment in "maceration" while trying to resist Rosamond's charms (p. 312).' Greenberg, 'Plexus and Ganglia', p. 50n.

26 Kitchel, *Quarry*, p. 26. John J. Bennett (ed.), *The Miscellaneous Botanical Works of Robert Brown*, 2 vols. (London: Hardwicke, 1866–68), I, pp. 463–86. Greenberg notes: 'The same volume also includes two papers on the structure of a newly classified "parasitic" plant, the Rafflesia, so designated after its discoverer, Sir Stamford Raffles, late Governor of the East India Company in Sumatra (pp. 367–431). Was it after this plant that the parasitic John Raffles was named?' Greenberg, 'Plexus and Ganglia', p. 50n.

27 Bennett, *Botanical Works of Robert Brown*, p. 465 – Greenberg's italics.

28 Gillian Beer, *Darwin's Plots: Evolutionary Narrative in Darwin, George Eliot and Nineteenth-Century Fiction* (London: Routledge and Kegan Paul, 1983).

29 Henry James, *Galaxy*, no. 15, 1873, pp. 424–8; R. H. Hutton, *Spectator*, no. 49, 1876, pp. 1131–3.

30 Charles Darwin, *On the Origin of Species* (London: 1859), p. 410; cited in Beer, *Darwin's Plots*, p. 150.

31 Sidney Colvin, *Fortnightly Review*, no. 13, 1873, pp. 142–7; Edward Dowden, *Contemporary Review*, no. 29, 1877, pp. 348–69.

32 Beer, *Darwin's Plots*, pp. 149–51.

33 Ibid., pp. 160, 161–2.

34 Ibid., pp. 164.

35 Ibid., pp. 167, 165–6.

36 Darwin, *The Origin of Species*, p. 415.

37 John Stuart Mill, *System of Logic: Ratiocinative and Inductive*, 2 vols. (London, 1843); G. H. Lewes, *The Foundations of a Creed* (London: 1873–75); 1:26.

38 John Tyndall, *On Radiation* (London: 1865), pp, 9–10.

39 Alexander Bain, *Mind and Body: The Theories of Their Relation* (London: 1873), p. 27.

40 Darwin, *The Origin of Species*, p. 171 – Beer's italics.

41 Ibid., p. 415.

42 Julia Wedgwood, 'The Boundaries of Science: A Second Dialogue', *Macmillan's Magazine*, vol. 4, 1861, p. 241.

43 Beer, *Darwin's Plots*, pp. 167–72.

44 Haight (ed.), *The George Eliot Letters*, IV, p. 49.

45 The editors of the Everyman edition, Margaret Harris and Judith Johnston, add the following explanatory note: '"that river of which Cyrus broke the strength" [is] the Gyndes, which Cyrus the Great, founder of the Persian empire, dispersed into 360 channels because one of his sacred white horses was drowned in it' [*M*, p. 793].

46 Beer, *Darwin's Plots*, pp. 179–80.

47 Tess Cosslett, *The 'Scientific Movement' and Victorian Literature* (Brighton: Harvester, 1982), p. 99.

48 Ibid., pp. 12, 21.

49 Ibid., pp. 94–6.

50 Ibid., p. 24.

51 Ibid., pp. 84, 88.

52 Ibid., pp. 89, 94.

53 Selma B. Brody, 'Physics in *Middlemarch*: Gas Molecules and Ethereal Atoms', *Modern Philology*, vol. 85, no. 1, August 1987, pp. 42–53.

54 Ibid., pp. 47–8.

55 Ibid., p. 47.

CHAPTER SIX

1 Jan B. Gordon, *Gossip and Subversion in Nineteenth-Century British Fiction* (London: Macmillan, 1996), pp. 279–80.

2 Lilian R. Furst, 'Struggling for Medical Reform in *Middlemarch*', *Nineteenth Century Literature*, vol. 48, no. 3, 1993 [pp. 341–61], p. 354.

3 Gillian Beer, *Arguing With the Past: Essays in Narrative from Woolf to Sidney* (London: Routledge, 1989), pp. 104–5.

4 U. C. Knoepflmacher, *Laughter and Despair: Readings in Ten Novels of the Victorian Era* (Berkeley: University of California Press, 1971), p. 188.

5 Ibid., p. 189.

6 Ibid., pp. 196–7.

7 Alexander Welsh, *George Eliot and Blackmail* (Cambridge, Mass.: Harvard University Press, 1985).

8 To Mrs Charles Bray, 4 September 1855. Gordon S. Haight (ed.), *The George Eliot Letters*, II, p. 214.

9 Welsh, *George Eliot and Blackmail*, pp. 124–5.

10 Mike Hepworth, *Blackmail* (London: Routledge, 1975), pp. 21–2.

11 *The Sociology of Georg Simmel*, trans. and ed. Kurt H. Wolff (New York: Free Press, 1964), p. 326.

12 Welsh refers us, here, to Kathleen Blake, '*Middlemarch* and the Woman Question', *Nineteenth-Century Fiction*, 31 (1976), pp. 285–312, and Sandra M. Gilbert and Susan Gubar, *The Madwoman in the Attic* (New Haven: Yale University Press, 1979), pp. 515–16.

13 Welsh, *George Eliot and Blackmail*, pp. 232–5.

14 Welsh notes: 'This judgment is now being seriously contested. Eugene Hollahan, "The Concept of 'Crisis' in *Middlemarch*", *Nineteenth-Century Fiction*, 28 (1974), pp. 453–7, argues that Ladislaw generates the plot of the novel as a whole; Gordon S. Haight, "George Eliot's 'eminent failure', Will Ladislaw", in *This Particular Web*, ed. Ian Adam, pp. 22–42, argues that he is "the true hero" and "the only coherent focus" of the Plot.' Welsh, *George Eliot and Blackmail*, p. 247n.

15 Ibid., pp. 246–7.

16 Ibid., p. 250.

17 Ibid., pp. 254–5.

18 Ibid., pp. 255, 275, 287.

19 Ibid., p. 75.

20 Ruth apRoberts, '*Middlemarch* and the New Humanity', in Gordon S. Haight and Rosemary T. Van Arsdel (eds.), *George Eliot: A Centenary Tribute* (London: Macmillan, 1982), [pp. 38–46], p. 43.

21 Suzanne Graver, *George Eliot and Community: A Study in Social Theory and Fictional Form* (Berkeley: University of California Press, 1984), p. 2.

22 Paul Ricoeur, 'The Question of Proof in Freud's Psychoanalytic Writings', *Journal of the American Psychoanalytical Association*, vol. 25, 1977, p. 862.

23 Welsh notes: 'Helen B. Lewis pursues this possibility in *Shame and Guilt in Neurosis* (New York: International Universities, 1971). She agrees with Eliot that women are more subject to shame than men are' (pp. 144–64). Welsh, *George*

Eliot and Blackmail, p. 156n.

24 Ibid., pp. 150–6.

25 Sidney Colvin, *Fortnightly Review*, no. 19, January, 1873; Henry James, *Galaxy*, March 1873; Anna T. Kitchel, 'Quarry for *Middlemarch*', A Supplement to *Nineteenth Century Fiction*, vol. 4 (1950), reprinted in *Middlemarch*, ed. Bert G. Hornback (New York: Norton, 1977), pp. 607–42.

26 Reva Stump, *Movement and Vision in George Eliot's Novels* (Seattle: University of Washington Press, 1959), pp. 138–54; Quentin Anderson, 'George Eliot in *Middlemarch*', in George R. Creeger (ed.), *George Eliot: A Collection of Critical Essays* (Englewood Cliffs, N.J.: Prentice-Hall, 1970), p. 148.

27 Knoepflmacher, *Laughter and Despair*, pp. 173–4; also 'Fusing Fact and Myth: The New Reality of *Middlemarch*', in Ian Adam (ed.), *This Particular Web* (Toronto: University of Toronto Press, 1975), pp. 70–7. This passage as a whole is taken from Welsh, *George Eliot and Blackmail*, pp. 221–3.

28 Beer, *Arguing With the Past*, p. 100.

29 Ibid., pp. 100–1.

30 Ibid., pp. 112–13.

31 Jeffrey Franklin, 'The Victorian Discourse of Gambling: Speculations on *Middlemarch* and *The Duke's Children*', *ELH*, vol. 61, 1994, pp. 899–921.

32 Ibid., pp. 900, 908.

33 Daniel Cottom, *Social Figures: George Eliot, Social History and Literary Representation* (Minneapolis: University of Minnesota Press, 1987), p. 175.

34 Edmund Burke, *Reflections on the Revolution in France*, ed. E.J. Payne (Oxford: Oxford University Press, 1921), p. 228.

35 Cottom, *Social Figures*, pp. 176–8.

36 Gordon, *Gossip and Subversion*, pp. 257–62.

37 Ibid., pp. 294, 238–9.

38 Ibid., p. 241.

39 Ibid., p. 252.

40 Ibid., pp. 263, 256.

41 Ibid., pp. 246–9.

WORKS CITED

Adam, Ian, 'The Structure of Realisms in *Adam Bede*', *Nineteenth Century Fiction*, vol. 30, no. 2, September 1975, pp. 127–49.

Adam, Ian, 'The Ambivalence of *The Mill on the Floss*', in Gordon S. Haight and Rosemary T. Van Arsdel (eds.), *George Eliot: A Centenary Tribute* (London: Macmillan, 1982), pp. 122–36.

apRoberts, Ruth, '*Middlemarch* and the New Humanity', in Gordon S. Haight and Rosemary T. Van Arsdel (eds.), *George Eliot: A Centenary Tribute* (London: Macmillan, 1982), pp. 38–46.

Auerbach, Nina, 'The Power of Hunger: Demonism and Maggie Tulliver', *Nineteenth Century Fiction*, vol. 30, no. 2, September 1975, pp. 150–7.

Auerbach, Nina, *Woman and the Demon: The Life of a Victorian Myth* (Cambridge, Mass.: Harvard University Press, 1982).

Auster, Henry, *Local Habitations: Regionalism in the Early Novels of George Eliot* (Cambridge, Mass.: Harvard University Press, 1970).

Barrett, Dorothea, *Vocation and Desire: George Eliot's Heroines* (London: Routledge, 1989).

Beer, Gillian, *Darwin's Plots: Evolutionary Narrative in Darwin, George Eliot and Nineteenth-Century Fiction* (London: Routledge and Kegan Paul, 1983).

Beer, Gillian, *Arguing With the Past: Essays in Narrative from Woolf to Sidney* (London: Routledge, 1989).

Bellringer, Alan W., *George Eliot* (London: Macmillan, 1993).

Blind, Mathilde, *George Eliot* (London: W. H. Allen, 1883).

Bloom, Harold (ed.), *George Eliot* (New York: Chelsea House, 1986).

Booth, Alison, *Greatness Engendered: George Eliot and Virginia Woolf* (Ithaca: Cornell University Press, 1992).

Brady, Kristin, *George Eliot* (London: Macmillan, 1992).

Brody, Selma B., 'Physics in *Middlemarch*: Gas Molecules and Ethereal Atoms', *Modern Philology*, vol. 85, no. 1, August 1987, pp. 42–53.

Carroll, David (ed.), *George Eliot: The Critical Heritage* (London: Routledge and Kegan Paul, 1971).

Cosslett, Tess, *The 'Scientific Movement' and Victorian Literature* (Brighton: Harvester, 1982).

Cottom, Daniel, *Social Figures: George Eliot, Social History and Literary Representation* (Minneapolis: University of Minnesota Press, 1987).

Dentith, Simon, *George Eliot* (Brighton: Harvester Press, 1986).

Eagleton, Terry, *Criticism and Ideology* (London: New Left Books, 1976).

Empson, William, *Some Versions of Pastoral* (Harmondsworth: Penguin, 1995).

Franklin, Jeffrey, 'The Victorian Discourse of Gambling: Speculations on *Middlemarch* and *The Duke's Children*', *ELH*, vol. 61, 1994, pp. 899–921.

Fraser, Hilary, 'St. Theresa, St. Dorothea, and Miss Brooke in *Middlemarch*', *Nineteenth Century Fiction*, vol. 40, no. 4, March 1986, pp. 400–11.

Fuchs, Eva, 'The Pattern's All Missed: Separation/Individuation in *The Mill on the Floss*', *Studies in the Novel*, vol. 19, Winter 1987, pp. 422–34.

Fuchs, Eva, 'Eliot's *The Mill on the Floss*', *The Explicator*, vol. 52, no. 1, pp. 79–80.

Furst, Lilian R., 'Struggling for Medical Reform in *Middlemarch*', *Nineteenth Century Literature*, vol. 48, no. 3, 1993, pp. 341–61.

Gervais, David, 'Televising "Middlemarch"', *English*, vol. 43, 1994, pp. 59–64.

Gilbert, Sandra and Gubar, Susan, *The Madwoman in the Attic: The Woman Writer and the Nineteenth-Century Literary Imagination* (New Haven: Yale University Press, 1984).

Goode, John, '*Adam Bede*', in Barbara Hardy (ed.), *Critical Essays on George Eliot* (London: Routledge and Kegan Paul, 1970), pp. 19–41.

Gordon, Jan B., *Gossip and Subversion in Nineteenth-Century British Fiction* (London: Macmillan, 1996).

Graver, Suzanne, *George Eliot and Community: A Study in Social Theory and Fictional Form* (Berkeley: University of California Press, 1984).

Greenberg, Robert A., 'Plexus and Ganglia: Scientific Allusion in *Middlemarch*', *Nineteenth Century Fiction*, vol. 30, no. 1, 1975, pp. 33–52.

Haight, Gordon S. and Van Arsdel, Rosemary T. (eds.), *George Eliot: A Centenary Tribute* (London: Macmillan, 1982).

Handley, Graham, *State of the Art: George Eliot* (Bristol: The Bristol Press, 1990).

Hardy, Barbara (ed.), *Critical Essays on George Eliot* (London: Routledge and Kegan Paul, 1970).

Heilman, Robert B., '"Stealthy Convergence" in *Middlemarch*', in Gordon S. Haight and Rosemary T. Van Arsdel (eds), *George Eliot: A Centenary Tribute* (London: Macmillan, 1982), pp. 47–54.

Hillis Miller, J., 'Narrative and History', *ELH*, vol. 41, 1972, pp. 455–73.

Hillis Miller, J., 'Optic and Semiotic in *Middlemarch*', in Harold Bloom (ed.), *George Eliot* (New York: Chelsea House, 1986).

Hillis Miller, J., 'Teaching *Middlemarch*: Close Reading and Theory', in Kathleen Blake (ed.), *Approaches to Teaching Eliot's* Middlemarch (New York: The Modern Language Association of America, 1990), pp. 51–63.

Hochman, Baruch, 'Recon/Decon/Structing *Middlemarch*', in Kathleen Blake (ed.), *Approaches to Teaching Eliot's* Middlemarch (New York: The Modern Language Association of America, 1990), pp. 39–50.

Homans, Margaret, 'Eliot, Wordsworth, and the Scenes of the Sisters' Instruction', *Critical Inquiry*, vol. 8, no. 2, 1981, pp. 223–41.

Homans, Margaret, 'Dinah's Blush, Maggie's Arm: Sexuality in George Eliot's Early Novels', *Victorian Studies*, vol. 36, no. 2, 1993, pp. 155–78.

Hulcoop, John F., '"This Petty Medium": In the Middle of *Middlemarch*' in Gordon S. Haight and Rosemary T. Van Arsdel (eds.), *George Eliot: A Centenary Tribute* (London: Macmillan, 1982), pp. 153–66.

Jacobus, Mary, 'Men of Maxims and *The Mill on the Floss*', in K. M. Newton (ed.), *George Eliot* (London: Longman, 1991), pp. 83–98.

Knoepflmacher, U. C., *Laughter and Despair: Readings in Ten Novels of the Victorian Era* (Berkeley: University of California Press, 1971).

Law, Jules, 'Water Rights and the "crossing o' breeds"', in Linda M. Shires (ed.), *Rewriting the Victorians: Theory, History and the Politics of Gender* (New York: Routledge, 1992), pp. 52–69.

Levine, George, *The Realistic Imagination: English Fiction from Frankenstein to Lady Chatterley* (Chicago: University of Chicago Press, 1981).

Martin, Carol A., *George Eliot's Serial Fiction* (Columbus: Ohio State University Press, 1994).

Pinney, Thomas (ed.), *The Essays of George Eliot* (London: Routledge and Kegan Paul, 1963).

Sedgwick, Eve Kosofsky, *Between Men: English Literature and Male Homosocial Desire* (New York: Columbia University Press, 1985).

Shires, Linda M. (ed.), *Rewriting the Victorians: Theory, History and the Politics of Gender* (New York: Routledge, 1992).

Shuttleworth, Sally, *George Eliot and Nineteenth-Century Science: The Make-Believe of a Beginning* (New York: Cambridge University Press, 1984).

Smith, David, 'Incest Patterns in Two Victorian Novels', *Literature and Psychology*, vol. 15, no. 3, Summer 1965, pp.135–62.

Spittles, Brian, *George Eliot: Godless Woman* (London: Macmillan, 1993).

Stephen, Leslie, *George Eliot* (London: Macmillan and Co. Ltd., 1902).

Thale, Jerome, *The Novels of George Eliot* (New York: Columbia University Press, 1959).

Van Ghent, Dorothy, '*Adam Bede*', in Harold Bloom (ed.), *George Eliot* (New York: Chelsea House, 1986), pp. 1–36.

Weed, Elizabeth, '*The Mill on the Floss* or the Liquidation of Maggie Tulliver', *Genre*, vol. 11, 1978, pp.427–44.

Welsh, Alexander, *George Eliot and Blackmail* (Cambridge, Mass.: Harvard University Press, 1985).

Wharton, Edith, 'George Eliot', *Bookman*, no. 15, May 1902, pp.247–51.

Wiesenfarth, Joseph, 'Antique Gems from *Romola* to *Daniel Deronda*', in Gordon S. Haight and Rosemary T. Van Arsdel (eds.), *George Eliot: A Centenary Tribute* (London: Macmillan, 1982), pp.55–63.

Williams, Raymond, 'Knowable Communities', in Harold Bloom (ed.), *George Eliot* (New York: Chelsea House, 1986), pp.81–97.

Woolf, Virginia, *Women and Writing* (London: The Women's Press, 1979).

Wormald, Mark, 'Microscopy and Semiotic in *Middlemarch*', *Nineteenth Century Literature*, vol. 50, no. 4, 1996, pp.501–24.

ACKNOWLEDGEMENTS

The editor and publisher wish to thank the following for their permission to reprint copyright material: Harvard University Press (for material from *George Eliot and Blackmail*); *Nineteenth Century Fiction* (for material from 'Plexus and Ganglia: Scientific Allusion in *Middlemarch*'; 'The Structure of Realisms in *Adam Bede*'; and 'The Power of Hunger: Demonism and Maggie Tulliver'); Macmillan (for material from *George Eliot: Gossip and Subversion in Nineteenth-Century British Fiction*; and *George Eliot: Godless Woman*); Routledge (for material from *Darwin's Plots: Evolutionary Narrative in Darwin, George Eliot and Nineteenth-Century Fiction*; 'Water Rights and the "crossing o' breeds"', in *Rewriting the Victorians: Theory, History and the Politics of Gender*; and *Arguing With the Past: Essays in Narrative from Woolf to Sidney*); Columbia University Press (for material from *Between Men: English Literature and Male Homosocial Desire*; and *The Novels of George Eliot*); Genre (for material from 'The Mill on the Floss* or the Liquidation of Maggie Tulliver'); *Victorian Studies* (for material from 'Dinah's Blush, Maggie's Arm: Sexuality in George Eliot's Early Novels'); The Modern Language Association of America (for material from 'Teaching *Middlemarch*: Close Reading and Theory', and 'Recon/Decon/Structing *Middlemarch*' in *Approaches to Teaching Eliot's* Middlemarch); Cambridge University Press (for material from *George Eliot and Nineteenth-Century Science: The Make-Believe of a Beginning*); *Studies in the Novel* (for material from 'The Pattern's All Missed: Separation/Individuation in *The Mill on the Floss*'); *Literature and Psychology* (for material from 'Incest Patterns in Two Victorian Novels'); New Left Books (for material from *Criticism and Ideology*); University of Minnesota Press (for material from *Social Figures: George Eliot, Social History and Literary Representation*); *English* (for material from 'Televising "Middlemarch"'); *The Explicator* (for material from 'Eliot's *The Mill on the Floss*'); University of California Press (for material from *Laughter and Despair: Readings in Ten Novels of the Victorian Era*); Harvester Press (for material from *George Eliot*; and *The 'Scientific Movement' and Victorian Literature*); Ohio State University Press (for material from *George Eliot's Serial Fiction*); Chelsea House (for material from '*Adam Bede*' and 'Knowable Communities', in *George Eliot*); The Women's Press (for material from *Women and Writing*).

There are instances where we have been unable to trace or contact copyright holders before our printing deadline. If notified, the publisher will be pleased to acknowledge the use of copyright material.

Editor's acknowledgements: I am most grateful to Alan Bellringer for encouraging me to contribute to this series and for putting me in contact with Richard Beynon. Gratitude is also due to Duncan Heath for his understanding and support. Substantial thanks are due to Linda Jones, to Tom Corns, and to the English Department Research Committee for resources facilitating the project's completion. As always, Scott Brewster has provided invaluable help and advice; I am, once again, in his debt. More still am I indebted to Bethany Grace, who spent the first six weeks of her life patiently watching her mother finish this book . . .

Lucie Armitt is Lecturer in English at the University of Wales, Bangor. She is the author of *Theorising the Fantastic* (Arnold 1996) and *Contemporary Women's Fiction and the Fantastic* (Macmillan 2000) and editor of *Where No Man Has Gone Before: Women and Science Fiction* (Routledge 1991).

INDEX

Columbia Critical Guides Series